Youard

PUNJABI

Punjabi is one of the more important regional languages
of India and Pakistan, and is especially widely used by
immigrants from those countries to Britain. This book
presents a simple everyday form of Punjabi based on the
standard Majhi dialect spoken in Lahore and Amritsar.
The main points of grammar and a basic vocabulary are
introduced in a series of graded lessons, each of which
is provided with keyed exercises. Particular attention is
given to explaining the details of the pronunciation and
a phonetic script is used which clearly represents these.
For those who want to be able to read Punjabi, there is
a chapter on the Gurmukhi script, but the book may be
used by those who wish only to learn to speak the
language.

TEACH YOURSELF BOOKS

PUNJABI

C. Shackle
B.A., B.Litt.

TEACH YOURSELF BOOKS
Hodder and Stoughton

First printed 1972
Fifth impression 1982

Copyright © 1972
Hodder and Stoughton Ltd.

This volume is published in the U.S.A. by David McKay Company Inc., 750 Third Avenue, New York, N.Y. 10017

ISBN 0 340 12464 4

Printed in Great Britain for
Hodder and Stoughton Educational,
a division of Hodder and Stoughton Ltd.,
Mill Road, Dunton Green, Sevenoaks, Kent,
by J. W. Arrowsmith Ltd., Bristol

Contents

Introduction

The Punjabi language

Punjabi is distantly related to English, being a member of the same Indo-European language-family. It is more closely connected with the other languages, known as Indo-Aryan, spoken in Pakistan and northern India, but most nearly resembles Hindi and Urdu, the national languages of India and Pakistan. The large number of English loan-words that have entered Punjabi in the last hundred years ease the task of the English-speaker who wants to learn the language, and he will also find the grammatical structure, with its genders, declensions, tenses, etc., largely familiar in form, especially if he has studied a language like Latin or German, although Punjabi grammar is much simpler than either of these !

The Punjab, where Punjabi is spoken, was one of the largest and richest provinces of British India : in 1947 it was divided between Pakistan and India. Today Punjabi is spoken by a majority of the inhabitants of West Pakistan in one form or another, although (because of the educational system there) most Pakistani Punjabis write in Urdu, the official language, not Punjabi. In India, Punjabi is most closely identified with the Sikhs, who are nearly all Punjabi-speakers, and for whom it has the authority of a scriptural language : they use the special Gurmukhi script for writing Punjabi. Besides the Sikhs, there are many Hindu Punjabi-speakers in India. Since April 1968, Punjabi has been the official language of the Indian state of Panjab. For those travelling or working in West Pakistan or north-west India, some knowledge of Punjabi is therefore a most useful asset.

Punjabis are among the most enterprising and adventurous peoples of India and Pakistan, and have emigrated from their homeland to many parts of the world, most notably to this country, where probably a majority of the immigrants from the two countries speak some form of Punjabi as their mother-tongue. The advantages of knowing some Punjabi to those who want to get into closer touch with Indian and Pakistani immigrants, whether for professional or just social reasons, will be obvious.

Punjabi literature has a tradition at least five hundred years old. Apart from some of the Sikh scriptures and other religious writing, there is some very fine poetry, generally simpler and easier to approach than that of many Oriental literatures. Nowadays there is an increasingly large output of novels, plays and short stories, some of them, especially the last, of a high standard.

The arrangement and use of this book

Perhaps the most difficult feature of the language to a beginner is the pronunciation, and the chapter on this should be read very carefully. A special phonetic script, used in the main part of the book, is introduced in this chapter. It is easy to learn, and is an accurate way of recording the sounds used in standard Punjabi. (It is basically the same as the script used in *Teach Yourself Urdu*, with some modifications for special Punjabi sounds.)

There follow 24 lessons, introducing the basic grammar and vocabulary, at the end of each of which there are exercises, to which a key is provided at the end of the

book. After working through these the learner should
have a good grasp of the grammatical forms of the
language and of the basic types of sentence construction.

The aim of this book is to present a simple, everyday
form of Punjabi of the kind used by townspeople of
some education, without dealing with very colloquial
or rustic forms on the one hand, or with a high-flown
literary language on the other. It is based on the
standard dialect of Lahore and Amritsar. There are,
however, many other dialects of Punjabi, as well as
some differences between Indian and Pakistani Punjabi :
an outline of these differences is given in Lesson 25.

For those who wish to read Punjabi, Lesson 26 deals
with the Gurmukhi script. If desired, this may be read
after the chapter on pronunciation, and the Gurmukhi
script used in the exercises. (The Urdu script, used for
writing Punjabi in Pakistan, is dealt with in *Teach
Yourself Urdu*, pp. xxxviii–xxxix.)

At the end of the book will be found a set of grammatical
tables, which it is hoped will prove useful as a
handy reference guide to Punjabi grammar. There are
also Punjabi–English and English–Punjabi vocabularies,
containing the words introduced in this book. In the
Punjabi–English vocabulary, Punjabi words are also
written in the Gurmukhi script, which should help
those who wish to practise writing the exercises in that
script.

Those who finish the book should be able to carry on
a simple conversation. But, as in learning to speak any
language, practice with a native speaker is invaluable,
both for acquiring a correct accent and for gaining
fluency. In any city in England there will usually be
Punjabi-speakers able and willing to help the learner
in this way.

If the chapter on the Gurmukhi script is also covered,
it should be possible to read newspaper articles and

similar pieces with the help of a dictionary, or of a
Punjabi-speaker to explain the less common words.
There are several Punjabi newspapers and magazines
published in this country. In reading, as in speaking,
practice is of course essential for those who wish to go
beyond the basic outlines of the language, which are all
that a book of this size and scope can hope to deal with.

Further reading

For those who wish to extend their knowledge of the
written language in a systematic way, the best book
available is Ved Prakash Vatuk, *Panjabi Reader*,
published in two volumes as Level I and Level II by the
Colorado State University Research Foundation in
America in 1964. After finishing this book, it should be
possible to begin on p. 87 of Level I. The two Punjabi
newspapers published weekly in London, the *Panjab
Times* and *Des Pardes*, will also be found useful by those
seeking to improve their ability to read the language.

Pronunciation

P1 The Roman Script

To be fully understood when speaking any language, one must distinguish between its basic sounds (phonemes). In the main part of this book, a phonetic script in Roman letters is used for writing Punjabi to help the learner acquire a reasonably accurate pronunciation, even without the help of a Punjabi-speaker. The notes in this chapter should first be read carefully, and the pronunciation exercises spoken aloud, until you are satisfied that you can make the necessary distinctions between the various sounds.

In the phonetic script used, each letter (or combination of two letters) has one sound only. Some special symbols have to be used in order to represent Punjabi sounds as accurately as possible, but these have been kept to a minimum, since the Roman script is only a beginner's aid, which leads on to the Gurmukhi script introduced at the end of this book.

P2 Vowels

There are ten vowels in Punjabi, written as follows :

/ə/ /a/	/y/ /i/	/w/ /u/	/e/ /əy/	/o/ /əw/

These are all pure vowels, like those of French or Italian, but unlike many English vowels, which are diphthongs (in which one vowel-sound glides off into another).

These ten vowels may be divided into five pairs. In the first three pairs the distinction is between a 'short' and a 'long' vowel, although it is the difference in the quality of the sounds rather than in length which is more important in Punjabi. In the fourth and fifth pairs the distinction is between a 'close' and an 'open' sound, all four vowels being 'long' rather than 'short'.

The pronunciation of these five pairs of vowels is approximately as follows :

First pair :   /ə/   as *a* in ' *a*rise ' or ' *a*bout '
                  /a/   as *a* in ' f*a*ther ' or ' b*a*th '
                              (in Standard English)

Second pair :   /y/   as *i* in ' b*i*t ' or ' m*i*ss '
                  /i/.   as *ea* in ' b*ea*t ' or ' s*ea*m '

Third pair :   /w/   as *u* in ' p*u*t ' or ' p*u*ss '
                  /u/   as *oo* in ' b*oo*m ' or ' f*oo*d '
                              (in Standard English)

Fourth pair :   /e/   as French *é* in ' *été* ' or ' bl*é* '
                           NOT as *ai* in ' m*ai*n ' or ' f*ai*l '
                              (which is a diphthong in
                              Standard English)

                  /əy/   between *e* as in ' m*e*t ' or ' f*e*tch '
                           and *a* as in ' h*a*t ' or ' h*a*nd '
                              (in Standard English)

Fifth pair :   /o/   as French *ô* in ' h*ô*te ' or ' n*ô*tre '
                           NOT as *oa* in ' f*oa*m ' or ' c*oa*l '
                              (which is a diphthong in
                              Standard English)

                  /əw/   as *o* in ' n*o*t ' or ' p*o*p '

Pronunciation exercise

Repeat the following pairs of words aloud, keeping the vowel sounds in each pair distinct:

1. /bəs/   *enough*   /bas/   *residence*
2. /dyn/   *day*   /din/   *religion*
3. /swt/   *son*   /sut/   *thread*
4. /de/   *give!*   /ləy/   *take!*
5. /so/   *that*   /səw/   *hundred*

P3 Nasalized Vowels

The seven 'long' vowels may all be nasalized, in which case they are written as follows:

/aŋ/	/iŋ/	/uŋ/	/eŋ/	/əyŋ/	/oŋ/	/əwŋ/

The symbol /ŋ/ is not a consonant, but indicates that the preceding vowel is nasalized, like the *n* in French 'bo*n*' or 'mai*n*'. It should be distinguished from the consonant /n/.

Pronunciation exercise

Distinguish aloud between the following pairs of words:

1. /na/   *not*   /naŋ/   *name*
2. /səman/   *luggage*   /səmaŋ/   *time*
3. /si/   *was*   /siŋ/   *boundary*
4. /sin/   *scene*   /siŋ/   *boundary*
5. /dosto/   *friends!*   /dostoŋ/   *from a friend*
6. /səw/   *hundred*   /səwŋ/   *sleep!*

P4 Diphthongs

When a 'short' vowel (/ə/, /y/ or /w/) is immediately followed by a 'long' vowel, a diphthong results: that is, there are two vowels in one syllable.

In the five common diphthongs written as /əi/, /əe/, /ya/, /yo/ and /yəw/ the first element is pronounced as a short /e/, whether this is written as /ə/ or as /y/. The symbol /ĕ/ will be used for this sound in this book when it is necessary to draw attention to the actual pronunciation of these five diphthongs, e.g.

/gəi/	she went	pronounced as /gĕi/
/gəe/	they went	pronounced as /gĕe/
/gya/	he went	pronounced as /gĕa/
/pyo/	father	pronounced as /pĕo/
/lyəwnda/	bringing	pronounced as /lĕəwnda/

Other diphthongs are pronounced as written, e.g.

/swal/	question	/jyunda/	living

When two or more ' long ' vowels follow one another, they fall into separate syllables (without there being any break or catch in the voice between them), e.g.

	/mai/	mother	(two syllables, /ma-i/)
but	/məi/	May	(one syllable, pronounced /mĕi/)

The same is true when ' long ' vowels and diphthongs come together in a word, e.g.

/hoya/	been	(two syllables, /ho-ĕa/)
/lyaiaŋ/	they brought	(three syllables, /lĕa-i-aŋ/)

Pronunciation exercise

Distinguish aloud between the following pairs of words :

1.	/talyaŋ/	locks	/taliaŋ/	keys
2.	/aya/	he came	/aiaŋ/	they came
3.	/məi/	May	/mai/	mother
4.	/pyo/	father	/pao/	put!
5.	/gəi/	she went	/tei/	twenty-three

P5 Consonants

There are thirty consonants and two semi-vowels in Punjabi. These may be arranged scientifically in the following tabular form :

		velar	palatal	retroflex	dental	labial
stops	voiceless	/k/	/c/	/t/	/t/	/p/
	aspirate	/kh/	/ch/	/th/	/th/	/ph/
	voiced	/g/	/j/	/ḍ/	/d/	/b/
nasals		/ṅ/	/ñ/	/ṇ/	/n/	/m/
flaps and trills				/ṛ/	/r/	
laterals				/ḷ/	/l/	
sibilants	voiceless		/ṣ/		/s/	
	voiced				/z/	
fricatives		/kh/				/f/
aspirate		/h/				
semi-vowels			/y/			/v/

There is no need to pay special attention to all the technical terms used to describe the different classes of consonant. What is necessary is to be able to distinguish between all the different consonants, in particular those which are shaded in the table. These are the sounds most difficult for English-speakers to produce, or to recognize in the speech of Punjabis. Particular attention is given to these sounds in the following pages, where the various consonants are discussed, beginning with the first four consonants in each of the five columns of the table.

Velar consonants

/k/ and /kh/

/kh/ is like the English *k* at the beginning of words, as
in ' *k*ill ' or ' *k*eep ', and is always pronounced with
strong aspiration. The closest English equivalent to
/k/ is the *k* in such words as ' s*k*ill ' or ' spea*k*ing ',
where the aspiration is much weaker. A simple test for
seeing whether one is pronouncing Punjabi /k/ and /kh/
correctly is to hold the hand in front of the mouth :
with /kh/ a strong puff of breath should be felt, but with
/k/ none at all. The same test may be carried out with
/c/ and /ch/, /t/ and /th/, /t/ and /th/, and /p/ and /ph/.

/g/   as English *g* in ' a*g*ree ' or ' a*g*ainst ' (without
       aspiration).

/ṅ/   as *ng* in ' ha*ng* ' or ' si*ng*er '.

Pronunciation exercise

Distinguish aloud between the following pairs of words :

1. /kari/   *effective*   /khari/   *small basket*
2. /yk/   *one*   /ykh/   *sugar-cane*
3. /kəm/   *work*   /gəm/   *sorrow*
4. /baṅg/   *cock-crow*   /baṅk/   *dissolute*

Palatal consonants

/c/ and /ch/

/ch/ is like the English *ch* at the beginning of such words
as ' *ch*urch ' or ' *ch*ild ', and always has strong aspiration.
/c/ is a much drier sound, never aspirated, and is something like *ty*. pronounced with the tip of the tongue down
behind the lower teeth.

/j/   again rather drier than English *j*, and more like *dy*,
       with the tip of the tongue down behind the lower
       teeth.

/ñ/   as *ni* in ' on*i*on ', or Spanish *ñ* in ' ma*ñ*ana '.

Pronunciation exercise

Distinguish aloud between the following pairs of words :

1.	/cal/	*movement*	/chal/	*jump*
2.	/cola/	*kind of coat*	/chola/	*kind of pulse*
3.	/cəñji/	*veil*	/jəñji/	*wedding-guest*
4.	/khəc/	*trouble*	/kəch/	*armpit*

Retroflex consonants

/t/ and /th/
These are the heavy *t*-sounds which are such an obvious
feature of ' Indian English '. They are produced by the
tip of the tongue being slightly rolled back to the roof
of the mouth (hence the linguist's term ' retroflex '), and
touching the top of the mouth just behind the teeth-
ridge. /t/ is a *t*-sound produced in this position without
aspiration, while /th/ has strong aspiration.

/ḍ/   the heavy *d*-sound of ' Indian English ', with the
       tongue in the same position as for /t/, and pro-
       nounced without aspiration.

/ṇ/   a nasal (*n*-sound) with the tongue in the same
       position as for /t/ and /ḍ/.

The long curling tails used in the Roman symbols for
these retroflex sounds may help to suggest the curled-
back position of the tongue. Be careful not to confuse
/ṇ/ with the symbol /ŋ/ used to mark the nasalization of
vowels (*cf.* P3).

Pronunciation exercise

Distinguish aloud between the following pairs of words :

1.	/ʈok/	*obstacle*	/ʈhok/ *shove*
2.	/ʈis/	*pain*	/ʈhis/ *hitting*
3.	/ɖəɳɖa/	*stick*	/ʈhəɳɖa/ *cold*
4.	/kəɳɖ/	*back*	/khəɳɖ/ *sugar*
5.	/maɳ/	*pride*	/maɳ/ *mother*

Dental consonants

/t/ and /th/
These sounds are quite different from /ʈ/ and /ʈh/, and
from the English *t*. They are produced with the tongue
flat and its edges touching the inside of the upper teeth
all round. (The *t* of French or Italian is produced in the
same way.) /t/ is pronounced with aspiration, while
/th/ has strong aspiration. Note that /th/ is nothing
like the English *th* in ' *th*in ' or ' *th*ere ', but is similar to
the *t-h* in ' boa*t*-*h*ouse '.

/d/   a dental *d* with the tongue in the same position as
        for /t/ and /th/, like the *d* of French or Italian.

/n/   as English *n*.

Pronunciation exercise

Distinguish aloud between the following pairs of words :

1.	/twk/	*verse*	/thwk/ *spit*
2.	/mət/	*religion*	/məth/ *advice*
3.	/thəm/	*pillar*	/dəm/ *breath*
4.	/sənt/	*holy man*	/sənd/ *tools*

Distinction of retroflex and dental

This diagram will help to show how the Punjabi
/t/, /d/, *etc.*, differ from /ʈ/, /ɖ/, *etc.*, and how both differ
from English *t* and *d* :

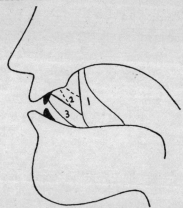

1. Position of tongue for Punjabi /t/ and /d/.
2. Position of tongue for English *t* and *d*.
3. Position of tongue for Punjabi /t/ and /d/.

Pronunciation exercise

Distinguish aloud between the following pairs of words :

1.	/tək/	*cut*	/tək/	*up to*
2.	/thok/	*shove*	/thok/	*heap*
3.	/dak/	*post*	/dakh/	*vine*
4.	/jəṇa/	*man*	/jəna/	*adultery*
5.	/bənda/	*being made*	/bənda/	*man*

Labial consonants

/p/ and /ph/

/p/ is pronounced without any of the aspiration which usually accompanies the English sound. /ph/ is a *p* with strong aspiration, like *p-h* in ' *top-hat* '. It should be pronounced in this way in those words written with it in the Roman script, although it is frequently interchangeable with /f/.

/b/   as English *b*, without aspiration.
/m/   as English *m*.

Pronunciation exercise

Distinguish aloud between the following pairs of words :

1.	/pət/	*honour*	/phət/	*split*
2.	/piṭha/	*ground*	/phita/	*ribbon*
3.	/pap/	*sin*	/bap/	*father*
4.	/pəmp/	*pump*	/əmb/	*mango*

Flaps and trills

/r/ and /ṛ/

/r/ is produced by the tip of the tongue just behind the
front teeth, with or without a short trill or tap. It is
quite different from the *r* of Standard English, although
similar to the Scottish *r*. It must be clearly pronounced
in all positions in a word. English-speakers usually have
difficulty in pronouncing /r/ after a ' long ' vowel, while
keeping the vowel-sound pure : Punjabi /der/ is pronounced as /de-/ + /-r/, and certainly does not rhyme
with English ' there '.

/ṛ/ is one of the most difficult sounds of Punjabi. It is
produced by the tongue being rolled back as for /ṭ/ or
/ḍ/, then quickly brought forward, to flap when the tip
touches the teeth-ridge. Alternatively, it may be
thought of as an *r*-sound produced in the same position
as /ṭ/ or /ḍ/. It is quite unlike both the English *r* and
the guttural French *r*.

Pronunciation exercise

Distinguish aloud between the following pairs of words :

1.	/de/	*of*	/der/	*delay*
2.	/pi/	*lover*	/piṛ/	*pain*
3.	/pir/	*holy man*	/piṛ/	*pain*
4.	/baraŋ/	*twelve*	/bəṛa/	*great*
5.	/pər/	*but*	/phəṛ/	*seize!*

Laterals

/l/ and /ḷ/

/l/ is the English clear *l*, like the first *l* in ' *l*ittle ', *never* like the second. /ḷ/ is an *l*-sound produced with the tongue rolled back as for /t/ or /ḍ/, and is again different from the second *l* in ' litt*l*e '. (Some Punjabi dialects do not have /ḷ/, using /l/ instead.)

Pronunciation exercise

Distinguish aloud between the following pairs of words :

1. /khali/   *empty*   /kaḷi/   *black*
2. /phwl/   *flower*   /pwḷ/   *bridge*

Other consonants

/s/   as English *s* in ' *s*eat ' or ' *s*oap ' ; never as *s* in ' ro*s*e '.

/z/   as English *z*.

/ṣ/   as English *sh* in ' *sh*ake ' or ' *sh*ut '. (Some Punjabis pronounce this as an *s* in the same position as /t/ or /ḍ/, but the first pronunciation is commoner, and easier for the English speaker.)

/kh/   a scrapy guttural sound, like the *ch* in Scottish ' lo*ch* ' or German ' A*ch*tung '.

/f/   a weaker sound than the English *f*, pronounced with the upper teeth lightly touching the middle of the lower lip.

/h/   as English *h*.

Substitutions

Many Punjabis always pronounce /z/ as /j/, and /kh/ as /kh/. This is especially true of uneducated people, and is also more common in India than in Pakistan. Also, many words spelt with /f/ may be pronounced with /ph/, and vice versa.

Semi-vowels

/**y**/ a weaker sound than the English *y*, pronounced
        with much less tension in the tongue. /**y**/ is not
        a common sound, and is used only at the begin-
        ning of a few words. (Remember that Punjabi
        /**y**/ is always a vowel.)

/**v**/ a weaker sound than the English *v*, being half-way
        between *v* and *w*. It is pronounced in the same
        way as Punjabi /**f**/, with the upper teeth lightly
        touching the middle of the lower lip.

Pronunciation exercise

Distinguish aloud between the following pairs of words :

1. /sadi/   *simple*   /ṣadi/   *wedding*
2. /sath/   *association*   /zat/ (or /jat/)   *caste*
3. /kaḷi/   *black*   /k̲h̲ali/ (or /khali/) *empty*
4. /ver/   *time*   /fer/ (or /pher/)   *again*
5. /y̲atra/   *pilgrimage*   /k̲h̲yal/ (or khyal/) *thought*

P6 Doubling of consonants

Consonants written as double are pronounced as such in
Punjabi, as they are in Italian. Sounds like /n/ or /s/
are simply pronounced for a longer time, like the *nn* in
' un*noticed* '. Other sounds are doubled by forming the
position for the consonant, holding this position briefly
and then articulating the sound. /kkh/ is something
like the *k-c* in ' boo*k-c*ase ', /pph/ like the *p-p* in ' lam*p-
p*ost ' and so on. Double consonants are not pronounced
at the end of words.

Pronunciation exercise

Distinguish aloud between the following pairs of words :

1. /hase/   *laughs*   /həsse/   *he may laugh*
2. /akhaṇ/   *I may say*   /əkkhaṇ/   *eyes*

3. /pwlaŋ/   *bridges*   /phwllaŋ/   *flowers*
4. /kəmaŋ/   *bow*   /kəmmaŋ/   *tasks*
5. /səji/   *decorated*   /səjji/   *right*

P7 Stress

The stressing of one syllable in a word is less strong in
Punjabi than it is in English, but is still quite noticeable.
As in English, the stress is normally on the first syllable.
In some words, however, the second syllable is stressed.
This is marked by the sign ‾ (macron) placed over the
vowel, as in the word /əsān/, *easy*.

As in English, ' short ' vowels in words which have
the second syllable stressed are often reduced to /ə/,
e.g. /kytāb/ or /kətāb/, *book*. Sometimes an initial vowel
may be lost altogether, *e.g.* /ykə̄tti/ or /kətti/, *thirty-one*.

Note : Vowels *after* the stressed syllable always keep
their full values in Punjabi and are not slurred as in
English.

Pronunciation exercise

Distinguish aloud between the following pairs of words :

1. /kəmmaŋ/   *tasks*   /kəmān/   *command*
2. /bəcca/   *child*   /bəcā/   *liberate*
3. /akhaŋ/   *I may say*   /əkhān/   *proverb*
4. /əsaŋ/   *by us*   /əsān/   *easy*
5. /swnya/   *heard*   /swṇāya/   *told*

P8 Tone

The use of tones, or different vocal pitches to distinguish
between different words that would otherwise sound the
same, is one of the most distinctive features of Punjabi.
The Punjabi tone-system is, however, much less complex
than that of Chinese, the best-known tone-language.
There are only two tones in Punjabi, both of which may
easily be learnt by an English-speaker, although it is

helpful to get a Punjabi to demonstrate the pronunciation of the low tone.

High tone

In syllables with high tone, the pitch of the voice rises
above its normal level, falling back to this in the following
syllable. In the phonetic script, high tone is written
with ´ (acute accent) over the vowel (or first vowel of a
diphthong), as in /énaŋ/, *these* or /náiŋ/, *not*.

The tone-bearing syllable always has the stress too,
so there is no need to mark the stress separately. Vowels
with high tone are usually pronounced a little shorter
than those with simple stress.

Diagrammatically, the rise and fall of the voice may
be shown as :

Normal pitch - - -

Low tone

At first, this is a little more complicated to produce than
the high tone. In syllables with low tone, the voice is
lowered below the normal pitch, rising back to this in
the following syllable. But the most distinctive feature
of the low tone is an initial tightening of the throat, and
the production of a slight glottal catch in the voice from
the throat before the vowel is pronounced. This glottal
catch serves to bring the pitch sharply down to the level
required for the pronunciation of the low tone.

Low tone is written in the phonetic script with
ˋ (grave accent) over the vowel (or first vowel of a
diphthong), as in /kòṛa/, *horse*, /tỳan/, *attention*, or
/pəṛàya/, *taught*. As with the high tone, the stress
always accompanies the low tone.

Diagrammatically, the fall and rise of the voice may
be shown as :

Normal pitch - - - /ʈa/ ⌐⌐ /an/ ⌐⌐ /pəʈ/ /ya/ ⌐⌐

/kò/ ⌐⌐ /tỳ/ ⌐⌐ /à/

(‖ shows the catch produced by the tightening of the throat.)

Possible position of stress or tone in a word

It may be helpful to summarize the possible positions of stress or tone in Punjabi words, and to show how they are written in the phonetic Roman script. There are nine possibilities, of which the fourth is much the most common :

(i) monosyllable with no accent *e.g.* /nuŋ/ *to*

(ii) monosyllable with acute accent = high tone
     e.g. /ó/ *this*

(iii) monosyllable with grave accent = low tone
     e.g. /tì/ *daughter*

(iv) polysyllabic word with no accent = stress on first
     syllable *e.g.* /mera/ *my*

(v) polysyllabic word with acute accent on first
    syllable = high tone (and stress) on that syllable
     e.g. /ódiaŋ/ *his*

(vi) polysyllabic word with grave accent on first
     syllable = low tone (and stress) on that syllable
     e.g. /kòʈa/ *horse*

(vii) polysyllabic word with macron on second
      syllable = stress on that syllable
     e.g. /əsmān/ *sky*

(viii) polysyllabic word with acute accent on second
       syllable = high tone (and stress) on that syllable
     e.g. /pərəẃṇa/ *guest*

(ix) polysyllabic word with grave accent on second
     syllable = low tone (and stress) on that syllable
     e.g. /pəʈàya/ *taught*

Pronunciation exercise

Distinguish aloud between the following pairs of words :

1.	/vèra/	year	/vərà/	make rain
2.	/ləbba/	got	/ləbà/	make get
3.	/kóṛa/	leper	/kòṛa/	horse
4.	/koṛa/	whip	/kòṛa/	horse
5.	/cəlṇa/	to go	/cèlṇa/	to suffer
6.	/pai/	she put	/pài/	brother
7.	/pəi/	that	/pèi/	mate!
8.	/sá/	breath	/sà/	rabbit
9.	/min/	Pisces	/míṇ/	rain
10.	/pənja/	claw	/pənjá/	fifty
11.	/peṭ/	stomach	/pèṭ/	offering
12.	/baraŋ/	twelve	/bárvaŋ/	twelfth
13.	/di/	of	/tì/	daughter
14.	/ṭhaṭh/	pomp	/tàt/	metal
15.	/rai/	mustard	/rái/	traveller

P9 English loan-words

During the last hundred years a very large number of English words have been borrowed by Punjabi, and many of these words will be encountered during the course of this book. Most of them have, however, been altered by Punjabi patterns of pronunciation, like loan-words in any language, and they should be pronounced in the Punjabi way as written in the phonetic script, not as they are in English.

Most of the changes such words undergo are fairly obvious, but the following points may be noted :

English *t*	becomes Punjabi /ṭ/.
English *d*	becomes Punjabi /ḍ/.
English *th* (as in ' *th*in ')	becomes Punjabi /th/ : remember this is a quite different sound.
English *th* (as in ' *the*re ')	becomes Punjabi /ḍ/.

English *r*   becomes Punjabi /r/, always
                                      pronounced.

As a general rule, try to pronounce these loan-words
as Indians who speak English with a heavy accent do,
and you will probably be more or less right !

Pronunciation exercise

First read the English word aloud, then the corresponding
Punjabi form in the second column. There *should* be
some difference between the two.

1. station   /steṣən/
2. telephone   /təylyfon/
3. road   /roḍ/
4. theatre   /thieṭər/
5. motor   /moṭər/
6. government   /gəwrmynṭ/
7. Southall   /səuthal/
8. London   /ləṇḍən/
9. England   /yṅgləȳṇḍ/

Lesson 1

1.1 There are four true personal pronouns :

/məyŋ/	I
/tuŋ/	you (singular)
/əsiŋ/	we
/twsiŋ/	you (plural)

1.2 Besides being used when speaking to more than one person, /twsiŋ/ is also used to show respect to a single person, like the French ' vous '. /tuŋ/ is normally used between close friends, and when addressing children or people much younger than, or of inferior status to, the speaker : otherwise /twsiŋ/ is used. In all cases of doubt it is better to be polite and use /twsiŋ/. To acquire the habit, /twsiŋ/ should be used in the exercises in this book, unless otherwise stated.

1.3 There are no special words corresponding to the English third person pronouns. Instead, the word for ' that ' is used, unless the physical or mental nearness of the person, object or idea referred to involves the use of the word for ' this '. These two words make no distinction for gender or for number :

/ó/ that, those : he, she, it, they
/é/ this, these : he, she, it, they (in cases where English ' this ' or ' these ' could be substituted for the pronouns)

1.4 The Present tense of the auxiliary verb is conjugated
with the pronouns as follows :

S.1. /məyŋ aŋ/   I am
  2. /tuŋ eŋ/   you are (singular)
  3. /ó e/   he, she, it is
      /é ve/   he, she, it is (for close person,
                     object, *etc.*)

P.1. /əsiŋ aŋ/   we are
  2. /twsiŋ o/   you are (plural, and singular for
                     respect)
  3. /ó ne/   they are
      /é ne/   they are (for close persons, objects,
                     etc.)

Note : To prevent a clumsy repetition of vowels,
the 3S. /e/ = ' is ' normally becomes /ve/ after a word
ending in /-e/.

1.5 In conversational Punjabi, word-order is fairly free,
but for a beginner it is safest to stick to the order normally used in writing and more formal speaking. The
basic rule is that the subject comes first in a sentence and
the verb last, *e.g.*

  /məyŋ əŋgrēz aŋ./   I am an Englishman.
  /ó pəñjābi ne./   They are Punjabi.

1.6 In questions, only the intonation is changed, not
the order of words. The voice rises in pitch on the
important word in the question, then falls after it. This
is different from English, in which the voice usually
rises at the end of a question, *e.g.*

        /pəñjābi/   Punjabi ?
  /twsiŋ/   Are you
           /o ?/

Contrast the intonation in a normal statement :

/twsiŋ/
    /pəñjābi/   You are Punjabi.
      /o./

1.7 When an interrogative word is used in a question, this normally comes immediately before the verb, *e.g.*

    /kəwŋ/
/ó əṅgrēz/   Who is that Englishman ?
      /e ?/
    /kýtthe/
/kytāb/   Where is the book ?
      /ve ?/

It will be seen that the subject comes first and the verb last in all these types of simple question.

1.8 There are no articles in Punjabi, so according to context,

    /kytāb/ = book, a book, the book.

Vocabulary

/məyŋ/	I	/kəwŋ/	who ?
/tuŋ/	you (sing.)	/ki/	what ?
/əsiŋ/	we	/kýtthe/	where ?
/twsiŋ/	you (plur., and sing. for respect)	/éthe/	here
		/óthe/	there
/ó/	that, those : he, she, it, they	/te/	and
		/pər/	but
/é/	this, these : he, she, it, they (where English ' this ' or ' these ' can be substituted for the latter)	/kytāb/	book
		/əkhbār/	newspaper
		/reḍyo/	radio
		/bəs/	bus
		/sṭeṣən/	station
		/əṅgrēz/	English(man)
		/pəñjābi/	Punjabi

Exercises

1A Translate into English :

(1) /kytāb éthe ve./   (2) /ó sṭeṣən e ?/   (3) /é əkhbār e./
(4) /twsiṇ kýtthe o ?/   (5) /ó pəñjābi ne./   (6) /əsiṇ
əṅgrēz aṇ./   (7) /é əṅgrēz kəwṇ e ?/   (8) /ó bəs e./   (9) /tuṇ
kəwṇ éṇ ?/   (10) /reḍyo éthe ve, pər kytāb óthe ve./

1B Translate into Punjabi :

(1) Where are you ?   (2) I am here.   (3) Is he English ?
(4) What is that ?   (5) It is a newspaper.   (6) The book is
there.   (7) Who is this ?   (8) Is he here ?   (9) Where are
they ?   (10) The Englishmen and the Punjabi are there.

Lesson 2

2.1 The Past tense of the auxiliary verb is conjugated as follows :

S.1.	/məyŋ sáŋ/	I was
2.	/tuŋ səyŋ/	you were (sing.)
3.	/ó si/	he, she, it was
	/é si/	he, she, it was (for close person, *etc.*)
P.1.	/əsiŋ saŋ/	we were
2.	/twsiŋ səw/	you were (plur., and sing. for respect)
3.	/ó sən/	they were
	/é sən/	they were (for close persons, *etc.*)

2.2 The negative of the past auxiliary is formed by placing the word /néiŋ/, *not*, immediately before the verb, *e.g.*

   /ó kytāb néiŋ si./   It wasn't a book.

The negative of the present auxiliary may be formed in the same way, by placing /néiŋ/ immediately before the verb, *e.g.*

   /é kytāb néiŋ e./   It isn't a book.

More commonly, /néiŋ/ is used alone, without a verb. The /néiŋ/ will still be at the end of the sentence, *e.g.*

   /é kytāb néiŋ./   It isn't a book.
   /ó əŋgrēz néiŋ./   He isn't English.

2.3 /haŋ/ is ' yes ', and /nə́iŋ/ is ' no '. In polite speech
these words are normally used with the word /ji/ : this
is an honorific particle, sometimes translated as ' sir ',
but /haŋ ji/ and /nə́iŋ ji/ (less commonly /ji haŋ/ and
/ji nə́iŋ/) are used much more widely than the English
' yes sir ' and ' no sir '. There is also a more colloquial
word for ' yes '—/aho/, used rather like the English
' yeah '. For /nə́iŋ/ in the sense of ' no ', /na/ may be
used. Both these words may be used with /ji/ : /aho ji/
and /na ji/ (never /ji aho/ or /ji na/).

2.4 As a general rule, adverbs of TIME precede adverbs
of PLACE, which in turn precede adverbs of MANNER.
Adverbs of time often precede even the subject, coming
first in the sentence, *e.g.*

/hwŋ tuŋ éthe kyoŋ eŋ ?/	Why are you here now ?
/kə́l məyŋ óthe saŋ./	Yesterday I was there,
	I was there yesterday.
/əj ó éthe nə́iŋ./	He is not here to-day.

Vocabulary

/nə́iŋ/	not, no	/kədoŋ/	when ?
/na/	no	/əj/	to-day
/haŋ/	yes	/kə́l/	yesterday
/aho/	yes, ' yeah '	/kyoŋ/	why ?
/ji/	honorific	/roʈi/	bread, food
	particle, some-	/paṇi/	water
	times = ' sir '	/boʈəl/	bottle
	or ' madam '	/mwṇḍa/	boy
/hwŋ/	now	/kwɽi/	girl
/os veɭe/	then, at that	/lal/	red
	time	/khali/	empty

Exercises

2A Translate into English :

(1) /kwɽi óthe nə́iŋ si./   (2) /é boʈəl khali e./   (3) /é kytāb

e ?/ (4) /néin ji, é kytāb néin./ (5) /kél mwnḍa kýtthe si ?/
(6) /tun pəñjābi en ?/   (7) /han ji, məyn pəñjābi an./
(8) /ó kəwn ne ?/ (9) /ó əṅgrēz ne, te kél óthe sən./
(10) /os veḷe twsin óthe kyon səw ?/

2B Translate into Punjabi :

(1) The bus is red. (2) Is that bottle empty ? (3) Where
is the bread ? (4) To-day the girl is not here. (5) But she
was here yesterday. (6) At that time the station was
not there. (7) Is that water ? (8) No, the bottle is
empty. (9) Why is the radio here ? (10) When were you
there ?   (11) The boy was English, but the girl was
not (English). (12) The bus is empty now.

Lesson 3

3.1 There are two genders, the masculine and the feminine. Two general rules may be given for determining the gender of a noun :

RULE 1 : Nouns denoting males are masculine : nouns denoting females are feminine.

RULE 2 : Nouns ending in /-a/ or /-aŋ/ are masculine : nouns ending in /-i/ or /-iŋ/ are feminine.

There are a few exceptions to the second rule, the most common being /paṇi/, *water*, which is masculine. Rule 1 takes precedence over rule 2, thus /pài/, *brother*, is masculine, not feminine. The gender of nouns not covered by either rule must simply be learnt as they are introduced in the vocabularies.

3.2 There are two classes of adjectives. The first are sometimes called 'red' adjectives, after the word /lal/, *red*, which belongs to this class. These are invariable in form, *e.g.*

/lal kələm/ (masc.)	red pen
/lal kytāb/ (fem.)	red book

The second class are known as 'black' adjectives, after the word /kaḷa/, *black*, which belongs to this category. This includes all adjectives ending in /-a/ in the masculine singular : these change to /-i/ for the feminine singular (*cf.* rule 2 given in the preceding paragraph), *e.g.*

/ka̧la kələm/ (masc.)   black pen
but   /ka̧li kytāb/ (fem.)   black book

3.3 Adjectives qualifying a noun precede it, as they do in English, *e.g.*

/é cənga mwŋḍa e./   He is a good boy,
                                         this is a good boy.

When the adjective is predicative, it follows the noun, but will of course come before the verb, *e.g.*

/é mwŋḍa cənga e./   This boy is good.

3.4 In English the normal reply to the question ' Is the bottle empty ? ' would be ' Yes, it is.' Punjabi usage is rather different. The normal reply to the question /botəl khali e ?/ would be /haŋ ji, khali e./ In other words, the subject, or the pronoun referring to the subject may be omitted, but the question must otherwise be answered in full.

3.5 In alternative questions of the type ' Is that a boy or a girl ? ', the Punjabi idiom is to put the auxiliary verb after the first alternative, *i.e.*

/ó mwŋḍa e jaŋ kwṛi ?/   not   /ó mwŋḍa jaŋ kwṛi e ?/

Vocabulary

/kytāb/	F.	book	/roṭi/	F.	bread
/əkhbār/	M.	newspaper	/paṇi/	M.	water
/reḍyo/	M.	radio	/botəl/	F.	bottle
/bəs/	F.	bus	/mwŋḍa/	M.	boy
/sṭeṣən/	M.	station	/kwṛi/	F.	girl
/kələm/	M.	pen	/bənda/	M.	man

/kəmra/ M.	room	/tiviŋ/ F.	woman
/kaḷa/	black	/vəḍḍa/	big
/cəṅga/	good	/choṭa/	small
/jaŋ/	or		

Exercises

3A Translate into English :

(1) /é cəṅga bənda e./ (2) /kytāb cəṅgi néiŋ si./ (3) /kél
tiviŋ kýtthe si ?/ (4) /vəḍḍa kəmra khali si./ (5) /é roṭi
cəṅgi e ?/ (6) /haŋ ji, cəṅgi e./ (7) /lal kytāb choṭi e./
(8) /məyŋ óthe saŋ, pər tuŋ kýtthe səyŋ ?/ (9) /ó kələm
kaḷa si jaŋ lal ?/ (10) /kaḷa si./ (11) /reḍyo cəṅga si./

3B Translate into Punjabi :

(1) This newspaper is big. (2) Where is that good boy ?
(3) The station was not big. (4) Was the room empty
yesterday ? (5) No, it wasn't. (6) That big man is
English. (7) Is the pen big or small ? (8) This water is
not good. (9) The book and the newspaper were there
yesterday. (10) The woman was small.

Lesson 4

4.1 There are three declensions of nouns. Once the gender of a noun is known, it is immediately clear which declension it belongs to, and how its plural is formed.

DECLENSION I : all masculine nouns of more than one syllable, ending in /-a/

PLURAL : change /-a/ to /-e/

| /mwŋɖa/ | boy | plural /mwŋɖe/ | boys |
| /bənda/ | man | /bənde/ | men |

DECLENSION II : all other masculine nouns

PLURAL : no change

| /kələm/ | pen, pens |
| /əkhbār/ | newspaper, newspapers |

DECLENSION III : all feminine nouns

PLURAL : add /-aŋ/

| /kwɽi/ | girl | plural /kwɽiaŋ/ | girls |
| /təyksi/ | taxi | /təyksiaŋ/ | taxis |

4.2 There are a number of small changes undergone by some nouns in Declension III in the plural :

(i) If the singular ends in a nasal vowel, the /-ŋ/ is dropped in the plural, *e.g.*

| /tiviŋ/ | woman | /tiviaŋ/ | women |

(ii) If the singular ends in /-a/ or /-aŋ/, the /-ŋ/ is dropped in the plural, and /-v-/ inserted before the /-aŋ/ to prevent two identical vowels coming together, *e.g.*

| /maŋ/ | mother | /mavaŋ/ | mothers |

(iii) If the singular has unstressed /-ə-/ in its final syllable, this is dropped in the plural, *e.g.*

| /botəl/ | bottle | /botlaŋ/ | bottles |

4.3 ' Red ' adjectives being invariable make no change for the plural. ' Black ' adjectives follow Declension I in the masculine and Declension III in the feminine, *e.g.*

Masc. (Declension I)	/vəḍḍa mwṇḍa/	big boy
	/vəḍḍe mwṇḍe/	big boys
Masc. (Declension II)	/vəḍḍa kələm/	big pen
	/vəḍḍe kələm/	big pens
Fem. (Declension III)	/vəḍḍi kytāb/	big book
	/vəḍḍiaŋ kytābaŋ/	big books

Note that one can often tell whether a noun of Declension II is singular or plural from the adjective accompanying it, as well as of course from the verb.

4.4 As already stated there are no articles in Punjabi (1.8). Sometimes, however, ' a ' may be translated as /yk/, which is the word for ' one ', *e.g.*

| /kél do mwṇḍe te yk kwṛi éthe sən./ | Yesterday two boys and a girl (*or* ' one girl ') were here. |

The rule is that when ' one ' could be used instead of 'a', /yk/ may be used.

4.5 There is no way of translating the English idiom ' there is ', ' there were ', *etc.* The Punjabi sentence in

30 PUNJABI

the last paragraph might also be translated ' There were
two boys and a girl here yesterday.'

Vocabulary

/təyksi/ F.	taxi	/tẁaḍa/	your (plur.,
/maṇ/ F.	mother		and sing. for
/kə̀r/ M.	house, home		respect)
/tez/	quick	/yk/	one, a, an
/mera/	my	/tyn/	three
/tera/	your (sing.)	/do/	two
/saḍa/	our	/car/	four

Exercises

4A Put into the plural :

(1) /mwnḍa choṭa e./   (2) /təyksi tez si./   (3) /é vəḍḍa
kə̀r e./   (4) /é tiviŋ əṅgrēz e./   (5) /məyŋ choṭa bənda aŋ./
(6) /kələm kaḷa e./   (7) /kə́l bəs kẖali si./   (8) /meri kytāb
kaḷi nə́iŋ./

(1) /hwṇ do banḍe éthe ne./   (2) /car kytābaŋ te yk
əkẖbār óthe sən./   (3) /mera kəmra kýtthe ve ?/   (4) /tẁaḍi
maŋ kýtthe ve ?/   (5) /ó botlaŋ kẖali ne./   (6) /é mere
kələm ne./   (7) /é tyn mwnḍe cəṅge ne./   (8) /é tera
reḍyo e ?/   (9) /haŋ ji, meri e./

4C Translate into Punjabi :

(1) The bus is quick to-day.   (2) Where are your books ?
(3) The rooms were empty then.   (4) The taxis are black,
but the buses are red.   (5) There were four books, two
newspapers and a pen here.   (6) Are those boys English ?
(7) No, they aren't.   (8) This is your house.   (9) Why were
the women here ?   (10) This isn't a good book.   (11) When
were the girls there ?   (12) Our mother is Punjabi,
but we are English.

Lesson 5

5.1 The basic form of the verb is the root. Verbs will be given in this form in the vocabularies, thus

/kər-/   do
/ja-/   go

5.2 The present participle is formed from the root in one of two ways :

1. Roots ending in a consonant add /-da/
   /kərda/   doing
2. Roots ending in a vowel add /-nda/
   /janda/   going

Note : All roots in /-a/, except /ja-/, *go*, and /kha-/, *eat*, form their present participle by changing this to /-əwnda/, *e.g.*

/a-/   come
/əwnda/   coming

5.3 The Present tense is formed by the present participle, which agrees with the subject in gender and number, like a 'black' adjective, and the present auxiliary.

	Masculine	*Feminine*	
S.1.	/məyŋ janda vaŋ/	/məyŋ jandi aŋ/	I go
2.	/tuŋ janda eŋ/	/tuŋ jandi eŋ/	you go (singular)
3.	/ó (é) janda e/	/ó (é) jandi e/	he, she, it goes

	Masculine	*Feminine*	
P.1.	/əsiŋ jande aŋ/	(/əsiŋ jandiaŋ aŋ/)	we go
2.	/twsiŋ jande o/	(/twsiŋ jandiaŋ o/)	you go (plur., and sing. for respect)
3.	/ó (é) jande ne/	/ó (é) jandiaŋ ne/	they go

Note : In the 1S. masculine, /v-/ is prefixed to the auxiliary to prevent two identical vowels coming together.

5.4 When the 2P. (/twsiŋ/-form) is used for respect in addressing a single person, the verb is always masculine, even when speaking to a woman, so

/twsiŋ roz ləndən jande o ?/ = Do you go to London every day ?
    (1) to one man, politely
    (2) to two or more men
    (3) *to one or more women, politely*

/twsiŋ roz ləndən jandiaŋ o ?/ = Do you go to London every day ? to two or more women (only)

Given the considerable inequality of status between the sexes in traditional Punjabi society, what could be more respectful in speaking to a woman than to treat her as a man ! The masculine form may also commonly be used by women in the 1P. (but never in the 1S.).

5.5 When ' to ' expresses motion to a place, it is not usually translated in Punjabi, *e.g.*

    /ó skul jande ne./   They go to school.

5.6 There are many compound verbs in Punjabi made

up of a noun in the singular immediately followed by the
verb, *e.g.*

/kəm kər-/	' do work ', *i.e.* work
/sygrəṭ pi-/	' drink cigarette ', *i.e.* smoke (cigarettes)
/khaṇa kha-/	' eat food ', *i.e.* eat

Vocabulary

/kər-/	do	/cá/ F.	tea
/ja-/	go	/kafi/ F.	coffee
/a-/	come	/sygrəṭ/ F.	cigarette
/kha-/	eat	/kəm/ M.	work
/pi-/	drink, smoke	/khaṇa/ M.	food
/kýtthoŋ/	where from ?	/dəftər/ M.	office
/kýddər/	where to ?	/tez/	quick, strong
/səda/	always		(of tea, *etc.*)
/kəde/	sometimes	/roz/	every day
/skul/ M.	school		

Exercises

5A Translate into English :

(1) /mwṇḍa roz skul janda e./ (2) /tyn tiviaŋ éthe kəm
kərdiaŋ ne./ (3) /é cá tez e./ (4) /bəs kýddər jandi e ?/
(5) /ləṇḍən jandi e./ (6) /twsiŋ khaṇa kýtthe khande o ?/
(7) /é kwṛi səda paṇi pindi e./ (8) /əsiŋ roz ləṇḍən əwnde
aŋ./ (9) /mera dəftər óthe néiŋ si./ (10) /ṭəyksiaŋ sṭeṣən
jandiaŋ ne./ (11) /ó əṅgrēz kəde kafi pinda e./ (12) /é
botlaŋ meriaŋ ne jaŋ twàḍiaŋ ?/

5B Translate into Punjabi :

(1) (To a woman) Where do you go every day ?
(2) (Woman answering) I go to London. (3) That girl
sometimes comes to school. (4) Where do the buses
come from ? (5) Do they eat here ? (6) When do you go

home every day ? (7) (To a child) Where is your school ?
(8) (To a little girl) Do you go to school every day ?
(9) This man always smokes cigarettes.   (10) This is
tea, not coffee. (11) Why do you smoke ? (12) Why do
you come to the office every day, and what work do
you do there ? (13) My mother sometimes drinks tea.

Lesson 6

6.1 The Imperfect tense, expressing habitual action in the past, is formed with the present participle, agreeing with the subject in gender and number, and the past auxiliary.

	Masculine	Feminine	
S.1.	/məyŋ janda saŋ/	/məyŋ jandi saŋ/	I used to go, I went (habitually)
2.	/tuŋ janda səyŋ/	/tuŋ jandi səyŋ/	you used to go (sing.)
3.	/ó (é) janda si/	/ó (é) jandi si/	he, she, it used to go
P.1.	/əsiŋ jande saŋ/	(/əsiŋ jandiaŋ saŋ/)	we used to go
2.	/twsiŋ jande səw/	(/twsiŋ jandiaŋ səw/)	you used to go (sing., and plur. for respect)
3.	/ó (é) jande sən/	/ó (é) jandiaŋ sən/	they used to go

6.2 The negative of the Imperfect is formed by reversing the order of the participle and the auxiliary, and pre-fixing /néiŋ/, *e.g.*

/ó ləŋḍən janda si./	He used to go to London.
/ó ləŋḍən néiŋ si janda./	He used not to go to London.

The negative of the Present is formed by prefixing /néiŋ/ : the auxiliary is usually dropped (*cf.* 2.2). *e.g.*

| /ó roz ləɳɖən janda e./ | He goes to London daily. |
| /ó roz ləɳɖən néiŋ janda./ | He doesn't go to London every day. |

6.3 /kəde/ means ' sometimes ' in an affirmative sentence, but ' never ' (' not any time ') in a negative one, *e.g.*

| /ó kəde cá pindi si./ | She used to drink tea sometimes. |
| /ó cá kəde néiŋ si pindi./ | She never used to drink tea. |

Note that in a negative sentence /kəde/ normally comes immediately before /néiŋ/.

6.4 Instead of prepositions, Punjabi has *post*positions, *i.e.* instead of ' from London ', or ' on the table ', one says ' London-from ' or ' table-on ', *e.g.*

| /bəs ləɳɖən toŋ əwndi e./ | The bus comes from London. |
| /reɖyo mez te ve./ | The radio is on the table. |

6.5 Two of these postpositions are normally abbreviated in speech, and often in writing :

(i) /wtte/, *on*, is usually shortened to /te/ (not to be confused with /te/, *and*).

(ii) /vyc/, *in*, is usually shortened to /yc/ or /cə/.

Vocabulary

/şəýr/ M.	city, town	/kwrsi/ F.	chair
/bəzār/ M.	market, ' the shops '	/rəý-/	live
		/toŋ/	from
/ʈren/ M.	train	/(wt)te/	on, by
/məzdūr/ M.	labourer, workman	/(v)yc/, /cə/	in
/gylās/ M.	glass	/naḷ/	with, by
/mez/ F. or M.	table	/kəde néiŋ/	never
		/əksər/	often, usually

Exercises

6A Put into the negative :

(1) /mwŋḍa roz skul janda e./   (2) /mwŋḍa roz skul
janda si./   (3) /tiviaŋ éthe kəm kərdiaŋ ne./   (4) /ó kəde
sygrət pinde sən./   (5) /əsiŋ roz ləŋḍən əwnde aŋ./   (6) /é
saḍe kəmre ne./   (7) /ó khaṇa khandi si./   (8) /məyŋ paṇi
pinda saŋ./

6B Translate into English :

(1) /əsiŋ roz bəzār jandiaŋ saŋ./   (2) /botəl te gylās mez
te ne./   (3) /é ṭren kýtthoŋ əwnda e ?/   (4) /şəýr toŋ
əwnda e./   (5) /twsiŋ bəs naḷ sṭeşən toŋ jande səw ?/
(6) /nə́iŋ ji, məyŋ bəs naḷ nə́iŋ saŋ jandi./   (7) /məzdūr
səda cá pinde sən./   (8) /é kwṛi ləŋḍən yc rəýndi e./
(9) /ó əksər ṭəyksi naḷ əwnda si./   (10) /ó bəzār kəde
nə́iŋ janda./   (11) /twsiŋ şəýr yc kəm kərde səw ?/
(12) /ṭren k̲h̲ali kəde nə́iŋ si./

6C Translate into Punjabi :

(1) Where were you living at that time ? (2) We were
living in London. (3) We often used to go to the shops.
(4) Did you go by bus ? (5) My mother used to go by
bus, but I sometimes went by train. (6) Were you working
in an office ? (7) No, I was a labourer. (8) Where is your
glass ? (9) It was on the table, but is not there now.
(10) Does he drink tea ? (11) He sometimes does, but he
usually drinks coffee. (12) Where is the big chair ?
(13) It's in the house now.

Lesson 7

7.1 When nouns are followed by postpositions, they must be put into what is called the *oblique* case. The other case, used without postpositions, is called the *direct* case : this has already been studied in the singular and plural (*cf.* 4.1).

The singular oblique case in the three declensions is formed as follows :

DECLENSION I nouns change /-a/ to /-e/

S. Direct /kəmra/   room
  Oblique /kəmre yc/ in the room

P. Direct /kəmre/   rooms

   DECLENSION II nouns and DECLENSION III nouns make no change

S. Direct	/kər/	house	/təyksi/ taxi
Oblique	/kər yc/	in the house	/təyksi yc/ in the taxi
P. Direct	/kər/	houses	/təyksiaŋ/ taxis

7.2 ' Black ' adjectives change /-a/ to /-e/ in the masculine singular oblique, like Declension I nouns : in the feminine they make no change, like Declension III nouns. The three words given above would be declined with /mera/, *my*, as follows :

	I	II	III
S. Dir.	/mera kəmra/	/mera kər̀/	/meri təyksi/
Obl.	/mere kəmre yc/	/mere kər̀ yc/	/meri təyksi yc/
P. Dir.	/mere kəmre/	/mere kər̀/	/meriaŋ təyksiaŋ/

Note that, while Declension II nouns do not change, the
adjective does. (' Red ' adjectives of course make no
change for the oblique.)

7.3 The words /ó/, *that*, and /é/, *this*, are usually unchanged in spoken Punjabi when used with a noun in
the singular oblique case, *e.g.*

/ó şəýr yc/   in that city
/é vəd̠d̠e kəmre yc/   in this big room

7.4 /kéṛa/ means ' which ? ', and is declined like a black
adjective, *e.g.*

/ó kéṛe kəmre yc rəýndi e ?/ Which room does she live
                                               in ?

Sometimes /kéṛa/ translates the English ' what ? ', when
this is equivalent to ' which ? ', *e.g.*

/twsiŋ kéṛi bəs naḷ   What (which) bus do you
   əwnde o ?/   come by ?

7.5 /kéṛa/ may also be used as an interrogative pronoun
meaning ' who ? '. In this usage it is as common as
/kəwṇ/, but remember it will decline for gender and
number, *e.g.*

/ó kéṛa e ?/ (/ó kəwṇ e ?/)   Who is that (man) ?
/ó kéṛiaŋ ne ?/ (/ó kəwṇ ne ?/) Who are those women ?

7.6   When the English ' what ? ' is not equivalent to
' which ? ', it is translated as /ki/, e.g.

/ó ki kəm kərda e ?/   What work does he do ?
                                (What's his job ?)

The oblique singular of /ki/ (and of /kəwn/) is /kys/, e.g.

/ó kys vel̯e jande sən ?/   What time used they to go ?

Vocabulary

/ciz/ F.	thing	/pə́r̯-/	read
/bək(ə)s/ M.	box	/lykh-/	write
/pəykət̯/ M.	packet	/ləmma/	long, tall
/cyt̯t̯hi/ F.	letter	/chot̯a/	small, short
/lyfāfa/ M.	envelope	/pwrāna/	old (of things)
/t̯ykət̯/ M.	ticket,	/bəẃt/	very
	postage-	/əndər/	inside
	stamp	/kér̯a/	which ? who ?
/kar/ F.	car	/kys vel̯e/	(at) what
/pyn̯d̯/ M.	village		time ? when ?
/yṅgləȳn̯d̯/	England	/jəldi/	quickly, early
M.			

Exercises

7A Translate into Punjabi :

(1) the little room : in the little room (2) the tall men :
from the tall man (3) the old house : inside the old
house (4) the black books : in the black book (5) your
car : on your car (6) my mother : with my mother
(7) the long letter : in the long letter (8) the big boxes :
from the big box

7B Translate into English :

(1) /t̀waḍi cyt̯t̯hi lyfāfe yc si./   (2) /tiviŋ pwrāne kə̀r yc
rəýndi e./   (3) /twsiŋ é pyn̯d̯ yc rəýnde səw ?/   (4) /nə́iŋ ji,
məyŋ ṣəýr yc rəýndi saŋ./   (5) /vəd̯d̯e lyfāfe yc kytāb e,

cyṭṭhi nɘiŋ./   (6) /mwŋḍa bɘẃt pwrāṇi kar naḷ ɘwnda si./
(7) /é lɘmme lyfāfe te tyn ṭykɘṭ ne./   (8) /é kí ciz e ?/
(9) /é bɘkɘs e, te bɘkɘs yc yk kɘlɘm e./   (10) /kéṛa kɘlɘm ?
saḍa e./   (11) /ó lɘmmi kwṛi kéṛi e ?/   (12) /mɘyŋ cyṭṭhi
lykhda saŋ./

7C Translate into Punjabi :

(1) Where are my stamps ?   (2) They are in the big red
envelope. (3) London is in England, and is a very big
city. (4) Do you live there ? (5) No, I used to live there at
that time, but now I live in a little village. (6) There are
four cigarettes in this packet, but I don't smoke. (7) What
time does the little bus come ? (8) It usually comes early.
(9) What is on the big table ? (10) There are two packets
there : in the red packet there is tea, and in the black
one coffee. (11) What time do you usually have (' drink ')
tea ? (12) I never have tea now.

Lesson 8

8.1 The oblique plural of nouns is formed in the following ways :

DECLENSION I nouns change /-a/ to /-yaŋ/

S. Dir.	/kəmṛa/	room
Obl.	/kəmṛe yc/	in the room
P. Dir.	/kəmṛe/	rooms
Obl.	/kəmṛyaŋ yc/	in the rooms

DECLENSION II nouns add /-aŋ/

S. Dir.	/kə̀r/	house
Obl.	/kə̀r yc/	in the house
P. Dir.	/kə̀r/	houses
Obl.	/kə̀raŋ yc/	in the houses

DECLENSION III nouns add /-aŋ/ as in the direct plural

S. Dir.	/həṭṭi/	shop
Obl.	/həṭṭi yc/	in the shop
P. Dir.	/həṭṭiaŋ/	shops
Obl.	/həṭṭiaŋ yc/	in the shops

Note that the oblique plural of all nouns always ends in /-aŋ/.

The same changes are undergone by nouns of Declension II in the oblique plural as those listed for Declension III nouns in 4.2, e.g.

/pəykət/ packet   /pəykṭaŋ yc/   in the packets

Also, nouns which have unstressed /-ə-/ in the final
syllable preceded by a double consonant both drop the
/-ə-/ and have a single consonant in the oblique plural,
e.g.

/pwttər/   son   /pwtraŋ toŋ/   from the sons

8.2 Some nouns of Declensions II and III really end in
a double consonant. Since, however, double consonants
are not pronounced at the end of a word, this only
becomes apparent when the ending /-aŋ/ is added, *e.g.*

> S. Dir.   /həth/ M.   hand
> P. Obl.   /hətthaŋ yc/   in the hands

> S. Dir.   /gəl/ F.   word, matter, thing
> P. Obl.   /gəllaŋ yc/   in the matters, *etc.*

Such words will be written as /hət(t)h/, /gəl(l)/ in the
vocabularies.

8.3 ' Black ' adjectives follow nouns of Declension III
in the feminine oblique plural, and may follow nouns of
Declension I for the masculine. More frequently, however, a ' black ' adjective with a masculine noun in the
oblique plural remains in the masculine oblique singular
form in /-e/. The three nouns given above will be declined with /mera/ as follows :

	I	II	III
S. Dir.	/mera kəmra/	/mera kèr/	/meri hətti/
Obl.	/mere kəmre yc/	/mere kèr yc/	/meri hətti yc/
P. Dir.	/mere kəmre/	/mere kèr/	/meriaŋ həttiaŋ/
Obl.	/mere kəmryaŋ yc/ (/meryaŋ kəmryaŋ yc/)	/mere kèraŋ yc/ (/meryaŋ kèraŋ yc/)	/meriaŋ həttiaŋ yc/

' Red ' adjectives are again unchanged.

8.4 /ó/, *that*, and /é/, *this*, become /ónaŋ/ and /énaŋ/
before nouns in the oblique plural. They have the same
pattern of declension as nouns of Declension II, *e.g.*

S. Dir.	/ó kə̀r/	that house
Obl.	/ó kə̀r yc/	in that house
P. Dir.	/ó kə̀r/	those houses
Obl.	/ónaŋ kə̀raŋ yc/	in those houses

8.5 /sǝk-/, *be able to*, is always used after the root of
another verb, *e.g.*

/əj ó a sǝkda e/   He is able to come to-day. (He can come
to-day.)

Vocabulary

/syk(k)h/ M.	Sikh	/pǝýla/	first
/hǝt(t)h/ M.	hand	/duja/	second, other
/kǝm(m) M.	work, job, task	/khǝrāb/	bad, rotten, ' no good '
/gǝl(l)/ F.	matter, word, thing	/thik/	right, correct
		/gǝlt/	wrong
/hǝṭṭi/ F.	shop	/sǝk-/	be able to
/əṅgrēzi/ F.	English language		(' can ')
		/bol-/	speak
/kalǝj/ M.	college	/pǝɽà-/	teach
/wstād/ M.	teacher	/lǝi/	for

Exercises

8A Translate into Punjabi :

(1) the other rooms : from the other rooms (2) inside
the old city : inside the old cities (3) the big colleges :
in the big colleges (4) these red buses : on these red
buses (5) the little office : in the little offices (6) the
first men : from the first men (7) with the tall boy :
with the tall boys (8) on the large hand : on the large
hands

8B Translate into English :

(1) /əngréz əngrēzi bolde ne./ (2) /ó vəḍḍe ṣəýr yc wstād
e, te óthe əngrēzi pəṛewͧnda e./ (3) /məyŋ pəñjābi néiŋ bol
səkdi./ (4) /é bənde kí kəm kərde ne ? məzdūr ne./
(5) /twàḍi gəl ṭhik e : é bəẃt cəṅgi cá e./ (6) /é pəñjābi
əkẖbār sykkhaŋ ləi e./ (7) /ónaŋ k̀raŋ yc kéṛe rəýnde
sən ?/ (8) /duje gylās mezaŋ te sən./ (9) /kwṛiaŋ é
kytāb néiŋ pəṛ səkdiaŋ./ (10) /saḍiaŋ cyṭṭhiaŋ duje
lyfāfyaŋ yc sən./ (11) /tͧwaḍe kaləj yc pəýla wstād kéṛa si ?/
(12) /məyŋ é khaɳa néiŋ kha sakda : bəẃt kẖərāb e./

8C Translate into Punjabi :

(1) In the other rooms there were four chairs and two
tables. (2) I can come to-day. (3) What's the matter ?
That black car is no good. (4) This teacher used to
teach English in those schools. (5) Sikhs never smoke.
(6) At that time these were my first tasks. (7) The
English is wrong in the newspapers. (8) Where does
this train come from ? (9) It comes from those towns.
(10) The labourers live in the old houses. (11) Which
rooms did those boys live in ? (12) She used to be able
to write a long letter every day.

Lesson 9

9.1 ' Black ' adjectives which end in nasalized /-aŋ/ keep their nasalization throughout, but are otherwise regular. /nəvaŋ/, *new*, declines as follows :

	Masculine	*Feminine*
S. Dir.	/nəvaŋ kəmra/	/nəviŋ həṭṭi/
Obl.	/nəveŋ kəmre yc/	/nəviŋ həṭṭi yc/
P. Dir.	/nəveŋ kəmre/	/nəviaŋ həṭṭiaŋ/
Obl.	/nəveŋ kəmryaŋ yc/	/nəviaŋ həṭṭiaŋ yc/
	(/nəvyaŋ kəmryaŋ yc/)	

9.2 The Present Continuous tense, corresponding to the English ' I am going ', *etc.*, is formed by the root of the verb plus the word /rýa/ agreeing with the subject in gender and number, followed by the present auxiliary.

	Masculine	*Feminine*	
S.1.	/məyŋ ja rýa vaŋ/	/məyŋ ja rói aŋ/	I am going
2.	/tuŋ ja rýa eŋ/	/tuŋ ja rói eŋ/	you are going (sing.)
3.	/ó (é) ja rýa e/	/ó (é) ja rói e/	he, she, it is going
P.1.	/əsiŋ ja rée aŋ/	(/əsiŋ ja róiaŋ aŋ/)	we are going
2.	/twsiŋ ja rée o/	(/twsiŋ ja róiaŋ o/)	you are going (plur., *etc.*)
3.	/ó ja rée ne/	/ó ja róiaŋ ne/	they are going

Note that the first element of the diphthong in all forms of /rýa/ is pronounced the same, as a short /ĕ/-sound (*cf.* P4), thus

MS. written as	/rýa/	pronounced as	/rĕa/
MP.	/rə́e/		/rĕe/
FS.	/rə́i/		/rĕi/
FP.	/rə́iaŋ/		/rĕiaŋ/

This /rýa/ is a form of the verb /rəý-/, *live*, used in a special idiomatic way.

9.3 When ' to ' expresses ' place to ' with a verb of motion it is not translated in Punjabi (*cf.* 5.5). But the noun is put into the oblique case, where this differs from the direct, as in Declension I, *e.g.*

/é mwṇḍa pəṭyāle ja rýa e./ This boy is going to Patiala.

9.4 The normal translation of the English ' to ' in other contexts is /nuŋ/, a postposition which of course puts the noun it accompanies into the oblique :

          /mwṇḍyaŋ nuŋ/   to the boys.

9.5 The pronouns with /nuŋ/ have some irregular forms :

S.1.	/məyŋ/	/məynuŋ/	to me
2.	/tuŋ/	/təynuŋ/	to you
3.	/ó/ /é/	/ónuŋ/ /énuŋ/ }	to him, her, it
P.1.	/əsiŋ/	/sanuŋ/	to us
2.	/twsiŋ/	/tẁanuŋ/	to you
3.	/ó/ /é/	/ónaŋ nuŋ/ /énaŋ nuŋ/ }	to them

When /ó/ and /é/, in the meanings of ' that ' and ' this ',
are used with a noun plus /nuŋ/, they are of course
simply in the oblique case, e.g.

/ónuŋ/	to him
/ó bənde nuŋ/	to that man

9.6 The English indirect object with verbs like ' give '
is translated as a noun or pronoun with /nuŋ/ in
Punjabi, e.g.

/ó məynuŋ kytābaŋ denda si./	He used to give me books.
/məyŋ mwŋḍe nuŋ əkẖbār denda vaŋ./	I give the boy a newspaper.

9.7 Note that the normal place for the direct object in
Punjabi is just before the verb, *unless* there is an
interrogative word in the sentence (*cf.* 1.7), e.g.

/ó roz dəftər toŋ é bəkəs ləynda e./	He takes this box from the office every day.

But

/tuŋ roz dəftər toŋ é bəkəs kyoŋ ləynda eŋ ?/	Why do you take this box from the office every day ?

The standard order is, therefore :

(i) Subject

(ii) Adverbs or adverbial phrases (a) of time
                                    (b) of place
                                    (c) of manner

(iii) Indirect object

(iv) Direct object

(v) Interrogative word

(vi) Verb

Vocabulary

/səbək/ M.	lesson	/de-/	give
/chwṭṭi/ F.	holiday	/ləy-/	take, buy, get
/pwttər/ M.	son	/pèj-/	send
/ṭi/ F.	daughter	/nəvaŋ/	new
/éthoŋ/	from here	/əwkha/	difficult
/óthoŋ/	from there	/dur/	far
/nuŋ/	to	/neṛe/	near (*postpn.*)

Exercises

9A Translate into Punjabi :

(1) in the long holiday : in the long holidays (2) the difficult lessons : in the difficult lessons (3) to the good son : to the good sons (4) near the little village : near the little villages (5) on the new box : in the new boxes (6) for the tall daughter : the tall daughters (7) to that big man : to those big men

9B Translate into English :

(1) /twsiŋ kýtthoŋ a ŕəe o ?/ (2) /məyŋ kaləj toŋ a rýa vaŋ./ (3) /ó kýtthe ve ?/ (4) /ó nəviŋ həṭṭi neṛe ve, pər saḍa kaləj bəẃt pwrāṇa e./ (5) /twsiŋ óthe kí kəm kərde o ?/ (6) /məyŋ hwṇ kaləj yc kəm nə́iŋ kərda, pər meri ṭi óthe kwṛiaŋ nuŋ əṅgrēzi pəṛəẃndi e./ (7) /chwṭṭiaŋ yc ó kýddər jandi e ?/ (8) /əksər ləṇḍən jandi e./ (9) /ó tẁaḍi maŋ nuŋ cyṭṭhi pèj rýa e./ (10) /é bəs ləṇḍən ja rə́i e ?/ (11) /nə́iŋ ji, é óthoŋ a rə́i e./ (12) /twsiŋ cá kýtthoŋ ləynde səw ?/ (13) /əsiŋ bəzār toŋ ləynde saŋ./ (14) /ó teri kafi pi rýa e./

9C Put these sentences into the Present Continuous tense :

(1) /ó mwṇḍyaŋ nuŋ səbək denda e./ (2) /əsiŋ cyṭṭhi pèjde aŋ./ (3) /mera pwttər éthoŋ ṭykəṭ ləynda e./ (4) /ó khaṇa khandiaŋ ne./ (5) /tuŋ kí kəm kərda eŋ ?/

(6) /məyŋ məzdūr nuŋ sygrəṭ denda vaŋ./   (7) /meri tĭ
óthoŋ əwndi e./   (8) /ó bənde əkẖbār péṛde ne./

9D Translate into Punjabi :

(1) Where is your son going ? (2) He is going to the new
college. (3) He gives lessons to the boys there. (4) I am
coming to your village for the holidays. (5) It is not very
far from here.   (6) Why is that girl smoking here ?
(7) I am sending them the packets. (8) This is a new
lesson, and it is very difficult. (9) We are working now,
but are going home early to-day. (10) The big man is
giving the little boy a letter. (11) He is giving us the
books. (12) My daughter is sending you stamps.

Lesson 10

10.1 The Past Continuous tense, corresponding to the English ' I was going ', *etc.*, is formed in the same way as the Present Continuous, except that the past auxiliary is used instead of the present, *i.e.*

	Masculine	*Feminine*	
S.1.	/məyŋ ja rýa saŋ/	/məyŋ ja rə́i saŋ/	I was going

               etc.

10.2 The Present and Past Continuous tenses are not usually used in the negative. Instead the ordinary Present and Imperfect negative forms are used, *e.g.*

/ó bár ja rýa e./	He is going out(side).
/ó bár nə́iŋ janda./	He isn't going out : he doesn't go out.
/ó əndər a rə́i si./	She was coming in(side).
/ó əndər nə́iŋ si əwndi./	She wasn't coming in : she used not to come in.

10.3 /da/ means ' of '. Since it is a postposition, the noun it follows will always be in the oblique case, *e.g.*

/mwŋḍe da/	of the boy, the boy's
/mwnḍyaŋ da/	of the boys, the boys'

/da/ is also declined like a ' black ' adjective, agreeing

in gender, number and case with the noun which
follows it, *e.g.*

/mwṇḍe di kytāb/   the boy's book, the book of the boy
/mwṇḍe de pyṇḍ yc/   in the boy's village, in the village
                     of the boy
/mwṇḍyaŋ diaŋ   the boys' chairs, the chairs of
  kwrsiaŋ/   the boys.

More than two words may be connected with /da/ in this
way : all but the last must be in the oblique case, *e.g.*

   /mwṇḍe de pyo da kèr/   the boy's father's house

Remember that the order of words in the /da/-construc-
tion is always the same as that in the English construction with the possessive ' 's ', and the opposite of
that with ' of '.

10.4 For the ' genitive ' of the four personal pronouns
the adjectives /mera/, /tera/, /saḍa/ and /tẁaḍa/ are
used. For the third person pronouns the following
forms are used :

Sing.   /óda/   (/éda/)   his, hers, its
Plur.   /ónaŋ da/   (/énaŋ da/)   theirs

10.5 In English there are four basic divisions of the
day, while in Punjabi there are only three :

     /səvēr/   morning
     /ṣam/   afternoon, evening (first part)
     /rat/   evening (second part), night

/ṣam/ is the time from noon until after sunset : in
general it is equivalent to both ' afternoon ' and
' evening '.

10.6 In many expressions of time, the English ' in ',
' at ' and ' on ' are all translated by /nuŋ/, *e.g.*

/ṣam nuŋ/	in the afternoon
/əytvar nuŋ/	on Sunday
/rat nuŋ/	at night

Even when there is no preposition in English, /nuŋ/ must
still normally be used in Punjabi, *e.g.*

/əj ṣam nuŋ/	this afternoon (' on to-day afternoon ')
/kə́l səvēr nuŋ/	yesterday morning (' on yesterday morning ')

Vocabulary

/səvēr/ F.	morning	/əytvar/ M.	Sunday
/ṣam/ F.	afternoon, evening	/somvar/ M.	Monday
/rat/ F.	night	/məngəl(var)/ M.	Tuesday
/pyo/ (Obl. Pl. /pevaŋ/) M.	father	/bár/	outside
		/zərūr/	certainly, of course
/pài/ M.	brother	/da/	of
/pəỳn/ F.	sister		

Exercises

10A Translate into Punjabi :

(1) the girl's hand : the girl's hands : the girls' hands :
on the girls' hands (2) my brother's office : my brothers'
office : my brothers' offices (3) inside her house : inside
their house : inside their houses : inside those houses
(4) the cities of England : from the cities of England :
from those cities of England (5) the village of this
woman : the villages of these women : in the villages
of these women (6) his little daughter's book : his little
daughters' books : in his little daughters' books (7) the
new houses of London : for the new houses of London
(8) the big box of black books : the big boxes of black
books : in the big boxes of black books

10B Translate into English :

(1) /tŵaḍi pəy̆ŋ kys veḷe a rə́i e ?/ (2) /ó əj rat nuŋ a
rə́i e./ (3) /te kýtthoŋ a rə́i e ?/ (4) /ó ónaŋ de pyo de kèr
toŋ a rə́i e./ (5) /əsiŋ məṅgəḷ ṣam nuŋ ónaŋ de pài de
kèr ja rə́e saŋ./ (6) /ṭren ṣəýr de ó sṭeṣən yc si./ (7) /twsiŋ
éthe khaṇa kha rə́e o ?/ (8) /nə́iŋ ji, məyŋ khaṇa nə́iŋ
khanda, cá pi rýa vaŋ./ (9) /é mwŋḍa mere pyo di
həṭṭi yc kəm kərda e./ (10) /ó somvar ṣam nuŋ óthoŋ
kytābaŋ ləy rə́e sən./ (11) /əksər ó zərür dəftər janda e,
pər hwŋ saḍi pəy̆ŋ de skul ja rýa e./ (12) /ó kwṛi da
dəftər meri maŋ de kèr toŋ dur e./

10C Translate into Punjabi :

(1) On Monday evening he was going home from the
office. (2) That man's son used to work in my father's
school. (3) This is the first new house of the old village.
(4) There was a table and four chairs in this room of the
teacher's daughter's house. (5) Yesterday morning I was
giving their brother a lesson. (6) He's certainly coming
with your brother now. (7) I used to get cigarette(s)
from this man's shop. (8) Their fathers' cars are outside.
(9) The boxes of glasses were in his sister's shop. (10) She
was going to the shops by bus this morning. (11) That
Sikh's sons were coming to school with my little brother.
(12) She was getting stamps for our letters on Tuesday
afternoon. (13) My sisters used to go to the college
every day, but this evening they are going to London.
(14) What his brother said was wrong : they never write
letters on Sunday. (15) Their daughters are not drinking
tea.

Lesson 11

11.1 The pronouns with /toŋ/, *from*, have some irregular forms :

S.1.	/məyŋ/	/məythoŋ/	from me
2.	/tuŋ/	/təythoŋ/	from you
3.	/ó/ /é/	/ós toŋ/ /és toŋ/ }	from him, her, it
P.1.	/əsiŋ/	/sathoŋ/	from us
2.	/tẇsiŋ/	/tẇathoŋ/	from you
3.	/ó/ /é/	/ónaŋ toŋ/ /énaŋ toŋ/ }	from them

Compare the forms with /nuŋ/ (9.5). /os/ and /es/ are strengthened forms of /ó/ and /é/, and may often be used instead of them in the oblique singular. /ó toŋ/ and /é toŋ/ are not usually used to mean *from him*, probably because they sound very like /óthoŋ/ and /éthoŋ/, meaning *from there* and *from here*.

11.2 With nearly all postpositions other than /nuŋ/, /toŋ/ and /da/ the pronouns must be put into the oblique singular of the masculine possessive, *e.g.*

> /mere ləi/   for me
> /tẇaḍe naḷ/   with you

But /ónaŋ/ and /énaŋ/ need not be in the possessive before postpositions, *e.g.*

/ónaŋ ləi/   or   /ónaŋ de ləi/   for them

11.3 Similarly, all nouns may have /de/ before most postpositions, *e.g.*

/kytābaŋ yc/	or	/kytābaŋ de vyc/	in the books
/mez te/	or	/mez de wtte/	on the table
/kwṛi naḷ/	or	/kwṛi de naḷ/	with the girl

Note that when a postposition has both a long and a short form, the former is normally used after /de/, as in the first two examples above.

On the whole, the forms without /de/ are more common.

11.4 Punjabi does not express the comparative and superlative degrees of adjectives by suffixes like the English -*er* and -*est*. Instead, the simple form of the adjective is used with the postpositions /toŋ/ or /naḷoŋ/, *than*, *e.g.*

/mwṇḍa kwṛi toŋ ləmma e./	The boy is taller than the girl.
/mwṇḍa kwṛi (de) naḷoŋ ləmma e./	
/ó məythoŋ syaṇa e./	He is cleverer than me.
/ó mere naḷoŋ syaṇa e./	
/é şəýr saḍe pyṇḍ toŋ bəẃt vəḍḍa e./	This city is much bigger than our village.

11.5 The construction is the same for the superlative, with the pronoun /sə́b/, *all*, used instead of the second noun, *e.g.*

| /ó sə́b toŋ pəỳṛa mwṇḍa si./ | He was the worst boy (literally, ' bad from all '). |
| /é kə̀r da sə́b toŋ cənga kəmra e./ | This is the best room in the house (literally, ' the house's best room '). |

11.6 /və́d/ and /kə̀t/ mean *more* and *less*, *e.g.*

| /twsiŋ mere pwttar toŋ və́d pə́ṛde o./ | You read more than my son. |

/əjkəl məyŋ sygrəţ kə̀ţ   Nowadays I smoke less.
pinda vaŋ./

But these words are not usually used in comparative
constructions of the kind illustrated in 11.4 and 11.5.

11.7 /bəɽa/ is an adjective meaning *great*. It is also
often used before another adjective to mean *very*,
like /bəẃt/, *e.g.*

/é bəẃt cəṅgi tiviŋ e./
/é bəɽi cəṅgi tiviŋ e./   She is a very good woman.

Very great is always /bəẃt bəɽa/, *e.g.*

/ó bəẃt bəɽa ḍakţər si./   He was a very great doctor.

11.8 When both /sə́b/, *all*, and /ó/ (or /é/) are used with
a noun, the order is the opposite of the English one, *e.g.*

/ó sə́b kytābaŋ nəviaŋ ne./   All those books are new.

Similarly with /sara/, *all, whole, e.g.*

/é sari zymĭŋ ónaŋ di e./   All this land is theirs.

Vocabulary

/ḍakţər/ M.	doctor	/pəỳɽa/	bad
/bəcca/ M.	child, boy	/syaŋa/	clever
/bəcci/ F.	child, girl	/sóna/	beautiful
/deş/ M.	country	/bəɽa/	great, very
/zymĭŋ/ F.	earth, land, ground	/sə́b/	all
/pàrət/	India	/sara/	whole, all
/pakystan/	Pakistan	/və́d/	more
/ləẁr/	Lahore	/kə̀ţ/	less
/əmrytsər/	Amritsar	/əjkəl/	nowadays
/édər/	(to) here, hither	/naloŋ/	than
/ódər/	(to) there, thither	/kevəl/	only

Exercises

11A Translate into Punjabi :

(1) The girl is very beautiful. (2) This girl is more beautiful than their sister. (3) She is the most beautiful girl in the school. (4) This is a very good book. (5) This book is much better than that. (6) These are the best books.

11B Translate into English :

(1) /ḍakṭər de bəcce bəṛe syaṇe ne./ (2) /əjkəl ónaŋ da pyo ləẁr de vyc rəýnda e./ (3) /ləṇḍən saḍe deş da séb toŋ vəḍḍa şəýr e./ (4) /pyṇḍ da skul tẁaḍe pài de kèr naḷoŋ choṭa si./ (5) /skul da séb toŋ syaṇa myṇḍa ódər ja rýa si./ (6) /tuŋ mere kələm naḷ kí lykh rýa səyŋ ?/ (7) /ódi séb toŋ vəḍḍi tì pəñjābi néiŋ péṛ səkdi./ (8) /é bəcci bəṛi sóṇi e, pər meri pəẏŋ toŋ syaṇi néiŋ./ (9) /énaŋ sykkhaŋ di zymīŋ əmrytsər de neṛe ve./ (10) /ləẁr pəñjāb da séb toŋ vəḍḍa şéyr e./ (11) /əjkəl saḍa ḍakṭər kèṭ əwnda e : ó kevəl somvar səvēr nuŋ a səkda e./ (12) /os toŋ syaṇa kéṛa e ?/

11C Translate into Punjabi :

(1) These four boys are not very clever. (2) Amritsar is much smaller than Lahore. (3) Why do you come here less nowadays ? (4) Where is that man's land ? (5) I cannot drink more than the doctor's son ; he is bigger than me. (6) Lahore is not far from Amritsar, but it is in Pakistan, and Amritsar is in India. (7) Our country is better and more beautiful than England. (8) All these pens are that boy's, but that (one) is yours. (9) Which is the oldest book ? (10) This book is newer than that. (11) Why were you getting bread there ? It's the worst shop in the town.

Lesson 12

12.1 The Future tense is formed by adding to the root of the verb a set of personal endings similar to the present auxiliary : to these endings in turn is added the syllable /-ga/, declined for gender and number.

	Masculine	*Feminine*	
S.1.	/məyŋ bolaṅga/	/məyŋ bolaṅgi/	I shall speak
2.	/tuŋ boleṅga/	/tuŋ boleṅgi/	you will speak
3.	/ó (é) bolega/	/ó (é) bolegi/	he, she, it will speak
P.1.	/əsiŋ bolaṅge/	(/əsiŋ bolaṅgiaŋ/)	we shall speak
2.	/twsiŋ bologe/	(/twsiŋ bologiaŋ/)	you will speak
3.	/ó (é) boləŋge/	/ó (é) boləŋgiaŋ/	they will speak

(i) Vowel-roots often insert /-v-/ before the endings of the Future to prevent awkward combinations of vowels. In the following examples only the masculine forms are given. /(v)/ indicates that the insertion is optional.

	/-a/ roots /ja-/, *go*	/-i/ roots /pi-/, *drink*	/-o/ roots /ho-/, *be*
S.1.	/javaṅga/	/pi(v)aṅga/	/hovaṅga/
2.	/ja(v)eṅga/	/pi(v)eṅga/	/hoveṅga/
3.	/ja(v)ega/	/pi(v)ega/	/hovega/
P.1.	/javaṅge/	/pi(v)aṅge/	/hovaṅge/
2.	/jaoge/	/pioge/	/hovoge/
3.	/ja(və)ŋge/	/pi(və)ŋge/	/ho(və)ŋge/

(ii) Roots in /-əy/ form their Future like /ləy-/, *take* :

S.1.   /ləvaṅga/   P.1.   /ləvaṅge/
2.   /lə(v)eṅga/   2.   /ləvoge/ or /ləwge/
3.   /lə(v)ega/   3.   /ləyṅge/

(iii) /de-/, *give*, usually shortens the vowel to /y/
(pronounced /ĕ/) before /-a/ and /-o/ :

S.1.   /dyaṅga/   P.1.   /dyaṅge/
2.   /deveṅga/   2.   /dyoge/
3.   /devega/   3.   /deṅge/

(iv) Roots in /-r/ and /-ɽ/ have the 3P. in /-n(ge)/,
not /-ŋ(ge)/, *e.g.*

/ó kəm kərənge/   they will work
/ó péɽənge/   they will read

12.2 The negative of the Future is formed simply by
putting /néiŋ/ before the verb, *e.g.*

/məyŋ ódər néiŋ javaṅgi./   I shan't go there.

12.3 Some verbal roots end in a double consonant, which
is kept before a vowel ending, but made single before
a consonant, *e.g.*

/ó mez te kytāb rəkhda e./   He puts a book on the
                              table.
/ó mez te kytāb rəkkhega./   He will put a book on the
                              table.

Such roots will be listed in the vocabularies with the
second consonant in brackets, like nouns ending in a
double consonant (8.2), thus, /rək(k)h-/.

12.4 Note the following adverbs of time :

    /pərsoŋ/   the day before yesterday
    /kél/   yesterday

/əj/	to-day
/kə́l/	to-morrow
/pərsoŋ/	the day after to-morrow

The meaning of /kə́l/ or /pərsoŋ/ is normally clear from the tense of the verb, e.g.

/kə́l ki vār si ?/	What day was it yesterday ?
/kə́l ki vār hovega ?/	What day will it be to-morrow ?

12.5 /apṇa/, *own*, is a reflexive possessive pronoun which refers to the subject of the sentence, e.g.

/ó apṇi kytāb pə́ṛ rýa si./	He was reading his (own) book.

But

/ó ódi kytāb pə́ṛ rýa si./	He was reading his (some-one else's) book.

When the possessor is the same as the subject of the sentence /apṇa/ must be used, e.g.

/məyŋ apṇi kytāb pə́ṛ rýa saŋ./   I was reading my book.

/məyŋ meri kytāb pə́r rýa saŋ/ would be bad Punjabi.
/məyŋ meri apṇi kytāb pə́ṛ rýa saŋ/ would mean ' I was reading *my own* book '.

12.6 /koi/ means *someone* and /kẃj/ *something*, e.g.

/koi édər a rýa e./	Someone is coming here.
/hwṇ məyŋ kẃj kha sakda vaŋ./	Now I can eat something.

In questions /koi/ and /kẃj/ translate the English *anyone* and *anything*, e.g.

/koi édər á rýa e ?/	Is anyone coming here ?
/twsiŋ kẃj khaoge ?/	Will you eat anything ?

62 PUNJABI

In negative sentences, they are equivalent to *no one* and *nothing*, e.g.

| /koi édər nə́iŋ əwnda./ | No one comes here. |
| /óthe kẃj nə́iŋ si./ | There was nothing there. |

12.7 /kẃj/ is not declined, but the oblique of /koi/ is /kyse/. This must not be confused with /kys/, the oblique of /kəwŋ/, *who* ? (7.6), e.g.

| /é kys da kə̀r e ?/ | Whose house is this ? |
| /é kyse da kə̀r nə́iŋ e./ | This isn't anyone's house. |

Vocabulary

/dost/ M.	friend	/vekh-/	see
/dyn/ M.	day	/rək(k)h-/	put
/var/ M.	day of week	/ho-/	be
/bẃd(var)/ M.	Wednesday	/lya-/	bring
		/koi/	someone
/virvar/ M.	Thursday	/kẃj/	something
/ṣwkkərvar/ M.	Friday	/apŋa/	' own '
		/kə́l/	yesterday, to-morrow
/ṣənychər-(var)/ M.	Saturday	/pərsoŋ/	day before yesterday, day after to-morrow
/dẃd(d)/ M.	milk		
/cini/ F.	sugar		
/vəẃṭi/ F.	wife		
/əgla/	next	/taiŋ/	until
/pychla/	last		

Exercises

12A Put into the Future :

(1) /kəl kəmra kḥali si./ (2) /é dẃd cə̀nga nə́iŋ./ (3) /ó éthe khaṇa khande ne./ (4) /əsiŋ ləŋḍən yc rə́ynde aŋ./ (5) /məyŋ bəs naḷ əwnda saŋ./ (6) /ó bəkəs pèj rýa si./

12B Translate into English :

(1) /óda dost əgle virvar nuŋ avega./ (2) /məyŋ kafi yc dẃd kəde nə́iŋ ṗinda./ (3) /ónaŋ di tì bəzār toŋ roṭi te cini lyavegi./ (4) /meri vəẃṭi pychle ṣənychər nuŋ óthoŋ a rə́i si./ (5) /pərsoŋ ó bənde apŋe bəccyaŋ de naḷ é kəm kərənge./ (6) /óthe məyŋ kẃj nə́iŋ saŋ vekh səkdi./ (7) /pərsoŋ məṅgəḷvar hovega./ (8) /tera dost apŋe pyo naḷoŋ ləmma e./ (9) /mwŋḍa dẃd kẏtthe rəkh səkega ?/ (10) /əsiŋ kevəl pərsoŋ taiŋ apŋe ṗài de kə̀r yc révaṅgiaŋ./ (11) /ó kyse da əkhbār pə́ṛ rẏa si./ (12) /kevəl do bənde te tyn mwŋḍe hovəŋge./

12C Translate into Punjabi :

(1) She will get sugar from her father's shop. (2) The teacher will come next Thursday afternoon. (3) Someone will bring bread the day after to-morrow. (4) Yesterday (it) was Saturday, and the day before yesterday (it) was Friday. (5) What day will it be to-morrow ? To-morrow it will be Monday. (6) In your brother's room I can see something on the table. (7) When will the girls go home ? (8) Someone was here last Wednesday. (9) He cannot do anything until to-morrow. (10) No one was reading yesterday's paper. (11) He won't drink milk. (12) His wife will certainly be a clever woman. (13) Now we shall be able to go to Lahore less.

Lesson 13

13.1 For the English verb *be*, Punjabi has both the auxiliary and the verb /ho-/, whose present participle is the irregular /hwnda/. The following tenses are therefore possible :

Present	/hwnda e/	/e/	is
Imperfect	/hwnda si/	/si/	was, used to be
Future		/hovega/	will be

The Present tense of /ho-/ is used only in statements of generally valid facts, *e.g.*

/həfte yc sət dyn hwnde ne./	There are seven days in a week.
/bəcce choţe hwnde ne./	Children are small.

Otherwise the auxiliary is used :

/pər é mwŋḍa ləmma e./	But this boy is tall.

13.2 There is no Punjabi verb equivalent to the English *have*. Instead, postpositions are used with the auxiliary verb or /ho-/ as follows :

(i) /da/ or the possessive pronouns, used with relatives :

/ódi kevəl yk pəy̆ŋ e./	He has only one sister. (Literally : ' There is only one sister of him.')

other human beings :

| /óthe mere ɖo ɖost sən./ | I had two friends there. |

parts of the body :

| /mwŋɖe da bəẇt vəɖɖa syr si./ | The boy had a very big head. |

immovable property :

| /óde pwttər de tyn kə̀r ne./ | His son has three houses. |

(ii) /koļ/, *beside*, used with movable property :

| /mere koļ yk kwrsi e./ | I have a chair. (Literally : ' Beside me is one chair.') |
| /mwŋɖe koļ kələm e./ | The boy has a pen. |

(iii) /nuŋ/, used with abstract nouns :

| /məynuŋ bəṛa şəwk si./ | I had a great desire. (Literally : ' To me was a great desire.') |

13.3   These constructions are also used in Punjabi where there is no *have* in English, *e.g.*

/sanuŋ wmēd e ky ó kə́l avega./	We hope that he will come to-morrow.
/ónuŋ pəta e ky twsiŋ ləŋɖən yc rəýnde o./	He knows that you live in London.
/mera k͟hyal e ky é gəļt e./	I think this is wrong.

The literal translations of these sentences are ' To us is hope that . . .', ' To him is a clue that . . .', ' My thought is that . . .'

Note that /ky/, *that*, is pronounced /kĕ/ : it is much less often omitted than *that* is in English.

13.4 /koi/ and /kẃj/ (*cf.* 12.6) are also used with nouns
as indefinite adjectives, meaning *some, any, etc., e.g.*

/óthe koi tiviŋ néiŋ si./	There was no woman there.
/mez te koi kytāb si./	On the table was a (' some ') book.
/mez te kẃj kytābaŋ sən./	On the table were some books.
/botəl yc kẃj dẃd si./	In the bottle was some milk.

/koi/ is generally used with singular nouns, /kẃj/ with
plural nouns and nouns which can have no plural, like
/dẃd/, /paṇi/, *etc.*

13.5 The distinction between adjectives and nouns is
less marked in Punjabi than in English. Many adjectives
can be used as nouns, *e.g.*

/bẃḍḍa nəwkər kəm kər rýa si./	The old servant was working.
/bẃḍḍa əkhbār péṛ rýa e./	The old man is reading the paper.

When ' red ' adjectives are used as nouns, they are
declined as nouns, *e.g.*

/é gərīb mwṇḍe di kytāb e./	This is the poor boy's book.
/é gərībaŋ di zymīŋ e./	This is the poor people's land.

Vocabulary

/nəwkər/ M.	servant	/bẃḍḍa/	old (of people)
/syr/ M.	head	/gərīb/	poor
/həfta/ M.	week	/tija/	third
/alu/ M.	potato	/cəwtha/	fourth
/şəwk/ M.	desire	/kynnaŋ/	how much,
/khyal/ M.	thought		how many
/pəta/ M.	' clue ', address	/kəi/	several, many
		/koḷ/	beside
/wmēd/ F.	hope	/heṭh/	under
/nədi/ F.	river	/ky/	that

/pəñj/	five	/sət(t)/	seven
/che/	six	/pəkā-/	cook

Exercises

13A Translate into Punjabi :

(1) We have two brothers. (2) They have five boxes.
(3) You have two shops. (4) The girl had this great hope.
(5) The old man has some land. (6) I had a black book.

13B Translate into English :

(1) /mera khyal e ky saḍa əgla səbək bəẃt əwkha hovega./
(2) /kə́l məyŋ tẃaḍe ləi alu pəkāvaṅgi./ (3) /tere koḷ
kynneŋ kələm ne ?/ (4) /mere koḷ koi kələm nə́iŋ,
kevəl é pwrāṇi cyṭṭhi e./ (5) /é alu gərīb de choṭe bəcce
de syr naḷoŋ vəḍḍa e./ (6) /ó deṣ diaŋ nədiaŋ bəẃt
vəḍḍiaŋ nə́iŋ hwndiaŋ./ (7) /məynuŋ pəta e ky ónaŋ
da koi nəwkər nə́iŋ si./ (8) /saḍe vəḍḍe pài da dost mez
heṭh kəm kər rýa e./ (9) /həfte da cəwtha dyn bẃdvar
hwnda e./ (10) /é bẃḍḍe nuŋ koi ṣəwk kəde nə́iŋ
hovega./ (11) /syaṇe mwnḍe de syr yc kəi khyal sən./
(12) /bẃḍḍe sykh di tì apṇa pəta lykh rə́i si./

13C Translate into Punjabi :

(1) How many days are there in a week ? (2) Is Sunday
or Monday the first day of the week ? (3) I think that
Sunday is the first day of the week. (4) Have you any
tea ? (5) Many men used to live in this beautiful house.
(6) Nowadays the old man is less poor : he has six
servants. (7) He was putting his letter under your
boxes. (8) The next bus will come to the village the day
after to-morrow in the morning. (9) No one can teach
these bad boys anything. (10) I hope that no one will
eat those new potatoes. (11) Beside that river my
father's old servant had a house. (12) He always comes
home on Friday but I know he won't be able to come
next week.

Lesson 14

14.1 The Imperative singular is the same as the root of the verb. In the plural /-o/ is added, *e.g.*

S. /a/ P. /ao/ come ! come in !

Some verbs have slightly irregular forms in the plural, similar to those in the Future (12.1) :

S. /ləẏ/ take ! /dé/ give ! /rəkh/ put ! /já/ go !
P. /ləẃ/ /dẏo/ /rəkkho/ /jáo/

Note that many short roots ending in a vowel have high tone in the Imperative : thus, /kha-/ has /khá/ and /kháo/.

14.2 The negative of the Imperative is formed by putting /na/, *not* (never /nə́iŋ/) before the verb, *e.g.*

/kəl na jáo./ Don't go to-morrow.

14.3 There is also a Future Imperative, implying that the action is not to be performed immediately, and thus rather politer than the ordinary Imperative. The singular adds /-iŋ/ to the root, and the plural /-yo/, *e.g.*

S. /rəkkhiŋ/ P. /rəkkhyo/ put ! (but not immediately)

This Future Imperative is not very commonly used. The most usual way of expressing a polite request is to use the plural of the simple Imperative, often with the honorific /ji/ (2.3) put after the verb, *e.g.*

> /ao ji !/   Please come in !

14.4 In addressing or calling to people, the vocative case may be used, although it is less commonly used by educated people. The vocative in the three declensions is formed as follows :

S. Dir.	/mwnḍa/	/pài/	/kwṛi/
Voc.	/mwnḍya/	/pàia/	/kwṛie/
P. Dir.	/mwnḍe/	/pài/	/kwṛiaŋ/
Voc.	/mwnḍyo/	/pàio/	/kwṛio/

It will be seen that masculine nouns add /-a/ and feminine nouns /-e/ in the singular, while all nouns add /-o/ in the plural.

‘ Black ’ adjectives are in the oblique case before nouns in the vocative, *e.g.*

> /pyare dosto/   dear friends !

A particle like /oe/, *oh* ! may be put before a noun in the vocative.

14.5 When a pronoun is the direct object of a verb it must be in the /-nuŋ/ form, *e.g.*

/énuŋ éthe na rakkho ji !/	Please don't put this here !
/məyŋ təynuŋ pəṛàvaṅga./	I will teach you.
/əsiŋ ónaŋ nuŋ kə́l lyavaṅge./	We'll bring them to-morrow.

14.6 With some verbs the direct object always has /nuŋ/, whether or not it is a pronoun, *e.g.*

/əsiŋ wstād nuŋ pwchdiaŋ saŋ./	We used to ask the teacher.
/ó mwnḍe nuŋ óthe wḍīk rýa e./	He's waiting for the boy there.
/meri tì nuŋ mylo !/	Meet my daughter !

Other verbs only have a direct object with /nuŋ/ if
that object is definite, *e.g.*

/ó nili kytāb nuŋ mez te   Put the (' that ') blue book
  rakkho !/   on the table !

But

/koi kytāb mez te rakkho !/   Put some book on the
                                          table !

14.7 It is not possible to give a set of simple rules which
will determine in all cases whether or not the direct
object should have /nuŋ/. Where there is both a direct
and an indirect object, only the latter can have /nuŋ/,
with the basic meaning of *to*, *e.g.*

/zəra məynuŋ ó lyfāfa dýo !/   Just give me that envelope !
/ó sanuŋ apɳa pəta zərūr   She will certainly send us
  pèjegi./   her address.

14.8 Notice these important uses of the word /kərke/ :

 (i) After nouns and pronouns it means *because of*, *e.g.*

    /es kərke/   because of this, therefore, so
    /míŋ kərke/   because of the rain

(ii) Used after some adjectives, it forms adverbs, *e.g.*

    /am/ general   /am kərke/ generally

Vocabulary

/zymīndar/ M.	farmer	/syaḷ/ M.	winter
/khet/ M.	field	/gərmiaŋ/ F. (Pl.)	summer
/rwk(k)h/ M.	tree	/tẁp(p)/ F.	sunshine
/pəttər/ M.	leaf	/bərf/ F.	snow, ice
/véra/ M.	year	/pyara/	dear, nice
/mèina/ M.	month	/kḥwṣ/	happy
/míŋ/ M.	rain	/bəmār/	ill

/am/	general	/baraŋ/	twelve
/khas/	special	/saf/	clean (*adj.*)
/pəy-/	fall	/saf kər-/	clean (*verb*)
/pwc(c)h-/	ask	/həra/	green
/wɖīk-/	wait for	/nila/	blue
/myl-/	meet	/kərke/	because of,
/ət(ʈ)h/	eight		' -ly '
/nəwŋ/	nine	/vəje/	o'clock
/dəs/	ten	/zəra/	just
/yaraŋ/	eleven		

Exercises

14A Translate into Punjabi, using singular and plural forms :

(1) Eat something !   (2) Meet the farmer !   (3) Have a cigarette !   (4) Just ask them !   (5) Go at ten o'clock !   (6) Take this paper !

14B Translate into English :

(1) /éthe gərmiaŋ vyc míŋ kə̀ʈ pəynda e./   (2) /əsiŋ tẁanuŋ ó vəɖɖe rwkh de heʈh wdīkange./   (3) /oe mwŋɖya, es kəmre nuŋ saf kəriŋ !/   (4) /vére de duje mə̀ine vyc car həfte hwnde ne./   (5) /saɖa pyara dost bəmār e : es kərke əsiŋ əgle mə̀ine nə́iŋ avange./   (6) /é sare khet ó gərīb zymīndar de nə́iŋ ho səkde./   (7) /am kərke bərf syaḷ yc və́d pəyndi e./   (8) /bənda kwɽi nuŋ yaraŋ vəje taiŋ sʈeʂən de neɽe wɖīk rýa si./   (9) /tẁp yc kəwŋ əngrēz khwʂ nə́iŋ hwnda ?/   (10) /ó khet yc dəs sykh apŋe hətthaŋ naḷ kəm kər rə́e sən./   (11) /é meri sə́b toŋ pyari tì e : zəra ónuŋ mylo ji !/   (12) /ó bəɽi khas kytāb e : ónuŋ kevəl syaŋiaŋ tiviaŋ pə́ɽ səkdiaŋ ne./

14C Translate into Punjabi :

(1) The leaves of that old tree are green in summer, but not in winter.   (2) The fourth field belongs to the old

farmer. (3) I hope that snow won't fall here next year.
(4) I don't know : that is why (' therefore ') I am
asking your mother. (5) Take that big blue book, but
don't write anything in it. (6) Nowadays he drinks less
coffee, especially at night. (7) I'll wait for you outside
until nine o'clock. (8) In this country there is more
sunshine in winter ; in the summer there is less because
of the rain (use /pəy-/). (9) He can put it in my room.
(10) I'll bring some sugar specially for your friend.
(11) These eight glasses are yours : please clean them
quickly. (12) I think that the girls will come at seven
o'clock on Saturday evening.

Lesson 15

15.1 The past participle (masculine singular) is formed by adding to the root the ending /-ya/ (pronounced /-ĕa/). This may be declined for gender and number as follows :

M.S.	(/a-/)	/aya/	come	(/vekh-/)	/vekhya/	seen
M.P.		/ae/			/vekhe/	
F.S.		/ai/			/vekhi/	
F.P.		/aiaŋ/			/vekhiaŋ/	

The declension is the same as for a ' black ' adjective, except that the masculine singular ends in /-ya/ instead of /-a/.

15.2 Some common verbs have irregular past participles, *e.g.*

M.S.	(/ja-/)	/gya/	gone	(/səwŋ-/)	/swtta/	slept
M.P.		/gəe/			/swtte/	
F.S.		/gəi/			/swtti/	
F.P.		/gəiaŋ/			/swttiaŋ/	

Like /gya/ are declined /lya/, /pya/ and /rýa/, the past participles of /ləy-/, /pəy-/ and /rəý-/.

15.3 Intransitive verbs form their Past tense simply with the past participle, which agrees with the subject in gender and number, *e.g.*

/ó kəl ləẃr gya./	He went to Lahore yesterday.
/kwṛi sət vəje taiŋ swtti./	The girl slept till 7 o'clock.

A very few transitive verbs (*i.e.* verbs which can have
a direct object) form their Past in the same way. The
most important of these are :

/bol-/	speak	/lya-/	bring
/myl-/	meet	/pẁl ja-/	forget
/sə́mj-/	understand		

/ó sanuŋ dəftər lyae./   They brought us to the office.
/tẁaḍi vəẃṭi pẁl gəi./   Your wife forgot.

Note that /məyŋ sə́mjya/ usually means *I understand*.

All other transitive verbs have a special construction
in the Past tense, which is explained in Lesson 17.

15.4 The negative of the Past is formed by putting
/nə́iŋ/ or /na/ before the verb, *e.g.*

/twsiŋ kyoŋ na ae ?/   Why didn't you come ?
/əsiŋ nə́iŋ sə́mje./   We don't (didn't) understand.

15.5 While the past auxiliary refers simply to a state in
the past, /hoya/, the Past of /ho-/, is used to indicate a
process, *e.g.*

/ó k̲h̲wṣ si./   He was happy.
/ó khwṣ hoya./   He was happy (when such-and-such
                          happened).

15.6 It has been remarked (11.3) that many postpositions may optionally have /de/ before them. There
is another class of postpositions which is normally
preceded by /toŋ/ : this /toŋ/ is seldom omitted. The
most important of these are :

/pəýlaŋ/	before	/bár/	outside
/bad/	after	/chwṭ/	besides
/bynāŋ/	without		

e.g. /dwpəýr toŋ pəýlaŋ/   before noon
     /ṣəýr toŋ bár/   outside the city

/bynāŋ/ is exceptional in that it may precede the noun, e.g.

/dẃd toŋ bynāŋ/ or /bynāŋ dẃd toŋ/ without milk

15.7 /hor/ means (an)other, while /duja/ means the other (or second), e.g.

| /hwŋ məyŋ hor kytāb lyavaṅga./ | Now I'll bring another book. |
| /hwŋ məyŋ duji kytāb lyavaṅga./ | Now I'll bring the other book. |

/hor koi/ means some(one) else, and /hor kẃj/, some(thing) else.

15.8 The oblique plural of /hor/ and /sớb/, when these are used as pronouns, are /hornaŋ/ and /sớbnaŋ/. /lokiŋ/, people, is treated as a masculine plural, and its oblique is /lokáŋ/.

Vocabulary

/lokiŋ/ M. Pl.	people	/wṭ(ṭ)h-/	rise, get up
		/pẁl ja-/	forget
/kwtta/ M.	dog	/sớmj-/	understand
/məkkhən/ M.	butter	/ho ja-/	become
		/jap-/	seem
/búa/ M.	door	/mar-/	hit, beat :
/bari/ F.	window		shut (door, window)
/dwpəýr/ F.	noon, midday	/lá-/	open (door, window)
/ớddi rat/ F.	midnight		
/təgɾa/	strong, fit	/pəýlaŋ/	before
/gənda/	dirty	/bad/	after
/hor/	other, else	/chwṭ/	besides
/fer/	again, then	/bynāŋ/	without
/səwŋ-/ (p.p. /swtta/)	sleep		

Exercises

15A Translate into Punjabi :

(1) Besides him. (2) Beside him. (3) Inside the house.
(4) Outside the house. (5) Before evening. (6) Without
any other girl.

15B Translate into English :

(1) /əsiŋ əytvar ṣam nuŋ ṫwaɖe dost de kə̀r gəe./ (2) /ó
kyoŋ pẉl gəiaŋ ?/ (3) /saɖi ti kə́l sət vəje toŋ pəýlaŋ
wṭṭhi./ (4) /ó bari lá rẏa e, te fer búa marega./ (5) /zymīn-
dar apṇe kwttyaŋ naḷ aya./ (6) /míŋ toŋ bad saɖe kə̀r
diaŋ sə́b bariaŋ bəẇt gəndiaŋ ho gəiaŋ./ (7) /é gəl toŋ chwṭ
sə́b ṭhik japda e./ (8) /bynāŋ ónaŋ lokaŋ toŋ twsiŋ óthe
kyoŋ rə́e ?/ (9) /óda kwtta roz dwpəẏr taiŋ səwnda e./
(10) /məyŋ nə́iŋ sə́mji : tẇaɖi gəl bəɽi əwkhi e./ (11)
/tiviŋ ónaŋ ləi məkkhəŋ te cini lyai./ (12) /mwŋɖa
ə́ddi rat toŋ bad ký́ddər ja səkya ?/

15C Translate into Punjabi :

(1) The girls came home late last night, but they got
up early this morning. (2) The old man seemed very
strong, but then he became ill. (3) Clever people will
never be able to understand this. (4) Shut the window,
and don't open the door ! (5) The farmer had one other
field outside the village. (6) I hope that the teacher
will beat that bad boy. (7) She used to go to the office
at 8 o'clock, but yesterday she went after 9 o'clock.
(8) I think someone else slept in your room on Thursday
night. (9) The river water seemed very dirty, so he
didn't go there. (10) My father's servant forgot everything else. (11) Snow fell this morning, so the old
woman couldn't go out of her house. (12) Why didn't
your Sikh friends speak Punjabi with me ?

Lesson 16

16.1 The Perfect tense of intransitive verbs is formed by using the past participle with the present auxiliary, *e.g.*

/ó bár gya e./   He has gone out.

In the negative, the auxiliary may be omitted, as in the Present, *e.g.*

/ó bár néiŋ gya./   He hasn't gone out. (Or ' He didn't go out.')

16.2 The Pluperfect tense of intransitive verbs is formed by using the past participle with the past auxiliary. This tense has very frequently the sense of a simple English past, *e.g.*

/ó bár gya si./   He went out. (Or ' He had gone out.')

In the negative, the auxiliary usually precedes the verb, as in the Imperfect, *e.g.*

/ó bár néiŋ si gya./ He didn't go out. (Or ' He hadn't gone out.')

16.3 The Future Perfect tense of intransitive verbs is formed by using the past participle with the Future of /ho-/, *e.g.*

/ó bár gya hovega./ He will have gone out.

In the negative, /néiŋ/ is put before the participle.

16.4 The Infinitive is formed by adding /-ṇa/ to the
root :

| /ja-/ | /jaṇa/ | to go |
| /vekh-/ | /vekhṇa/ | to see |

(i) Roots in /-r/ and /-ṛ/ add /-na/ (cf. 12.1), as do those
in /-ṇ/ :

| /kər-/ | /kərna/ | to do |
| /swṇ-/ | /swṇna/ | to hear, listen |

(ii) Roots in double consonants have a single one before
the ending (cf. 12.3) :

| /rək(k)h-/ | /rəkhṇa/ | to put |

(iii) All roots in /-a/, except /ja-/ and /kha-/, change this
to /-əw/ before the infinitive ending (cf. 5.2) :

| /pəṛà-/ | /pəṛəẁṇa/ | to teach |
| /lya-/ | /lyəwṇa/ | to bring |

16.5 The Infinitive may be used as a noun, e.g.

| /cùth bolṇa pəÿṛa e./ | It is wrong to lie. |
| /nəẁṇa cənga e./ | It is good to wash. |

16.6 It may also be used as a polite imperative. It is
especially common in public notices and official instruc-
tions. For the negative, /na/ is used, e.g.

/éthe səmān na rəkhṇa !/   Don't put luggage here !

16.7 The Infinitive is used with the verbs /cá-/, want,
and /ṣwru kər-/, begin, e.g.

| /ó kél əwṇa cəẁnde ne./ | They want to come to-morrow. |
| /ó cyṭṭhi lykhṇi kədoṇ ṣwru kərega ?/ | When will he begin to write the letter ? |

The Infinitive declines for gender and number like
a ' black ' adjective, and *must* always agree with its
object, as in the second sentence above.

16.8 Notice these constructions with /nuŋ/ and /a-/ :

/ónuŋ pəñjābi néiŋ əwnda./ He doesn't know Punjabi.
(Literally : ' Punjabi
doesn't come to him.')

/sari kytāb məynuŋ yad si./ I remembered the whole
book. (Literally : ' The
whole book came to me
in memory.')

/sanuŋ koi gəl néiŋ si sə́mj We didn't understand
əwndi./ anything. (Literally :
' No thing was coming to
us in understanding.')

The same construction is used with /lə́b(b)-/, *get, find* :

/ónuŋ təyksi néiŋ lə́bbi./ He didn't get a taxi.

/myl-/ may be used like /lə́b(b)-/ in this way, with
the same meaning. When /myl-/ means *meet*, its construction is quite normal (*cf.* 14.6, 15.3).

16.9 The word /təràŋ/, *way, manner*, is very commonly
used after pronouns and adjectives to form adverbs, *e.g.*

/es təràŋ/ in this way, /kys təràŋ/ in which way ?
thus how ?

/cəngi təràŋ/ in a good
way, well

Vocabulary

/naŋ/ M. name /tòbi/ M. washerman
/səmān/ M. luggage /gwsəlkhana/ bathroom
/kəpṛa/ M. cloth M.

/əsmān/ M.	sky	/həvāi jàz/ F.	aeroplane
/pəñchi/ M.	bird	/cəwṛa/	broad, wide
/səṛək/ F.	road, street	/səcca/	true
/cá-/	want, wish	/vaṅg/	like
/şwru kər-/	begin	/bylkwl/	quite
/twr-/	go (along), walk	/əcəɲcet/	suddenly
/tò-/	wash (clothes, *etc.*)	/léb(b)-/ (p.p. /lébba/)	get, find (*cf.* 16.8)
/nà-/ (p.p. /nàta/)	wash (one-self), bathe	/myl-/	get, find (*cf.* 16.8)
/wḍ(ḍ)-/	fly	/cùth bol-/	tell a lie, tell lies, lie
/ɣad a-/	remember (*cf.* 16.8)	/mən(n)-/	believe
/sə́mj a-/	understand (*cf.* 16.8)	/swn-/	hear, listen to
/təràṇ/ F.	way, manner	/syk(k)h-/	learn

Exercises

16A Translate into English :

(1) /ó tiviṇ nuṇ khaṇa pəkəw̄ṇa né̇iṇ əwṇda./ (2) /éthe naṇ te pəta lykhṇa./ (3) /mwṇḍa duje gwsəlkhane yc nàta hovega./ (4) /ó bylkwl səcci gəl e./ (5) /əcəɲcet sare pəñchi əsmān yc wḍṇa şwru kərde ne./ (6) /məyṇ reḍyo kəde né̇iṇ swṇna cəẃnda vaṇ : os te səda cùth bolde ne./ (7) /tẁaḍa dost həvāi jàz naḷ kyoṇ né̇iṇ si aya ?/ (8) /é sóni kytāb ónaṇ nuṇ kys təràṇ myḷi ?/ (9) /ó syaṇi kwṛi əṅgrēzi cəṅgi təràṇ sykhṇi cəẃnda si./ (10) /kə́l meri vəẃti kəpṛe tòṇe şwru kəregi./ (11) /es təràṇ japda e ky ónaṇ nuṇ apṇe pài da pəta ɣad né̇iṇ si aya./ (12) /zəra meri gəl swṇo : saḍa pwrāṇa wstād ləṇḍən gya e./ (13) /ónuṇ bəs né̇iṇ si myḷi : es kərke ó pyṇḍ di cəwṛi səṛək te twr rýa si./ (14) /ó saḍe naḷ ódər jaṇa cəẃnda si, pər əcəɲcet ó bəmār pya./ (15) /kwṛi

ódər zərūr gəi si, pər zymīndar da pəta ónuŋ nə́iŋ lə́ḅḅa: es kərke ónuŋ nə́iŋ si myḷi./

16B Translate into Punjabi :

(1) The aeroplane was flying in the blue sky like a bird. (2) I want to believe you, but I think that you are lying (use /tuŋ/). (3) It is quite true that the old man never went there. (4) Where did you get this beautiful cloth from ? (5) I found it in the old market yesterday morning. (6) My little daughter is beginning to wash clothes like a washerman. (7) The bathroom has got very dirty : clean it this afternoon. (8) I hope that he has remembered the name of the street now. (9) It is difficult to wash without water. (10) Which college do the cleverest boys want to study in ? (11) The poor man didn't understand anything in the newspaper. (12) It is wrong to speak in this way, but the boy doesn't know English. (13) How will they begin to work without it ? (14) We don't know, but we want to ask your sister. (15) It has become very difficult to put any luggage in the little room.

Lesson 17

17.1 In the tenses formed with the past participle (Past, Perfect, Pluperfect and Future Perfect), transitive verbs other than those mentioned in 15.3 have a special construction. The logical subject is put into the oblique case and takes the postposition /ne/, *by*. The participle agrees in gender and number with the object, and the verb is in the third person, *e.g.*

/tòbi ne kəpṛe tòe./	The washerman washed the clothes. (' By the washerman the clothes were washed.')
/mwnḍe ne pəñjābi sykkhi e./	The boy has learnt Punjabi.
/ónaŋ ne apṇa kèr bəṇāya si./	They had built their own house.
/ḍakṭər ne é fylmaŋ vekhiaŋ hoŋgiaŋ./	The doctor will have seen these films.

Note that /ne/, like /da/, /nuŋ/ and /toŋ/, always comes immediately after the noun.

17.2 When the object has /nuŋ/, the verb is always third person masculine singular, *e.g.*

/óne dujiaŋ kytābaŋ nuŋ mez te rəkkhya./	He put the other books on the table.

But

/óne kẃj kytābaŋ mez te   He put some books on the
rəkkhiaŋ./   table.

Similarly, when there is no object, the verb will
always be third person masculine singular, *e.g.*

/óne vekhya si ?/   Did he see ?

17.3 The four personal pronouns never take /ne/, a
special agent case being used instead :

/məyŋ/	/məyŋ/	by me
/tuŋ/	/tuŋ/	by you
/əsiŋ/	/əsaŋ/	by us
/twsiŋ/	/twsaŋ/	by you

The two singular pronouns have the same form in the
agent case as in the direct case, but the construction is
the same, *e.g.*

/məyŋ tyn sóṇiaŋ kwṛiaŋ   I saw three beautiful
vekhiaŋ./   girls.
/twsaŋ saḍa kwtta vekhya e ?/ Have you seen our dog ?

Note that /ó/ and /é/ do take /ne/.

17.4 The Infinitive is used in a number of constructions
implying advisability or necessity :

(i) Subject with /nuŋ/, Infinitive followed by /cáida e/,
it is necessary. This gives the sense of the English *ought
to, e.g.*

/məynuŋ kél jaṇa cáida e./   I ought to go to-morrow.
                             (Literally : ' To go
                             to-morrow is necessary to
                             me.')

/məynuŋ kél jaṇa cáida si./   I ought to have gone
                             yesterday.

/ónuŋ əŋgrēzi sykhṇi   He ought to learn English.
cáidi e./

When there is no Infinitive, /cáida e/ can be translated
as *want*, e.g.

/sanuŋ roṭi cáidi e./   We want some bread.

(ii) Subject with /nuŋ/, Infinitive followed by /pəy-/,
fall, *lie*. This gives the sense of the English *have to*, e.g.

/kə́l sanuŋ jaṇa pəvega./   We shall have to go to-morrow.
/ónaŋ nuŋ mwṛna pya./   They had to come back.

(iii) Subject with /ne/ (or in agent case), Infinitive
followed by auxiliary or /ho-/. This also gives the sense
of the English *have to* or *must*, but is weaker in its
suggestion of duty or obligation than (ii), e.g.

/kwṛi ne jaṇa e./   The girl has to go (must go).
/məyŋ cyṭṭhi lykhṇi e./   I must write a letter.

17.5 Nouns in the oblique singular followed by the
postposition /toŋ/ may instead be put into the ablative
singular, which is formed as follows :

Dir. S.	/mwnḍa/	/ṣəýr/	/həṭṭi/
Abl. S.	/mwnḍyoŋ/	/ṣəýroŋ/	/həṭṭioŋ/

e.g.   /ṣəýr toŋ bár/ or /ṣəýroŋ bár/   outside the city

With most nouns, the oblique form with /toŋ/ is more
common than the ablative. There is no ablative plural.

17.6 Similarly, many postpositions may take this
ablative ending /-oŋ/, e.g.

/əndər/   inside   /əndroŋ/   from inside
/kwṛi skul əndroŋ nykli./ The girl came out from
                           (inside) the school.

/wtte/   on   /wttoŋ/   from on
/óne əkhbār mez wttoŋ lya./ He took the book from
                            (on) the table.

/(v)yc/   in   /(vyc)coŋ/   from in, among

/énaŋ kəpɽyaŋ vyccoŋ məyŋ   I won't take any of (from
  koi nə́iŋ ləvaṅga./   among) these clothes.

Sometimes virtually no difference is made to the
meaning of a postposition by the addition of the /-oŋ/,
e.g.

/pəýlaŋ/	or	/pəýloŋ/	before
/pyccher/	or	/pycchoŋ/	after
compare /kəd/	or	/kədoŋ/	when ?

17.7 The particle /vi/, *too, also, even;* always follows the
word which it emphasizes. It can never come first in
a sentence, *e.g.*

/kwɽiaŋ vi aiaŋ./   The girls came too. (Even the girls
                        came.)

/məyŋ vi vekhya./   I saw too. (Even I saw.)

17.8 The particle /hi/ (sometimes colloquially /i/)
similarly follows the word which it emphasizes. It may
sometimes be translated as *indeed,* but most often
corresponds to a heavy stress in English, *e.g.*

  /kwɽiaŋ hi aiaŋ./   The *girls* came.
  /məyŋ hi vekhya./   *I* saw.

Note that in Punjabi the voice rises on words or
phrases followed by /vi/ or /hi/, instead of the heavy
stress used in English, *e.g.*

  /kwɽiaŋ hi/
/kə́l/   The *girls* came yesterday.
            /aiaŋ./
/kə́l hi/
      /kwɽiaŋ/   *Yesterday* the girls came.
            /aiaŋ./

Vocabulary

/şəb(ə)d/ M.	word	/dəs(s)-/	tell
/pəyse/ M.Pl.	money	/swṇā-/	tell (story)
/thəyli/ F.	bag, purse	/bəṇā-/	make, build
/kàṇi/ F.	story	/nyk(ə)l-/	go out
/fyl(ə)m/ F.	film	/mwṛ-/	return,
/boli/ F.	language		come back,
/əmīr/	rich		go back
/səwkha/	easy	/thoṛa/	little, few
/myṭṭha/	sweet	/bəẃt sara/	many, a lot
/kər-/ (p.p.	do		of
/kita/)		/hor/	more
/kha-/ (p.p.	eat	/əje/	still, yet
/kháda/)		/vi/	too, also,
/pi-/ (p.p.	drink		even
/pita/)		/hi/, /i/	' indeed '
/de-/ (p.p.	give	/vyccoṇ/, /coṇ/	from in,
/dytta/)			among : of
/ləy-/ (p.p.	take	/sámṇe/	in front of
/lya/)		/pycche/	after,
/kəẃ-/ (p.p.	say		behind
/kẃa/)			

Exercises

17A Put into the Past :

(1) /məyṇ mwṇḍa vekhda vaṇ./   (2) /məyṇ mwṇḍa vekh
səkda vaṇ./   (3) /tòbi kəpṛe ləynda e./   (4) /tòbi kəpṛe
lyəwnda e./   (5) /twsiṇ kafi pinde o P/   (6) /ó məynuṇ
pəyse dendi e./   (7) /əsiṇ é mez nuṇ bəṇəw̄ndiaṇ aṇ./
(8) /bənda khaṇa khanda e./   (9) /mwṇḍa kwṛi nuṇ
kəẃnda e./   (10) /mwṇḍa pəñjābi bolda e./   (11) /ó
əṅgrēzi pəṛəẃnde ne./   (12) /tuṇ mere dost nuṇ mylda eṇ./

17B Translate into English :

(1) /əmīr ne tẁanuṇ kynneṇ pəyse dytte sən P/   (2) /óne
əje vi é kəm nə́iṇ kita./   (3) /twsaṇ apṇi thəyli kẃtthe

rəkkhi ?/ (4) /məyŋ búe de sámŋe hi ónaŋ nuŋ wḍīkna c./
(5) /əmīraŋ nuŋ pəyse nə́iŋ cáide./ (6) /mere nəwkər nuŋ
hor pəyse deŋe pəynge./ (7) /tiviŋ ne apŋiaŋ dostaŋ nuŋ
fyləm di sari hi kàŋi swŋāi hovegi./ (8) /ónaŋ ne búa
marya, pər hwŋ məyŋ bari ləẃŋi e./ (9) /fer wstād ne
mwŋḍe nuŋ hor bəẃt sare şəbəd dəsse./ (10) /óne kwrsi
bəŋəw̄ŋi şwru kər dytti./ (11) /əsaŋ ónaŋ diaŋ gəllaŋ
nə́iŋ mənniaŋ./ (12) /saḍe pyo ne həvāi jàz naḷ əwŋa
cáya, par ónuŋ pəyse nə́iŋ sən lə́bbe./

17C Translate into Punjabi :

(1) You ought to put all this money in your purse.
(2) I think that your language is much sweeter than
ours. (3) I had to learn Punjabi quickly, but now I know
(it) well. (4) Even the clever girl did not know, so they
all asked the teacher. (5) The old farmer gave us some
bread. (6) The boy has brought you more butter from
his village. (7) These clothes are *very* old. You ought
not to give them to the poor. (8) He told me that this
long story is quite true. (9) He became ill, but he still
taught the boys English. (10) He has taken a lot of
money out of my purse. (11) They began to speak their
own language. (12) She said that Punjabi is *much* easier
than English.

Lesson 18

18.1 For the Oblique Infinitive, the final /-a/ of the Infinitive is dropped :

Inf.	/jaṇa/	/vekhṇa/	/kərna/	/rəkhṇa/
Obl. Inf.	/jaṇ/	/vekhən/	/kərən/	/rəkkhən/

Note that /ə/ is inserted to help the pronunciation after consonant roots.

18.2 The Oblique Infinitive is used with /ləg(g)-/ in the sense of *begin to*, and /de-/ in the sense of *allow to*, e.g.

| /ó jaṇ ləgge./ | They began to go. |
| /ónaŋ ne sanuŋ jaŋ dytte./ | They allowed us to go. |

18.3 The Oblique Infinitive is naturally used before postpositions. The following examples illustrate some of its more important uses :

(i) With /nuŋ/, indicating purpose :

| /ó bari marən nuŋ wṭṭhya./ | He got up to close the window. |

With verbs of motion, like /ja-/, the /nuŋ/ may be omitted (*cf.* 9.3), *e.g.*

| /ó paṇi piŋ gya./ | He went to drink (some) water. |

(ii) With /ləi/, also indicating purpose :

| /ó pəyse kəmə̄w̄ŋ ləi kəm kər rýa si./ | He was working to earn money. |
| /əsaŋ ónaŋ nuŋ əwŋ ləi kýa./ | We told them to come. (Literally : ' We said to them for coming.') |

(iii) With /da/ :

/bənde nuŋ mwɽən di koi wmēd néiŋ si./	The man had no hope of returning.
/ónuŋ əṅgrēzi péɽən da şəwk si./	He wanted to study English, he enjoyed studying English.
/məyŋ cyţţhi lykhən di koşyş kiti./	I tried to write a letter.

(iv) With /kərke/ :

| /bəmār hoŋ kərke ó néiŋ aya./ | Because he was ill he didn't come. (Literally : ' Because of being ill . . .') |

The Oblique Infinitive is also used with other post-positions. Note that it makes no change for gender or number, unlike the ordinary Infinitive.

18.4   /ap/ is a reflexive pronoun, meaning *self*, *e.g.*

| /əsiŋ ap gəe./ | We went ourselves. |
| /mwŋḍa ap aya e./ | The boy has come himself. |

(i) The possessive form of /ap/ is /apŋa/, *own* (12.5). The masculine oblique singular /apŋe/ is also used with postpositions, like /mere/, /saḍe/, *etc.*

| /ónaŋ ne bylli nuŋ apŋe naḷ lya./ | They took the cat with them(selves). |

(ii) When /nuŋ/ follows /ap/, the usual form is /apŋe ap nuŋ/, e.g.

/ó apŋe ap nuŋ bəɾa admi   He thinks himself a great
səmjda e./   man.

/apŋe ap nuŋ/ may also mean by oneself, e.g.

/ó apŋe ap nuŋ ʈhik ho   He got better by himself,
gya./   it got right by itself.

(iii) /apo vyc/ means among ourselves, among them-selves, etc., e.g.

/twsiŋ apo vyc kyoŋ gəllaŋ   Why were you talking
kər róe səw ?/   among yourselves ?

18.5 When the idea of motion to a person is to be expressed, the postposition /kol/ is used, not /nuŋ/, e.g.

/məyŋ wstād kol gya./   I went to the teacher.

Similarly, the idea of from a person is expressed by /koloŋ/, the ablative form of /kol/ (17.6), e.g.

/óne mwŋɖe koloŋ kələm   He took a pen from the
lya./   boy.

18.6 In expressions like a pound of butter, a cup of tea, /da/ is not used :

/yk pəwŋɖ məkkhən/   a pound of butter
/yk pyala cá/   a cup of tea
but /cá da pyala/   a teacup

18.7 The names of the months are English loan-words, listed in the vocabulary. Dates are expressed by using the ordinal /pəýli/ for the first of the month, and the cardinals /do/, /tyn/, etc., for the other days, e.g.

/pəýli jwlāi nuŋ/   on the first of July
/des sətĕmbər nuŋ/   on the tenth of September

/pəýli/ is feminine because /tərīkh/, date, is also feminine.

18.8 /vari/ means *turn* or *time*, like the French *fois*, e.g.

/əsaŋ ónuŋ kynniŋ vari pwchṇa hovega ?/	How many times (how often) will we have to ask him ?
/məyŋ ó fyləm do vari vekhi e./	I have seen that film twice.
/hwṇ twàḍi vari e./	Now it is your turn.

Other uses of the English word *time* are covered by /vəkət/ or /veḷa/.

Vocabulary

/admi/ M.	man, person	/bəyṭh ja-/	sit down
/səẃra/ M.	father-in-law	/khlo-/ (p.p. /khlota/)	stand
/jwāi/ M.	son-in-law	/khlo ja-/	stand up
/pyala/ M.	cup	/kəmā-/	earn
/pəwnḍ/ M.	pound	/ləg(g)-/ (p.p. /ləgga/)	begin
/səs(s)/ F.	mother-in-law	/kéḍ(ḍ)-/	put out, pull out
/núŋ/ F.	daughter-in-law	/chəḍ(ḍ)-/	leave
/bylli/ F.	cat	/səmj-/	think, consider
/siṭ/ F.	seat	/koşyş kər-/	try
/tərikh/ F.	date	/gəllaŋ kər-/	talk
/vari/ F.	turn, time	/vyá kər-/	marry
/əg(g)/ F.	fire	/jəlā-/	light, make burn
/gərəm/	warm, hot		
/tyar/	ready	/koḷoŋ/	from (people)
/thəŋḍa/	cold		
/ap/	self	/vəl/	towards
/bəyṭh-/ (p.p. /bəyṭha/)	sit		

MONTHS

/jənvəri/ F.	January	/jwlāi/ F.	July
/fərvəri/ F.	February	/əgəst/ M.	August
/marəc/ M.	March	/sətɔ̄mbər/ M.	September
/əprəȳl/ M.	April	/əktūbər/ M.	October
/məi/ F.	May	/nəvɔ̄mbər/ M.	November
/jun/ M.	June	/dəsɔ̄mbər/ M.	December

Exercises

18A Translate into English :

(1) /meri səs ne məynuŋ wɖīkən ləi kẏa si./   (2) /məyŋ
apṇi tì naḷ ónuŋ vyá kərən dytta./   (3) /bənde ne əg
jələ̄wŋ di koṣys kiti, pər nə́iŋ jəlā səkya./   (4) /tiviŋ
bəythṇa cə́wndi si, pər ónuŋ siṭ nə́iŋ lə́bbi./   (5) /ó khlo
gya, te cá bəṇə̄wŋ ləgga./   (6) /twsəŋ kys tərīkh nuŋ
jaṇa e ?/   (7) /tẇaḍa dost nəwŋ dəsɔ̄mbər nuŋ əwŋ di
koṣyṣ kərega, pər ho səkda e ky bərf kərke ó nə́iŋ a
səkega./   (8) /twsiŋ zəra bəyth jao, te əsiŋ ap kəmra tyar
kəraṅge./   (9) /ódi maŋ te səs kyse hor tiviŋ naḷ gəllaŋ
kər rə́iaŋ sən./   (10) /ónaŋ ne hor pəyse kəmə̄wŋ ləi
bəṛiaŋ koṣyṣaŋ kitiaŋ./   (11) /gərəm ho jaŋ di wmēd naḷ
óne búa marya te fer əg de sámṇe hi bəyth gəi./   (12) /əsiŋ
nəwkər nuŋ do gylās dẇd lyəwn ləi kə́vaṅge./   (13) /ó admi
thoṛe pəyse kəmə̄wnde ne : es kərke lokiŋ ónaŋ nuŋ
gərīb sə́mjde ne./   (14) /bylli kèroŋ nykəlṇa nə́iŋ si
cə́wndi, pər əcəṇcet tẇaḍe pwttər ne ónuŋ kə́ḍḍya./   (15)
/sanuŋ ṭhəṇḍa dẇd cáida e, pər óne sanuŋ kevəl gərəm
paṇi piṇ dytta./

18B Translate into Punjabi :

(1) He began to talk to his son-in-law. (2) The girl tried
to come on 1st June. (3) After eating three pounds of
butter the little boy became ill. (4) I told him to sit
there, but he wanted to stand. (5) The boy hoped to
leave his book there. (6) After getting married, he met

his father-in-law (for) the first time. (7) The clever little girl got ready to go by herself. (8) That poor man wanted to leave his country, and tried to come to England. (9) He didn't allow his daughter to light the fire. (10) Besides that, he didn't take anything from us. (11) On 11th August, he had to go to the other village twice. (12) How many days are there in October ? (13) The man brought us a cup of tea himself. (14) They think themselves clever, but they told us that fire is cold and ice is hot. (15) His daughter-in-law tried to talk to the old man before asking him. (16) Because it was late, the farmer was walking quickly towards his fields.

Lesson 19

19.1 The conjunctive participle is formed by adding /ke/ to the root of the verb :

/ja-/	/ja ke/	having gone
/pwc(c)h-/	/pwch ke/	having asked

The conjunctive participle is indeclinable. It often corresponds to an English finite verb followed by *and, e.g.*

/ó cá pi ke cəla gya./ He drank the tea and went off. (Having drunk the tea, he went off.)

Sometimes the conjunctive participle is equivalent to an English adverb, *e.g.*

/ó həs ke bolya./ He spoke laughingly. (He laughed and spoke.)

19.2 Some conjunctive participles are idiomatically used in special ways :

(i) /rəl ke/, from /rəl-/, *meet*, usually means *together* :

/məyŋ ónaŋ naḷ rəl ke aya./ I came together with them.

(ii) /jaŋ ke/, from /jaŋ-/, *know*, means *knowingly, on purpose* :

/óne jaŋ ke kwtte nuŋ marya./ He hit the dog on purpose.

(iii) /chəd ke/, from /chəd(ḍ)-/, *leave*, in the phrase /es nuŋ choḍ ke/, *leaving this aside, apart from this.*

(iv) /kərke/, from /kər-/, *do* (see 14.8).

These participles may also be used in their original meanings, *e.g.*

/óne kəm kər ke fyləm vekhi./	He saw a film after work. (Having worked he saw a film.)

19.3 The verbal agent is formed by adding to the oblique infinitive the suffix /-vaḷa/, which is declined like a ' black ' adjective. The verbal agent has three main uses :

(i) As a verbal noun, like English words in *-er*, *e.g.*

/ó lykhəŋvaḷa e./	He is a writer.
/fyləm vekhəŋvaḷyaŋ ne hor pəyse nóiŋ sən dytte./	Those who were watching the film (' the film-lookers ') didn't pay any more money.

(ii) As an adjective with another noun, corresponding to an English relative clause :

/kòṛa kà khaŋvaḷa janvər hwnda e./	The horse is an animal which eats grass (a grass-eating animal).
/kəm kərənvaḷiaŋ kwṛiaŋ ne sanuŋ vekhya./	The girls who were working saw us.

(iii) As a sort of future participle, meaning *about to* :

/gəḍḍi ṭwrənvaḷi e./	The train is about to start.
/məyŋ janvaḷa saŋ./	I was about to go.

19.4 /-vaḷa/ may also be added to nouns in the oblique case, giving a sense of connexion or association, *e.g.*

/nilian əkkhan vaḷa/	a man with blue eyes
/kwtte vaḷi/	a woman with a dog
/mwnḍe vaḷi kàni/	a story with a boy in it, story about a boy

It may be added to adverbs with a similar sense :

| /bár vaḷa kénd/ | the outside wall |

19.5 /jýa/ may be used after adjectives, giving the sense of the English suffix *-ish*, *e.g.*

| /cyṭṭa jýa kagəz/ | whitish paper |

/jýa/ declines like /gya/ (15.2). In words like /kýo jýa/, *what sort of ?*, *etc.*, only the second part declines.

19.6 Note the following fractional numbers :

/édda/	half
/səva/	one and a quarter
/ḍéṛ/	one and a half
/ṭài/	two and a half

For other fractions, the following are used with a cardinal number :

/səva/	a quarter more than
/sáḍe/	a half more than
/pəwṇe/	a quarter less than

e.g.

| /səva tyn/ | $3\frac{1}{4}$ | /sáḍe dəs/ | $10\frac{1}{2}$ |
| /pəwṇe che/ | $5\frac{3}{4}$ | (*i.e.* six less a quarter) | |

Smaller fractions may be expressed with the word /hyssa/, *part* :

| /ónan da tija hyssa/ | a third (part) of them |

19.7 One of the most common uses of the fractional numbers is to express time, when used with /vəje/, o'clock :

/kynneŋ vəje ne ?/	What time is it ?
/səva vəja e./	It is 1.15.
/pəwɲe nəwŋ vəje./	8.45.
/sáḍe yaraŋ vəje./	11.30.

Note that fractional numbers up to /ḍéṭ/ are singular, others plural.

Vocabulary

/hyssa/ M.	part	/bənd kər-/	shut
/bag/ M.	garden	/məṅg-/	ask for, order
/kénd/ M.	wall	/həs(s)-/	laugh
/kagəz/ M.	paper	/ro-/	cry
/kòṛa/ M.	horse	/jaɲ-/	know
/janvər/ M.	animal	(p.p.	
/rwpya/ M.	rupee	/jata/)	
/vaḷ/ M.Pl.	hair	/pəw̃ñc-/	arrive
/pəyr/ M.	foot	/vəṛ-/	enter
/mún/ M.	face, mouth	/céṛ-/	go up, rise,
/ək(k)h/ F.	eye		mount
/gəḍḍi/ F.	train	/ləý-/	go down
/kà/ F.	grass	(p.p.	
/chət/ F.	roof, ceiling	/ləttha/)	
/pəwṛi/ F.	ladder, step,	/əjýa/	such
	stair	/éo jýa/	this sort of,
/cyṭṭa/	white		like this
/wcca/	high	/óo jýa/	that sort of,
/nivaŋ/	low		like that
/bənd/	shut	/kýo jýa/	what sort of ?
/məna/	forbidden	/ykko jýa/	the same (sort
/cəla ja-/	go off, go		of), alike
	away	/kyoṅky/	because
/khól-/	open	/rəl ke/	together

Exercises

19A Translate into Punjabi :

(1) 11.15. (2) 2.45. (3) 12.30. (4) 9.45. (5) 1.30. (6) £1·75
(7) £3·50. (8) £2·50. (9) 4¾. (10) 1¼. (11) Half a glass
of milk. (12) A glass and a half of milk. (13) A quarter
of the people.

19B Translate into English :

(1) /ó bag a ke apṇi núṇ nuŋ mylya, te fer rəl ke sṭeṣən
cəle gəe./ (2) /əsiŋ pəwṛiaŋ te céṛ ke yk choṭe jə́e kəmre
vyc vəṛe./ (3) /zəra məynuŋ ó tài rwpəe vaḷa dýo./ (4) /os
wcce kə̀r di chət wtte əsaŋ do nile jə́e pəñchi vekhe./
(5) /səvə̄r de sáḍe sət vəje ó məzdūr bag yc kəm kərna
ṣwru kərəŋge./ (6) /óne kyse duje həṭṭi vaḷe koḷoŋ éo
jýa kagəz lya hovega./ (7) /saḍa kalyj pəwṇe əth vəje
bənd hwnda e./ (8) /tuŋ jaŋ ke apṇa səmān mere pəyr te
rəkkhya ?/ (9) /choṭe mwṇḍe ne ro ke yk ləmmi jə́i
kàṇi swṇəw̄ṇi ṣwru kiti./ (10) /kəpṛe tòŋvaḷi tiviŋ ne
óde koḷoŋ kẃj nə́iŋ məṅgya./ (11) /sanuŋ rəl ke ə́wŋ
di wmə̄d si, pər mere dost nuŋ roṭi vaḷe koḷ jaṇa pya./
(12) /os nuŋ chəḍ ke hor sə́b kẃj saf japda e./ (13) /es
bag yc kà te pəyr rəkhṇa məna e./ (14) /bəs ṭwrənvaḷi hi
si, pər fer səva vəje taiŋ sṭeṣən yc rə́i./ (15) /ó kə́nd
bəṇəw̄ṇvaḷyaŋ naḷ həs ke gəllaŋ kər rýa si./

19C Translate into Punjabi :

(1) I told him to come yesterday at a quarter to two.
(2) What sort of house do you want to live in ? In one
with a green roof. (3) People who live in London do this
every day. (4) The sick man got up and came down the
stairs this morning. (5) He asked us (*use* /koḷoŋ/) for
some water to wash his hair. (6) She laughed and told
us that it is forbidden to sit on the grass. (7) He closed
the shop and went home at half past five. (8) I need a
ladder, because I have to go up on the roof. (9) The

girl with beautiful eyes sat down on the low wall. (10) He
opcned his purse and gave the poor man one and a half
rupees. (11) His son and my son-in-law are quite alike.
(12) We think that garden with the trees in it is very
beautiful. (13) A tallish man was walking down the
street with the big houses in it. (14) Putting his hands
over (/te/) his face, he began to cry. (15) The chair-
maker arrived home at 1.30 and asked for his midday
meal.

Lesson 20

20.1 The cardinal numbers from 1–100 are less simple than in most European languages, since each number must be learnt separately, although there are certain regularities. The numbers are as follows:

1 /yk/	23 /tei/	45 /pəñjtāḷi/
2 /do/	24 /cə́vvi/	46 /chətāḷi/
3 /tyn(n)/	25 /pə́ñji/	47 /səntāḷi/
4 /car/	26 /chəbbi/	48 /əṭhtāḷi/
5 /pəñj/	27 /sətāi/	49 /wnȳñja/
6 /che/	28 /əṭhāi/	50 /pəñjá/
7 /sət(t)/	29 /wnə̄tti/	51 /ykvə̄ñja/
8 /ət((ṭ)h/	30 /tí/	52 /bəvə̄ñja/
9 /nəwŋ/	31 /ykə̄tti/	53 /tərvə̄ñja/
10 /dəs/	32 /bətti/	54 /cwrə̄ñja/
11 /yaraŋ/	33 /teti/	55 /pəcvə̄ñja/
12 /baraŋ/	34 /cəwti/	56 /chəpə̄ñja/
13 /teraŋ/	35 /pəynti/	57 /sətvə̄ñja/
14 /cəwdaŋ/	36 /chətti/	58 /əṭhvə̄ñja/
15 /pəndraŋ/	37 /səynti/	59 /wnáṭh/
16 /soḷaŋ/	38 /əṭhə̄tti/	60 /sət(t)h/
17 /sətāraŋ/	39 /wntāḷi/	61 /ykáṭh/
18 /əṭhāraŋ/	40 /caḷi/	62 /báṭh/
19 /wnni/	41 /yktāḷi/	63 /tréṭh/
20 /ví/	42 /bətāḷi/	64 /cəẃnṭh/
21 /ykki/	43 /tərtāḷi/	65 /pəýnṭh/
22 /bai/	44 /cətāḷi/	66 /chýaṭh/

67 /sətáṭh/	79 /wnāsi/	90 /nəvve/
68 /əṭháṭh/	80 /əssı/	91 /ykānveŋ/
69 /wnə̄ttər/	81 /ykāsi/	92 /banveŋ/
70 /səttər/	82 /byasi/	93 /tyrānveŋ/
71 /ykə̀ttər/	83 /tyrāsi/	94 /cwrānveŋ/
72 /bə̀ttər/	84 /cwrāsi/	95 /pəcānveŋ/
73 /tyə̀ttər/	85 /pəñjāsi/	96 /chyanveŋ/
74 /cəvə̀ttər/	86 /chyasi/	97 /sətānveŋ/
75 /pəñjə̀ttər/	87 /sətāsi/	98 /əṭhānveŋ/
76 /chyə̀ttər/	88 /əṭhāsi/	99 /nəṛȳnveŋ/
77 /sətə̄ttər/	89 /unānveŋ/	100 /səw/
78 /əṭhə̄ttər/		

Note that 19, 29, . . . 89 are of the same pattern as the following series. The prefix /wn-/ means *one less than*.

20.2 /yk/ is indeclinable. The other numbers, when used with a noun in the oblique case, may add /-aŋ/ for their oblique form. Those numbers ending in /-a/ add /-ŋ/, and those in /-aŋ/ are unchanged.

/nəvaŋ kwṛiaŋ naḷ/	with the 9 girls
/soḷaŋ admiaŋ da/	of 16 men
/bəvə̄ñjaŋ sykkhaŋ ləi/	for 52 Sikhs

20.3 For higher numbers the following words are used :

/həzār/	1,000
/lək(k)h/	100,000 (lac)
/kərōṛ/	10,000,000 (crore)

Thus 123,456,789 is /baraŋ kərōṛ cəwti lək̇h chəpə̄ñja həzār sət səw wnānveŋ/. In India this figure would be written as 12,34,56,789, showing the crores and lacs instead of millions.

With /səw/ and the above three numbers, the fractional numbers are very commonly used wherever possible, e.g.

/tài səw/ (/do səw pəñjá/)	250
/səva che həzār/ (/che həzār do səw pəñjá/)	6,250
/ḍéṛ kərōṛ/ (/yk kərōṛ pəñjá ləkh/)	15,000,000

20.4 The lower numbers have emphatic forms :

/ykkoi/	just one
/doveŋ/	both
/tynne/	all three
/care/	all four

20.5 The first four ordinal numbers are irregular. Thereafter the suffix /-vaŋ/ is added to the cardinal, and the ordinals are declined like /nəvaŋ/ (9.1).

/pəýla/	first	/chevaŋ/	sixth
/ḍuja/	second	/sətvaŋ/	seventh
/tija/	third	/əṭhvaŋ/	eighth
/cəwtha/	fourth	/navaŋ/	ninth
/pəñjvaŋ/	fifth	/dəsvaŋ/	tenth

From *11th* upwards, the ordinals have high tone :

/yárvaŋ/	eleventh	/bárvaŋ/	twelfth

20.6 There is no true indirect speech in Punjabi. /ky/, *that*, usually introduces direct speech, like inverted commas in English, e.g.

/óne kýa si ky məyŋ pəñjābi aŋ./	He said, ' I am Punjabi.' He said that he was Punjabi.
/óne sanuŋ pwcchya ky ó kýtthe ne./	He asked us, ' Where are they ? ' He asked us where they were.

Sometimes the pronoun is altered after /ky/ as in English, but the verb is usually the same as in the direct speech, so the first sentence could be :

/óne kýa si ky ó pəñjābi e./	He said that he was Punjabi.

20.7 There are two relative pronouns, both meaning *who, which, that* :

(i) /jéṛa/, declined like a ' black ' adjective (*cf.* /kéṛa/, 7.4).

(ii) /jo/, which declines as follows (*cf.* /kəwn/ and /ki/, 7.6) :

S.Dir.	/jo/	P.Dir.	/jo/
S.Obl.	/jys/	P.Obl.	/jýnaŋ/

20.8 The relative pronoun is usually ' picked up ' in the main clause by /ó/, *e.g.*

/məyŋ ó bənde nuŋ néiŋ pəchāŋda, jéṛa a rýa e./
Or /jéṛa bənda a rýa e, məyŋ ónuŋ néiŋ pəchāŋda./
I don't recognize the man (that man), who is coming.

Notice the order of the second sentence ' Which man is coming, I do not recognize him '. This pattern is more common in Punjabi than the first, which is closer to the English order.

The relative adverbs (/jýtthe/, *where, etc.*) are used in the same way :

/jýtthe ó rəýnda e, óthe hor   No one else can live where
koi néiŋ rəý səkda./   he does.

Sentences of the type ' I know who you are ' will be translated with /ky/ and an interrogative pronoun (*cf.* 20.6) :

/məyŋ jaŋda vaŋ ky twsiŋ   (' I know, " Who are you ? " ')
kéṛe o./

Vocabulary

/dərzi/	M.	tailor	/myŋt/	M.	minute
/koṭ/	M.	coat	/skyŋt/	M.	second
/mil/	M.	mile	/naṣta/	M.	breakfast
/kəýŋṭa/	M.	hour	/aŋḍa/	M.	egg

/kaṇṭa/ M.	fork	/pa-/	put (in), wear
/cəmməc/ M.	spoon	/naṣta kər-/	have breakfast
/chwri/ F.	knife	/vərt-/	use
/kəyñci/ F.	scissors	/kəm a-/	be useful
/dáṛi/ F.	beard	/véḍ(ḍ)-/	cut
/pəgṛi/ F.	turban	/kheḍ-/	play
/wṅg(ə)l/ F.	finger	/jo/	who, which, that
/pəyni/ F.	penny		
/duṇa/	double	/jéṛa/	who, which, that
/tiṇa/	triple		
/taza/	fresh	/jýtthe/	where
/béa/	stale	/jýtthoŋ/	from where
/nykka/	little, small	/jýddər/	(to) where
/syu-/ (p.p. /sita/)	sew	/jədoŋ/	when
		/odoŋ/	then
/pəchāṇ-/ (p.p. /pəchāta/)	recognize	/còṭpət/	immediately
		/kw/	about (used after numbers)
/ḍyg(g)-/	fall		
/ləmma pəy-/	lie down	/pəre/	beyond

Exercises

20A Translate into Punjabi :

(1) 5,500. (2) 12,827. (3) 125. (4) 2,750. (5) 987,654,321.
(6) 250,000. (7) 10 villages. (8) In 10 villages. (9) All 4
villages. (10) In just one village. (11) On the 13th day.
(12) On the 13th of February.

20B Translate into English :

(1) /jys kəpṛe nuŋ twsiŋ kəyñci naḷ véḍ rée səw, ó mera
si./ (2) /vəḍḍi mez te nəwkər ne pəynti cəmməc, wntaḷi
kaṇṭe te báth chwriaŋ rəkkhiaŋ./ (3) /yk kəỳṇṭe vyc
səth mynṭ hwnde ne, te tyn həzār che səw skynṭ./

(4) /əmrytsər ləẃroŋ tí kw mil dur e, pər doveŋ ṣəýr pəñjāb yc ne./ (5) /əsiŋ kevəl ónaŋ sykkhaŋ nuŋ pəchāŋ səkde aŋ, jéṛe dáṛi te pəgṛi rəkhde ne./ (6) /ví nuŋ məyŋ dẃdvaḷe koḷoŋ əṭhāraŋ aŋḍe məṅge sən, jýnaŋ vyccoŋ koi vi taza néiŋ si./ (7) /əytvar nuŋ ónaŋ səttaŋ məzdūraŋ nuŋ duṇe pəyse mylde ne./ (8) /niveŋ kə́nd pəre tynne bəcce kheḍ rə́e sən./ (9) /jýddər məyŋ ja rə́i aŋ, ódər twsiŋ kyoŋ jaṇa cəẃnde o?/ (10) /sanuŋ ṭhik pəta néiŋ si ky ónaŋ ne naṣta kita e jaŋ néiŋ./ (11) /jys sṭeṣən vəl gəḍḍi ṭwr rə́i si, óthe meri səs məynuŋ wḍīk rə́i si./ (12) /pàrət yc lokiŋ wṅgḷaŋ naḷ khaṇa khande ne, te kaṇṭe kə̀ṭ vərtde ne./ (13) /jo kagəz twsiŋ bəzāroŋ lyae o, ó kyse dyn kəm avega./

20C Translate into Punjabi :

(1) I told him myself that we would certainly come on the 25th. (2) The tailor with the little shop sewed the coat which he is wearing to-day. (3) After having breakfast, the old woman lay down again, because she was ill. (4) There are 100 pence in a pound. (5) Even before the beginning of winter, the leaves had fallen off the trees. (6) The dog, the cat and the horse are all four-footed animals. (7) The letter which you wrote on the 12th came on the 21st. (8) After half an hour she went to get some fresh bread herself. (9) When I began to tell him the story, he immediately said that he had heard it before. (10) He was trying to cut the bread with the knife which your father gave me. (11) The poor man put a little sugar in his tea, and began to eat the stale bread. (12) I asked her how she had got those £250. (13) Both brothers came with their six sisters to see the old film. (14) The brother who lives in London told us he had seen the film six times.

Lesson 21

21.1 The past participle of any verb may be used with /hoya/, the past participle of /ho-/, as an adjective denoting a state, *e.g.*

/məyŋ thəkya hoya saŋ./   I was tired.
/kwɽi bəyṭhi hoi e./   The girl is sitting down ('seated').

When such a past participle with /hoya/ is used before a noun, it is often equivalent to an English relative clause (*cf.* the use of the verbal agent, 19.3):

/swtta hoya mwŋḍa ó kəmre   The boy who was asleep was
   vyc si./   in that room.

Sometimes the present participle is used with /hoya/ in this way:

/rondi hoi kwɽi maŋ koḷ gəi./   The weeping girl went to her mother.

21.2 The Passive is formed by using the past participle with /ja-/, declined regularly, *e.g.*

/éthe pəñjābi boli jandi e./   Punjabi is spoken here.
/kənək véḍḍi gəi e./   The wheat has been cut (harvested).
/é kýa néiŋ ja səkda./   This cannot be said.

21.3 The Passive is considerably less common than in

English. It is never used when the verb has a direct
object, *e.g.*

> The boy hit the dog.
> (or) The dog was hit by
> the boy.

> /mwŋḍe ne kwtte nuŋ marya./

The only alternative method of expression in Punjabi
is to change the order of the words, and say /kwtte nuŋ
mwŋḍe ne marya./ This reversed word-order sometimes
corresponds to an English passive.

Note that /ne/ does not mean *by* with a passive verb.
/ne/ is only used as the sign of the agent with the past
(active) tenses of transitive verbs (17.1).

21.4 An English impersonal passive is often expressed
in Punjabi by an active verb in the third person plural,
with no subject expressed, *e.g.*

> /kəýnde ne ky . . ./   It is said that . . .

Of course, this could also be translated as /kýa janda
e ky . . ./

21.5 There are quite a number of pairs of verbs in
which the first, with a short vowel, is intransitive and
the second, with a long vowel, is transitive, *e.g.*

/twt(ṭ)-/ break (*intr.*)	/toṛ-/ break (*trans.*)
/pàŋḍa twṭṭa./	The pot broke.
/óne pàŋḍe nuŋ toṛya./	He broke the pot.

Sometimes the first member of the pair may be
equivalent to an English passive, *e.g.*

/ó kytābaŋ vecda e./	He sells books.
/éthe kytābaŋ vykdiaŋ ne./	Books are sold here.

21.6 By adding /-ā/ to the root of most verbs, causal

verbs may be formed. Some examples of causal verbs have already been introduced :

/péṛ-/	read	/pəṛà-/	teach, cause to read
/swŋ-/	hear	/swŋā-/	tell, cause to hear

Note that the stress (or tone) shifts on to the second syllable in causal verbs, and that high tone becomes low. A long vowel in the simple verb is shortened in the causal.

Examples of the use of causal verbs are :

/məyŋ es nuŋ ṭhik kəraṅga./	I'll put this right (I'll mend this).
/məyŋ es nuŋ ṭhik kərāvaṅga./	I'll have this put right (mended).
/óne paṇi pita./	He drank some water.
/əsaŋ ónuŋ paṇi pyāya./	We gave him some water to drink.
/mwŋḍé khyddo naḷ kheḍ ŕáe sən./	The boys were playing with the ball.
/ó mwŋḍyaŋ nuŋ khyddo naḷ khyḍā ŕáya si./	He was making the boys play with the ball.

21.7 By adding /-vā/ to the root of some verbs, double causals may be formed, with the sense of ' getting someone else to do something ', *e.g.*

/óne é kytāb péṛi./	He read this book.
/wstād ne ónuŋ é kytāb pəṛài./	The teacher taught him this book. (The teacher made him read this book.)
/məyŋ wstād koḷoŋ ónuŋ é kytāb pəṛvài./	I got the teacher to teach him this book.

Notice the use of /koḷoŋ/ in the last sentence, literally ' I got him taught this book from the teacher '. The agent through whom the action denoted by double causals is performed takes either /te/ or /koḷoŋ/, as here.

21.8 The actual meaning of verbs in /-ā/ and /-vā/ depends on whether the basic root is transitive or intransitive. The following patterns occur :

(i) intransitive (short vowel)	/tw̧ʈ(ʈ)-/	break
transitive (long vowel)	/toɽ-/	break
causal (in /-ā/ or /-vā/)	/tw̧ɽ(v)ā-/	have broken
(ii) intransitive	/bəŋ-/	be made, become
transitive (in /-ā/)	/bəŋā-/	make
causal (in /-vā/)	/bəŋvā-/	have made
(iii) transitive	/péɽ-/	read
causal (in /-ā/)	/pəɽà-/	make read, teach
double causal (in /-vā/)	/pəɽvà-/	have taught

Vocabulary

/malyk məkān/ M.	landlord	/eveŋ/	thus, in this way, for no reason
/pànḍa/ M.	pot, (sauce)pan	/jyveŋ/	as, in which way
/phəl/ M.	fruit		
/phwl(l)/ M.	flower	/kyveŋ/	how ? in which way ?
/gwlāb/ M.	rose		
/seb/ M.	apple	/məsaŋ/	scarcely, hardly
/malʈa/ M.	orange		
/kərāya/ M.	vent, fare	/kynnaŋ cyr/	for a long time
/khyddo/ M.	ball		
/kənək/ F.	grain, wheat, corn	/səgoŋ/	but (rather)
		/na (hi) . . .	neither . . .
/wmər/ F.	age	na (hi) . . .	nor . . .
/swkka/	dry	/tw̧ʈ(ʈ)-/	break (*intr.*)
/pəkka/	ripe, cooked	(p.p.	
/kəcca/	raw, unripe	/tw̧ʈʈa/)	

/toṛ-/	break (*trans.*)	/thək-/	be tired
/vyk-/	be sold	/pẏj(j)-/	be wet
/vec-/	sell	/vəkhā-/	show
/jag-/	wake up (*intr.*)	/swṭ(ṭ)-/	throw
/bəŋ-/	be made, become	/cwk(k)-/	lift, pick up
		/nəs(s)-/	run
/khẇl(l)-/	open (*intr.*)	/moṛ-/	turn, return (*trans.*)
/pək(k)-/	cook (*intr.*), ripen	/akh-/	say
/pèr-/	fill (*intr./ trans.*)	/əkhvā-/	be called
		/bwlā-/	call, summon

Exercises

21A. Translate into Punjabi :

(1) to wake up (*intr.* and *trans.*), to have woken up. (2) to cook (*intr.* and *trans.*), to have cooked. (3) to return (*intr.* and *trans.*), to have returned. (4) to hear, to tell, to have told. (5) to write, to make write, to have (something) written.

21B Translate into English :

(1) /teri tì di kynniŋ wmər e ? mera khyal e ky məsaŋ cəwdaŋ véryaŋ di hovegi./ (2) /es phəl nuŋ pəñjābi yc kí akhde ne ? énuŋ seb kəýnde ne./ (3) /apŋe pwtraŋ naḷ rəl ke zymīndar pəkkiaŋ hoiaŋ kəŋkaŋ véḍ rýa si./ (4) /məyŋ óde koḷoŋ é cyṭṭhi lykhvāi, te lyfāfe yc pwai./ (5) /kél rat nuŋ óne apŋi swtti hoi vəẇṭi nuŋ tyn vari jəgāi./ (6) /əsaŋ khaŋ de kəmre vyc vəṛ ke khẇlli hoi bari nuŋ marya si./ (7) /əj bəzār yc na hi cini na hi məkkhəŋ kyse nuŋ ləbba./ (8) /eveŋ japda si jyveŋ ó sanuŋ apŋi nəviŋ kytāb vəkhəw̄ŋi cəẇnda si./ (9) /əcəŋcet do admi khetaŋ vəloŋ nəs ke ae./ (10) /jýnaŋ lokaŋ de koḷ bəẇt sare pəyse hwnde ne, ónaŋ nuŋ əmīr kəýnde

ne./ (11) /tuŋ ónaŋ məzdūraŋ koḷoŋ é wcca kénd kyoŋ
bənvā rýa eŋ ? eveŋ hi !/ (12) /jys kèr yc saḍe dost kynnaŋ
cyr rəýnde sən, ónuŋ malyk məkān ne vecya e./ (13) /é
saḍa apṇa kèr néiŋ : malyk məkān nuŋ kərāya deṇa
pəynda e./

21C Translate into Punjabi :

(1) He immediately sat down on the wet grass. (2) What
is this beautiful flower called ? It is called a rose.
(3) I'll get the girl to tell you that story about the four
birds. (4) That saucepan is not only old but broken too.
(5) Show us how one should throw the ball. (6) He is
neither old nor ill, but he couldn't lift this little box.
(7) He said that he had thirty full bottles and didn't
want (any) more. (8) His daughter-in-law was about
35 years old at that time. (9) After the fire was lit,
their clothes quickly became dry. (10) Wheat is generally
harvested in September here. (11) They laughed and
told us that no newspapers were sold in the village.
(12) These oranges were put on the table by the boy
you think the nicest of all.

Lesson 22

22.1 Several compound verbs, made up of a noun (or adjective) and a verb, have been met with (*cf.* 5.6), *e.g.*

/khaṇa kha-/	eat
/ṣwru kər-/	begin
/bənd kər-/	shut

In compounds of this kind, /kər-/ is the root most commonly used. To form parallel intransitive verbs, /ho-/ is used instead of /kər-/, *e.g.*

/óne fyləm vekhṇi ṣwru kiti./	He began to watch the film.
/fyləm ṣwru hoi./	The film began.

22.2 There is another important type of compound verb in which the first element is a verbal root. Various verbs are used as the second member of the compound, of which the most common are /ja-/, /de-/ and /ləy-/ : when used in such compounds, these verbs lose their ordinary meaning, but serve to strengthen or intensify the meaning of the first verb. It is often difficult to translate the difference in meaning between the simple verb and its intensive compound form, but in the latter greater stress is laid on the completeness of the action.

(i) /ja-/ is used with all intransitive verbs :

/ó kwrsi te bəyṭha./	He sat on the chair.
/ó kwrsi te bəyṭh gya./	He sat down on the chair.
/ó kél aya./	
/ó kél a gya./	He came yesterday.

(ii) /de-/ is used with all transitive verbs (including causals) :

/məyŋ cyṭṭhi pèjaṅga./	I will send the letter.
/məyŋ cyṭṭhi pèj dyaṅga./	I will send off the letter.
/óne sanuŋ kələm dytta./	He gave us a pen.
/óne sanuŋ kələm de dytta./	

In compounds with /de-/, there is often also an idea of action directed outwards in another's interest :

/óda naŋ lykho./	Write his name.
/óda naŋ lykh dýo./	Write down his name (for me).

(iii) /ləy-/ is used with transitive verbs, but is less common than /de-/ : besides suggesting completeness, it usually gives the idea of action directed towards the subject :

/óda naŋ lykh ləẃ./	Write down his name (for your own use).
/óne kytāb ləi./	He took the book.
/óne kytāb ləy ləi./	

22.3 It is often not easy to see when an intensive compound should be used, and when the simple verb would be more appropriate. The following rules may be given :

(i) Intensive compounds are normally found only as finite verbs, *i.e.* as the main verbs in sentences or clauses.

(ii) Even as finite verbs, they are rare in negative sentences (in which the idea of completeness is necessarily lacking), and are not very common in questions.

(iii) In statements and commands, they are very common, especially when the completeness of the action is to be stressed.

22.4 Some nouns have a locative plural case in /-iŋ/, with the basic meaning of *in*. The locative plural is used in the following ways :

(i) To express place *in* :

/khetiŋ/	in the fields
/ódi apṇi hətthiŋ/	in his own hands, with his own hands
/sə́bniŋ thaiŋ/	in all places, everywhere

(ii) To express time *at* or *in* :

/ratiŋ/	at night(s)
/óniŋ dyniŋ/	in those days
/hər pəñjiŋ vériŋ/	every five years

(iii) To express the price *for* which something is got :

| /é məynuŋ dəsiŋ rwpəiŋ mylya./ | I got this for 10 rupees. |

(iv) In some compound verbs with /pəy-/, *fall* :

/sociŋ pəy-/	' fall into thoughts ', become thoughtful
/gəlliŋ pəy-/	' fall into words ', start talking
/nəzriŋ pəy-/	' fall into sights ', be seen, appear

22.5 Before a noun in the locative plural, numerals have the ending /-iŋ/, and pronouns also end in /-iŋ/ (/óniŋ/, /sə́bniŋ/, *etc.*). Adjectives end either in /-i/, or in /-e/, the oblique masculine form, before masculine nouns :

| /nange pəyriŋ phyr-/ | go around barefoot (on bare feet) |

22.6 A very few nouns also have a locative singular in /-e/, commonly used only in a few phrases, *e.g.*

/kə̀re/	at home
/dyne/	by day
/səvēre/	in the morning
/kəcche mar-/	put under the arm (literally : ' in the armpit ')

22.7 The demonstrative pronouns have the following emphatic forms :

S.Dir.	/ói/	/éi/
Obl.	/ose/	/ese/
P.Dir.	/ói/	/éi/
Obl.	/ónaŋ hi/	/énaŋ hi/

These have the basic meanings of *that very* and *this very* :

| /ose veḷe/ | at that very time |
| /ese kərke/ | for this very reason |

But they often translate the English *same* :

| /kə́l ói kwṛi a gəi si./ | Yesterday the same girl came. |

22.8 The auxiliary verb has two emphatic forms. commonly used only in the third person :

		First form	*Second form*	
Present :	3S.	/həy ve/	M. /həyga/	F. /həygi/
	3P.	/həy ne/	/həyge/	/həygiaŋ/
Past :	3S.	/həy si/	/siga/	/sigi/
	3P.	/həy sən/	/sige/	/sigiaŋ/

There is little difference in meaning between the two forms : they are used where in English there would be a heavy stress on the auxiliary :

| /ó vi sykh həyga./ | Even he *is* a Sikh. |
| /ó te syaṇa həysi./ | Well, he *was* clever. |

Note that /te/, like /vi/ and /hi/ (17.7, 17.8), follows the word which it emphasizes. It can sometimes be translated as *well*. (This /te/ is of course quite different from /te/, *and*, or /te/, *on*.)

Vocabulary

/kərəmcari/ M.	employee	/mar swt(t)-/	kill
/kwli/ M.	porter	/kəcche mar-/	put under the arm
/mwsəlman/ M.	Muslim	/lá-/	take off (clothes)
/karkhana/ M.	factory	/phyr-/	turn, wander about
/buṭ/ M.	shoe, boot		
/pasa/ M.	side, direction	/bə́n(n)-/ (p.p. /bə́dda/)	tie
/thaŋ/ F.	place		
/nəwkri/ F.	employment, job	/gwac-/	be lost
		/sociŋ pəy-/	become thoughtful
/pwls/ F.	police		
/əlmāri/ F.	cupboard	/gəlliŋ pəy-/	start talking
/va/ F.	wind		
/vəkhra/	different, separate	/nəzriŋ pəy-/	appear, be seen
/nəǹga/	bare, naked	/vəg-/	flow, blow (wind)
/khəbba/	left		
/səjja/	right	/rwk-/	stop (*intr.*)
/ḍúǹga/	deep	/rok-/	stop (*trans.*)
/ói/	that very, the same	/ləṛ-/	fight, quarrel
/éi/	this very, the same	/(di) thaŋ/	instead of
		/(di) ráiŋ/	by means of
/hər/	every	/vapəs/	back
/hər koi/	everyone	/te/	well (*emphatic*)
/mər-/ (p.p. /moya/)	die		

Exercises

22A Translate into English :

(1) /əj ṣam nuŋ óne tẁaḍiaŋ kytābaŋ kəcche mar ke ləy

ləiaŋ./ (2) /ó buṭ lá ke nəǹge pəyriŋ phyr rýa si./ (3) /mere
səẃre ráiŋ ose karkhane yc ónuŋ cəǹgi jéi nəwkri myli./
(4) /pychle dyniŋ ónaŋ di sə́b toŋ nykki tì mər gəi./
(5) /apṇa səmān bə́n ke kwli bwlao! nə́iŋ ji, énuŋ éthe
hi rəýŋ dýo./ (6) /pəñje mwsəlman mwṇḍe apo vyc
ləṛən ləgge./ (7) /dwpəýriŋ kə̀r a ke óne khaṇa kha
lya si./ (8) /ó nəwkər koḷon apṇe kəpṛe əlmāri yc rəkhvā
deŋgiaŋ./ (9) /fer pwls vaḷa óniŋ pəyriŋ vapəs mwṛ ke
ose pyṇḍ taiŋ pəẃñc gya./ (10) /khəbbe həth naḷ óne
apṇiaŋ sariaŋ cizaŋ zymīŋ toŋ cwk ləiaŋ./ (11) /twsiŋ
óthe nəzriŋ nə́iŋ səw pəe: kyoŋ ? məyŋ dəftər jaṇa si./
(12) /jys veḷe va vəgəŋ ləggi, ose veḷe əsiŋ sə́b əndər
cəle gəe./ (13) /məyŋ kərəmcari ho ke tẃanuŋ hor kẃj
nə́iŋ dəs səkda./ (14) /səjje pasyoŋ ói admi a rýa e,
jys ne nəviŋ həṭṭi bəŋvā dytti si./

22B Translate into Punjabi :

(1) The police asked them who had killed the little boy.
(2) The old man sitting on the chair was deep in thought
(' in deep thoughts '). (3) Well, he *is* a Pakistani, so he
will certainly be a Muslim. (4) Everybody was happy
talking to their old friends. (5) I read her letter
yesterday : now I'll read it out to you. (6) We got the
same sort of chair for only sixty rupees. (7) They said
they would get the window mended to-morrow afternoon.
(8) There are 350 employees in the factory the rich man
had built beyond the river. (9) The newspaper you
have asked for got lost the day before yesterday.
(10) He tried to lift the big box with both hands.
(11) He said that it was the same thing, but it now
seems as if it *is* quite a different matter. (12) She gave
the woman who was crying some tea to drink. (13) I
recognized the old Sikh who had started talking to the
policeman. (14) He went out of the house at a quarter
past eleven, and still hasn't come back.

Lesson 23

23.1 The Present Subjunctive is the same in form as the Future (12.1) without the final suffix /-ga/, except in the first person plural :

	/bol-/	/ja-/	/ləy-/
S.1.	/bolaŋ/	/javaŋ/	/ləvaŋ/
2.	/boleŋ/	/ja(v)eŋ/	/lə(v)eŋ/
3.	/bole/	/ja(v)e/	/lə(v)e/
P.1.	/bolie/	/jaie/	/ləie/
2.	/bolo/	/jao/	/ləvo/ or /ləw/
3.	/bolaŋ/	/ja(və)ŋ/	/ləyŋ/

The second person plural is the same as the plural Imperative (14.1), but has no high tone.

The negative of the Present Subjunctive is always formed with /na/, never with /néiŋ/.

23.2 The Present Subjunctive is used in sentences of the following kind, in which there is usually some idea of doubt :

/cəlie !/	Let's go !
/hwŋ məyŋ kí kəraŋ ?/	Now what am I to do ?
/ó kyte bəmār na hove./	Perhaps he's ill.
	(Literally : ' May he not be anywhere ill.')

23.3 The Present Subjunctive is most commonly used, however, in subordinate clauses, where there is some idea

of doubt, desire or necessity. It is only occasionally
that it can be translated by *may be, should, etc.*, in
English. Compare the following examples :

/kwṛi kəýndi e ky ó ṭwr jave./	The girl says that he is to go away.
but /kwṛi kəýndi e ky ó twr janda e./	The girl says that he is going away.
/mera ji kərda si ky kəm kəraŋ./	I wanted to work. (Literally : ' My heart was making that . . .')
/ónaŋ nuŋ cyṭṭhi pèj dýo taŋ jo ó gwsse na hoŋ./	Send them a letter, so that they won't be angry.
/ó pàveŋ məynuŋ sədde, taŋ vi məyŋ néiŋ jaṇa./	I won't go, although he may invite me.
/je məyŋ ódər javaŋ, taŋ ónuŋ zərūr mylaṅga./	If I go there, I will certainly meet him.

23.4 /pàŋveŋ/, *although*, is usually ' picked up ' in the
main clause by /taŋ vi/, *even then, still* : /je/ or /jekər/, *if*,
is usually ' picked up ' by /təŋ/, *then*. In Punjabi it is
/pàŋveŋ/ or /je/ that may be dropped, rather than
/taŋ (vi)/, *e.g.*

/ónuŋ pwch ləw, taŋ kẁj néiŋ akhega./	(If) you ask him, he won't say anything.

23.5 To express habitual action, three constructions are
used :

(i) The present participle with /hwnda/, the present
participle of /ho-/, *e.g.*

/əjkəl məyŋ paṇi pinda hwnda vaŋ./	Nowadays I always drink water.

(ii) The present participle with /rəýnda/, the present
participle of /rəý-/, *e.g.*

/os veḷe məyŋ ódər janda rəýnda saŋ./	At that time I used to make a habit of going there.

This construction must not be confused with the Present and Imperfect Continuous (9.2, 10.1) :

/os veḷe məyŋ óder ja rẏa   At that time I was going
saŋ./   there.

(iii) The gerund with /kər-/. The gerund is the same in form as the masculine singular past participle : but it is indeclinable, and is always formed regularly, whether or not the past participle is regular :

/ónaŋ de koḷ jaya kəro !/   Keep on going to them !

23.6 The verb /ləg(g)-/ has already been introduced in the sense of *begin* (18.2). Its basic meaning is *be attached to*, and it is used in a wide variety of idiomatic expressions, of which the most important are :

(i) With various abstract nouns, often equivalent to the English *feel* :

/tẁanuŋ gərmi ləgdi e ?/   Are you feeling hot ?
                           (Literally : ' Is heat
                            attached to you ? ')
/məynuŋ pẁkh ləgdi e./   I am (feeling) hungry.

(ii) Again with /nuŋ/ (*cf.* 16.8), equivalent to the English *seem* or *suit* :

/ó fyləm məynuŋ bwri ləgdi   That film seemed bad to me.
si./   I disliked that film.
/éo jẏa ḍres ónuŋ cəṅga   This sort of dress suits her.
ləgda e./   She likes this sort of dress.

(iii) With /cyr/ or /der/, *time, delay*, meaning *take time* :

/é kynnaŋ kw cyr ləggega ?/   About how long will this
                              take ?
/ə́dda kəẏnṭa ləggega./   It will take half an hour.

(iv) In various other constructions :

/kwñji ta̱ḻe yc ləgdi e./	The key fits the lock.
/kə̀r yc əg ləg gəi e./	The house has caught fire.
/hwŋ hor kəmmaŋ yc ləgga hoya e./	Now he is engaged in other tasks.

The transitive of /ləg(g)-/ is /la-/, literally meaning *attach* :

/óne ké̱nd te sucna la dytti./	He put up a notice on the wall.
/ónaŋ ne kə̀r yc əg lai e./	They have set fire to the house.

23.7 Just as /twsiŋ/ is used when addressing a single person respectfully, the third person plural may be used in order to refer to a single person, to whom one wishes to show respect or honour :

/ó bəẃt bəɽe admi sən./	He was a very great man.

The masculine plural will be used, even if a woman is being referred to (*cf.* 5.4). This use of the third person plural is less common than the standard use of /twsiŋ/.

To show respect to one's own or others' parents, /pyta (ji)/ is used instead of /pyo/ and /mata (ji)/ for /maŋ/, *e.g.*

/mere pyta ji sən pə̱ýṇṭh yc óder gəe sən./	My father went there in '65.

Vocabulary

/synema/	cinema	/gwá̱ṇḍi/	M.	neighbour
(Decl. II) M.		/d̠res/	M.	dress
		/ta̱ḻa/	M.	lock
/pyta/	father	/gwrdwara/		gurdwara,
(Decl. II) M.	(respectful)	M.		Sikh temple
		/cẏr/	M.	time, delay
/pərəẃ na/	M. guest	/der/	F.	time, delay

/mata/ F.	mother (respectful)	/enaŋ/	so, so much, so many
/sucna/ F.	notice	/onaŋ/	so, so much, so many
/kwñji/ F.	key		
/gərmi/ F.	heat	/jynnaŋ/	as, as much, as many
/sərdi/ F.	cold		
/sərdiaŋ/ F.Pl.	winter	/kyte/	somewhere, anywhere
/pẅk(k)h/ F.	hunger	/kýdre/	somewhere, anywhere
/tré/ F.	thirst		
/bwra/	bad	/kyte na/,	perhaps
/wdās/	sad	/kýdre na/	(with Pres. Subj.)
/razi/	happy, satisfied	/pàŋveŋ/	although, even if
/sən/	year (used before dates)	/pàŋveŋ ... pàŋveŋ .../	whether ... or ...
/ləg(g)-/	' be attached to ' (23.6)	/je/, /jekər/	if
/la-/	attach, put on (23.6)	/taŋ/	then
		/taŋ vi/	even then, still
/səd(d)-/	call, invite	/taŋ jo/	so that
/ḍər-/	fear, be afraid	/jo koi/	whoever
/ji kər-/	want	/jo kẅj/	whatever
/gwsse ho-/	be angry	/tək/	until

Exercises

23A Translate into English :

(1) /lokiŋ ónaŋ de pyta nuŋ ram sýṅ kərke sədde sən./
(2) /jo kẅj os əlmāri yc hove, ó sə́b mata ji nuŋ de dýo./
(3) /pàŋveŋ məynuŋ pẅkh nə́iŋ si ləgdi, taŋ vi ji kərda si ky ónaŋ de naḷ khaṇa khavaŋ./ (4) /əsiŋ dərdiaŋ saŋ ky ó bəcce nuŋ na mare./ (5) /gwrdware de kə́nd te yk sucna la dytti gəi si, taŋ jo sare ṣəýr dyaŋ sykkhaŋ nuŋ é pəta hove./ (6) /sərdiaŋ hoŋ, gərmiaŋ hoŋ, óne kəde

peyriŋ kẃj nóiŋ si paya./ (7) /bag yc tẃp pəyŋ kərke
sare pərəẃŋyaŋ nuŋ gərmi ləg rɵi si./ (8) /óde gwáɳḍi
apo vyc gəllaŋ kərde hwnde sən./ (9) /duje synema yc
ói fyləm ləg rɵi e, jéṛi əsaŋ sən əṭhvɵ̃ñja yc vekh ləi si./
(10) /məynuŋ ónaŋ nuŋ myləɳ da ṣəwk te həyve. cəŋga
fer, cəlie !/ (11) /je twsiŋ mere naḷ ao, taŋ ó sanuŋ
khaɳa zərūr khwa devegi./ (12) /jynnaŋ i cyr ləg jave,
onaŋ i cyr məyŋ éthe bəyṭhaṅga./ (13) /pychli vari ó
kytāb məynuŋ eniŋ cə̀ṅgi nɵiŋ si ləgdi./ (14) /pyta ji
é gəl swn ke kýdre gwsse na hoɳ./

23B Translate into Punjabi :

(1) They said that this key doesn't fit the lock of the
bathroom door. (2) Perhaps she will be sad when she
sees us. (3) I didn't like the dress my sister wore so
much. (4) They told me of their own accord that the
gurdwara was built in 1884. (5) Please tell them to keep
on coming till next October. (6) He tried to make her
happy, but she went on crying. (7) I must wait here,
although your friend may take a long time. (8) All the
people in the village used to call her ' mother '. (9) If
you are thirsty, I will give you some tea to drink.
(10) Whether you like it or not, it is still her most
beautiful dress. (11) The guest whom they invited was
not anywhere to be seen. (12) I wanted to go this
evening, but he said it would take an hour and a half.
(13) She was afraid that the neighbours would not
believe this. (14) If he comes on the 30th, ask him
whether he has met that girl or not.

Lesson 24

24.1 The Past Subjunctive is the same as the present participle, declined for gender and number, but with no auxiliary :

MS.	/janda/	FS.	/jandi/
MP.	/jande/	FP.	/jandiaŋ/

The negative of the Past Subjunctive always has /na/. This avoids confusion with the negative of the Present with /nə́iŋ/ and the auxiliary omitted (6.2).

24.2 The Past Subjunctive is commonly used only in conditional sentences, in which the fulfilment of the condition is impossible :

/je twsiŋ ónuŋ maf kərde, taŋ cəṅga hwnda./	If you had forgiven him, it would have been a good thing.
/məynuŋ pəta hwnda, taŋ duji vari na janda./	If I knew, I would not go again (a second time). If I had known, I would not have gone again.

24.3 The present participle passive is formed by adding /-ida/, declined for gender and number, to the root. In standard Punjabi, however, the construction with the past particple and /ja-/ (21.2), is normally used for the Passive, and the participle in /-ida/ has the sense of desirability :

/é gəl swŋidi e./	This is worth hearing.
/eveŋ nə́iŋ jaida./	One should not go like this.

Compare /cáida e/, *it is necessary*, from /cá-/, *want*
(17.4).

24.4 In the Present tense, a special form of the participle'
ending in /-na/ instead of /-da/, is commonly used in
speech, but only in the 1S., 2S. and 1P. :

/məyŋ bolna vaŋ/	/məyŋ bolni aŋ/	I speak
/tuŋ bolna eŋ/	/tuŋ bolni eŋ/	you speak
/əsiŋ bolne aŋ/	(/əsiŋ bolniaŋ aŋ/)	we speak

This form is not used in the negative, or in the
Imperfect. The ordinary forms in /-da/ are always
correct, even in the three persons of the Present given
above.

24.5 The present adverbial participle is formed by
adding /-(n)dyaŋ/ (sometimes /-(n)de/) to the root : in
other words, it is like a masculine oblique plural of the
present participle. It is used in the following ways :

(i) To mean *while* :

/ləŋḍən yc rə́yndyaŋ məyŋ ónuŋ mylda hwnda saŋ./	While living in London, I used to keep meeting him.

In this usage, it is commonly doubled for emphasis :

/ónaŋ ne əwndyaŋ əwndyaŋ sanuŋ kýa./	They told us on the way. (Literally : ' while coming, coming '.)

(ii) With /hi/ or /sar/ to mean *as soon as* :

/óne əwndyaŋ hi sanuŋ pwcchya./	As soon as he came, he asked us.
/óne jagdyaŋ sar surəj vekhya./	As soon as he woke up, he saw the sun.

(iii) With /nuŋ/ to mean *for* (a time) :

/məynuŋ é dwai pindyaŋ   I've been taking this medicine
tyn həfte ho gəe./   for three weeks.
(Literally: 'To me ... three
weeks have become.)

(iv) With /vekh-/ :

/məyŋ ó gəḍḍi nuŋ jandyaŋ I saw that train going.
vekhya./

24.6 The past adverbial participle is formed by adding
/-yaŋ/ (sometimes /-c/) to the root, and is used most
often in the following two constructions :

(i) With /bynāŋ/ to mean *without* :

/mere vəl vekhyaŋ bynāŋ ó He went off without looking
cəla gya./   at me.

(ii) With /nuŋ/ to mean *since* (*cf.* (iii) above) :

/óde jənəm hoyaŋ yk véra A year has passed since his
ho gya e./   birth.

24.7 The repetition of words is a very common feature
of Punjabi, and is used to express various shades of
meaning :

(i) Adjectives and adverbs are repeated to indicate
distribution over time or space, or over a number of
objects :

/deş de vəḍḍe vəḍḍe şəýr/ the country's large cities
/həwḷi həwḷi bolo !/   Speak slowly !

(ii) Numerals are repeated to give a distributive
sense :

/ónaŋ nuŋ tyn tyn dýo !/ Give them three each !

(iii) Some pronominal adjectives are repeated with /da/ in the middle : this emphasizes the distribution :

/óthe sare da sara vəkət   The whole time I was there
məyŋ saŋ te mera dost./   with my friend.

(iv) In the conjunctive participle, the root may be repeated, emphasizing continuance of the action through time (*cf.* 24.5 (i)) :

/soc soc ke kəm kəro !/   Work thoughtfully (carefully) !
/akh akh ke/   having said over and over again

(v) Adjectives are sometimes repeated to give the sense of the English *nice and* . . . :

/thəŋɖa thəŋɖa paṇi/   nice cold water

24.8 Slightly different from this repetition of the same word is the use of pairs of words together, often similar in sound :

(i) Almost any noun may be used with a jingle-word beginning with /ṣ-/, otherwise meaningless, to indicate a spreading out of the sense. This usage is definitely colloquial and rather jocular :

/roti ṣoti/   bread and so on, ' grub '
/phwl ṣwl/   flowers and that sort of thing

(ii) Some adjectives are commonly followed by another similar in sound or meaning, to emphasize the sense :

/thik thak/   quite O.K.
/sýdda sada/   quite straightforward (' straight and simple ')
/razi bazi/   very happy, quite content
/saf swthra/   very clean
/mənnya pərmənnya/   (very) famous

(iii) In the conjunctive participle the root is often followed by an echo-root, otherwise meaningless, giving a slight emphasis : this is a rather colloquial usage :

/moṭ maṛ ke/	having turned
/swṇ səṇ ke/	having heard

(iv) The past participle of a verb may be used with the past participle of the causal to express the idea of all ready for use :

/bəṇya bəṇāya/	ready made

24.9 To form feminine nouns from masculine ones, the following patterns should be noted :

(i) Masculines in /-a/ form their feminine in /-i/ : this is by far the most common pattern :

/dada/	grandfather (father's father)	/dadi/	grandmother (father's mother)
/kòṛa/	horse	/kòṛi/	mare
/bylla/	tom-cat	/bylli/	cat

With inanimate nouns, the feminine denotes a diminutive of the masculine :

/soṭa/	big stick	/soṭi/	little stick
/buṭa/	tree	/buṭi/	shrub, plant

(ii) Masculines in /-i/ form their feminine in /-əṇ/ :

/tòbi/	washerman	/tòbən/	washerwoman
/mali/	gardener	/malən/	gardener's wife

(iii) Masculines ending in a consonant form their feminines in /-i/, /-ṇi/ or /-āṇi/ :

/tərkhāṇ/	carpenter	/tərkhāṇi/	carpenter's wife
/uṭh/	camel	/uṭhṇi/	she-camel
/nəwkər/	servant	/nəwkrāṇi/	maid

Vocabulary

/dada/ M.	grandfather (paternal)	/loɽ/ F.	need
/nana/ M.	grandfather (maternal)	/khəbər/ F.	news
/caca/ M.	uncle (father's brother)	/məsīt/ F.	mosque
		/mwk-/	finish, end (*intr.*)
/mama/ M.	uncle (mother's brother)	/mwkā-/	finish, end (*trans.*)
/potra/ M.	grandson (son's son)	/jwab de-/	answer, dismiss
/dótra/ M.	grandson (daughter's son)	/kəm yc la-/	employ
		/maf kər-/	forgive
/saḷa/ M.	brother-in-law (wife's brother)	/soc-/	think
		/sámb-/	take care of, look after
/tərkhāŋ/ M.	carpenter	/lwk-/	hide (*intr.*)
/mali/ M.	gardener	/lwkā-/	hide (*trans.*)
/buṭa/ M.	tree	/lwk chyp ke/	secretly
/soṭa/ M.	big stick	/myl- jwl-/	resemble
/uṯh/ M.	camel	/mwft/	free, gratis
/jənəm/ M.	birth	/véla/	free, unoccupied
/mwl(l)/ M.	price	/kəlla/	alone
/məwka/ M.	opportunity	/mənnya pərmēnnya/	famous
/jwab/ M.	answer	/həwḷi/	slowly, softly
/dwk(k)h/ M.	sorrow, pain	/məgər/	after
/dwai/ F.	medicine	/bare (yc)/	about
/vél/ F.	leisure, free time	/hwŋe/	right now, immediately
		/kèṭṭokèṭ/	at least
		/náiŋ taŋ/	otherwise

Exercises

24A Translate into English :

(1) /ónaŋ cizaŋ da mwl car car rwpǝe ve, pǝr mǝyŋ
tẁanuŋ é mwĩt de dyaṅga./ (2) /óne potriaŋ dótriaŋ
nuŋ bag yc kheḍdyaŋ vekhya./ (3) /ódi saḷi de vyá
hoyaŋ nuŋ sǝt mèine ho gǝe ne./ (4) /énaŋ vǝḍḍe vǝḍḍe
ṣǝ́yraŋ yc rǝýndyaŋ óda ji kǝrda si ky ó apṇe deṣ mwṛ
jave./ (5) /jekǝr mere dade kǝlle mwkǝ̃lle na hwnde,
taŋ nǝwkrāṇi nuŋ kǝm yc na lǝwnde./ (6) /maĩ kǝro, ǝj
roṭi ṣoṭi nǝ́iŋ cáidi./ (7) /je ónuŋ yṅglǝýŋḍ jaŋ da mǝwka
na mylda, taŋ es veḷe hor da hor hi hwnda./ (8) /bynaŋ
bolyaŋ ó hǝwḷi hǝwḷi mǝsīt vǝl ṭwr pya./ (9) /hǝr roz
mǝyŋ ónaŋ nuŋ dǝsni aŋ ky hwṇe ódi koi loṛ nǝ́iŋ./
(10) /mǝnne pǝrmǝ̃nne ḍakṭraŋ ne bǝmāraŋ nuŋ ói dwai
pya dytti e./ (11) /jǝdoŋ óde cheveŋ bǝcce da jǝnǝm
hoya, taŋ tǝrkhāṇi nuŋ kèr de choṭe choṭe kǝmmaŋ toŋ
vél nǝ́iŋ si lǝ́bbi./ (12) /soṭe nuŋ toṛ taṛ ke ó nǝs gya, te
buṭyaŋ pycche lwkǝŋ di koṣyṣ kiti./ (13) /ónuŋ é kytab
pǝ́rdyaŋ kǝ̀ṭṭokǝ̀ṭ ṭài kǝỳnṭe ho gǝe hoṅge./ (14) /kàṇi
mwkdyaŋ sar mera potra sǝwŋ gya./

24B Translate into Punjabi :

(1) As soon as I saw him I recognized his uncle. (2) The
gardener and his wife took care of all the garden jobs,
otherwise we should not have lived in that big house.
(3) If she hadn't told you, I would have answered
myself. (4) It will be about fourteen years since I saw
a camel. (5) Nowadays he is busy with various important
(/bǝṛe bǝṛe/) jobs, but everyone needs time off. (6) She
got the carpenter to make them one chair each.
(7) Having reached the village, I saw the farmer working
in the fields. (8) In 1944, he secretly went round many
of the cities of India. (9) As soon as she heard this sad
story, his grandmother died. (10) Read this book care-

fully, otherwise it won't be of any use. (11) My grandson hid the knife in the cupboard without telling anybody anything. (12) She was tired after telling her grandchildren so many long stories. (13) His aunt was born in 1929, and died last May. (14) Although they are alike, those two men are not brothers.

Lesson 25

Varieties of Punjabi

25.1   As was explained in the Introduction, the Punjabi taught in this book is the standard Punjabi, based on the Majhi (/**máji**/) dialect of the central area which includes the cities of Lahore and Amritsar.

25.2   This standard language is used by educated people, but dialects are still much stronger in Punjabi than in English, and even educated speakers retain features of pronunciation and words characteristic of their own dialects. Thus, in the Malvai dialect spoken in the southern part of Indian Punjab, the word /**apaŋ**/ is used instead of the standard /**əsiŋ**/ for *we,* while in many dialects spoken in the western Punjab (in Pakistan) the word for *three* is not /**tyn**/ but /**trəy**/ (*cf.* the French *trois*).

25.3   Besides these dialect variations, there is naturally some difference between spoken Punjabi and the formal written language. In this book a middle course between the two has been kept, with rather more emphasis on the spoken language. One important feature of the written language, also used in formal speech, is the use of a different form of the present auxiliary (1.4) :

	Spoken form	*Written form*	
S.1.	/məyŋ aŋ/	/məyŋ haŋ/	I am
2.	/tuŋ eŋ/	/tuŋ həyŋ/	you are

	Spoken form	*Written form*	
S.3.	/ó e/	/ó həy/	he, she, it is
P.1.	/əsiŋ aŋ/	/əsiŋ haŋ/	we are
2.	/twsiŋ o/	/twsiŋ ho/	you are
3.	/ó ne/	/ó hən/	they are

There are some other minor differences : for instance,
/os/ and /es/ are much commoner for the oblique forms
of the demonstratives in writing, while /ó/ and /é/ are
commoner in speaking (11.1).

25.4 The most important division, however, is that
between the Muslim Punjabi of Pakistan and the Sikh
and Hindu Punjabi of India. The difference between
these is almost entirely one of vocabulary, Pakistani
Punjabi using many words drawn from Urdu, Persian
and Arabic, where Indian Punjabi has words taken from
Hindi and Sanskrit. The basic vocabulary used in
everyday life is more or less common to both, but for
most abstract subjects different sets of words are used.
As one would expect, the differences are greater in
writing than in speech, and are more noticeable with
educated speakers, especially when they are discussing
abstract subjects. In this book the Indian Punjabi word
has generally been used, where variants exist, but the
most widely understood word has been preferred, even
though it may originally be an Arabic rather than a
Sanskrit word.

25.5 Some examples of the differences between Pakistani
and Indian Punjabi words, arranged by subject, will
give some idea of the nature of the division :

(i) The most obvious differences are in religious
terminology. These differences extend over a wide field.
For example, the Sikh greeting is

/sət sri əkāl/   True is the Timeless One (God)

whereas Muslims greet one another by saying

   /səlām ələȳkwm/   Peace be upon you

Because Friday is the Muslim Sabbath, the words for
two days of the week are different :

Thursday   /jwmerat/   F.   not   /virvar/   M.
Friday   /jwma/   M.   not   /ṣwkkərvar/ M.

(ii) Many terms of politeness and respect are also
different, *e.g.*

Indian Punjabi	Pakistani Punjabi	
/ykbāl ji/	/ykbāl sáb/	Mr. Iqbal
/pyta ji/	/valyd sáb/	father (*cf.* 23.7)
/mata ji/	/valda/	mother (*cf.* 23.7)
/tə̀nvad/	/ṣwkria/	thank you !

(iii) Nearly all words to do with language and literature are different : this is not so strange when one
remembers that the Sikh and Muslim Punjabi literary
traditions are different, and they use two different
scripts. Some examples are :

Indian Punjabi		Pakistani Punjabi		
/ṣəbəd/	M.	/ləfəz/	M.	word
/əkkhər/	M.	/hərəf/	M.	letter
/ənvād/	M.	/tərjwma/	M.	translation
/kəvyta/	F.	/ṣəyri/	F.	poetry

(iv) Many terms of politics and administration are
different :

Indian Punjabi		Pakistani Punjabi		
/raṣṭərpəti/	M.	/sədər/	M.	president
/məntri/	M.	/vəzīr/	M.	minister
/səbà/	F.	/məjlys/	F.	assembly

(v) Finally, there are many general pairs of words, where the Pakistani word (generally of Arabic or Persian origin) is understood and sometimes used in India, while the Indian word (usually of Sanskrit origin) is not used in Pakistan, *e.g.*

Indian Punjabi	Pakistani Punjabi (also used in India)	
/jətən kər-/	/koşyş kər-/	try
/ərémb kər-/	/şwru kər-/	begin
/kevəl/	/syrəf/	only
/pàg/ M.	/hyssa/ M.	part

Lesson 26

The Gurmukhi Script

26.1 In India Punjabi is normally written in the Gurmukhi script (/**gwrmwkhi lypi**/). Like the Devanagari script used for writing Hindi, to which it is closely related, Gurmukhi is written from left to right. Once the sounds of Punjabi have been mastered, it is quite an easy script to learn, the main difficulty being the writing of the two tones.

26.2 There are thirty-five letters (/əkkher/) in the alphabet (/vərəŋmala/), and these are scientifically arranged in seven groups of five letters each, the five middle groups corresponding to the five columns of the pronunciation table on p. 5. The letters, with their names and sound-values, are:

	Letter	Name	Value
1.	ੳ	/uɽa/	see 26.4
2.	ਅ	/əyɽa/	see 26.4
3.	ੲ	/iɽi/	see 26.4
4.	ਸ	/səssa/	/s/
5.	ਹ	/haha/	/h/ or tone
6.	ਕ	/kəkka/	/k/
7.	ਖ	/khəkkha/	/kh/

	Letter	*Name*	*Value*
8.	ਗ	/gəgga/	/g/
9.	ਘ	/kə̀gga/	/k/ or /g/ + tone
10.	ਙ	/ṅəṅa/	/ṅ/
11.	ਚ	/cəcca/	/c/
12.	ਛ	/chəccha/	/ch/
13.	ਜ	/jəjja/	/j/
14.	ਝ	/cə̀jja/	/c/ or /j/ + tone
15.	ਞ	/ñəña/	/ñ/
16.	ਟ	/təyṅka/	/ṭ/
17.	ਠ	/ṭhəṭṭha/	/ṭh/
18.	ਡ	/ḍəḍḍa/	/ḍ/
19.	ਢ	/tə̀ḍḍa/	/ṭ/ or /ḍ/ + tone
20.	ਣ	/ŋaṇa/	/ŋ/
21.	ਤ	/tətta/	/t/
22.	ਥ	/thəttha/	/th/
23.	ਦ	/dədda/	/d/
24.	ਧ	/tə̀dda/	/t/ or /d/ + tone
25.	ਨ	/nənna/	/n/
26.	ਪ	/pəppa/	/p/
27.	ਫ	/phəppha/	/ph/
28.	ਬ	/bəbba/	/b/
29.	ਭ	/pə̀bba/	/p/ or /b/ + tone
30.	ਮ	/məmma/	/m/
31.	ਯ	/yəya/	/y/
32.	ਰ	/rara/	/r/
33.	ਲ	/ləlla/	/l/ or /l̤/
34.	ਵ	/vəvva/	/v/
35.	ੜ	/ɽaɽa/	/ɽ/

Five letters are written with dots below to represent additional sounds :

	Original letter	*Value*	*Dotted letter*	*Name*	*Value*
4.	ਸ	/s/	ਸ਼	/ṣəṣṣa/	/ṣ/
7.	ਖ	/kh/	ਖ਼	/k͟h͟ək͟h͟k͟h͟a/	/k͟h͟/
8.	ਗ	/g/	ਗ਼	/gəgga/	/g/
13.	ਜ	/j/	ਜ਼	/zəzza/	/z/
27.	ਫ	/ph/	ਫ਼	/fəffa/	/f/

The difference between /g/ and /g/ may be ignored, while /k͟h͟/, /z/ and /f/ are often pronounced as /kh/, /j/ and /ph/ respectively (*cf.* p. 11.).

26.3 .For the vowels special signs (/ləgaŋ matraŋ/) are used, written before, after, above or below the consonant :

Vowel-sign	*Sign written with* ਕ */k/*	*Position in which written*	*Name*	*Value*
none	ਕ	—	/mwkta/	/ə/
ਾ	ਕਾ	after	/kənna/	/a/
ਿ	ਕਿ	before	/sẏari/	/y/
ੀ	ਕੀ	after	/bẏari/	/i/
ੁ	ਕੁ	below	/əwṅkəṛ/	/w/
ੂ	ਕੂ	below	/dwləẏṅkṛe/	/u/
ੇ	ਕੇ	above	/laŋ/	/e/
ੈ	ਕੈ	above	/dwlāiaŋ/	/əy/
ੋ	ਕੋ	above	/hoṛa/	/o/
ੌ	ਕੌ	above	/kənəw̄ṛa/	/əw/

Note that there is no means of telling whether or not
a consonant is followed by /ə/, (except at the end of a
word, since no word ends in /-ə/).

26.4 Where a vowel does not follow a consonant it
must be written with one of the first three letters of the
alphabet, known as 'vowel-bearers'. Each vowel-
bearer is used only with certain vowel-signs, as follows :

Vowel-sign	Vowel-bearer	Sign + Bearer	Value
-	ਅ	ਅ	/ə/
ɪ	ਅ	ਆ	/a/
f	ੲ	ਇ	/y/
ੀ	ੲ	ਈ	/i/
-	ੳ	ਉ	/w/
ੂ	ੳ	ਊ	/u/
ੇ	ੲ	ਏ	/e/
ੈ	ਅ	ਐ	/əy/
ੋ	ੳ	ਓ	/o/
ੌ	ਅ	ਔ	/əw/

In dictionaries and the Punjabi–English vocabulary at
the end of the book, words are arranged first in order of
letters and then in order of vowel-signs. Since the three
vowel-bearers are letters, the order of words is as
follows :

ਉ ਊ ਓ ਅ ਆ ਐ ਔ ਇ ਈ ਏ ਸ ਸਾ ਸਿ ਸੀ ਸੁ ਸੂ
ਸੇ ਸੈ ਸੋ ਸੌ ਹ ਹਾ ਹਿ ਹੀ ਹੁ ਹੂ ਹੇ ਹੈ ਹੋ ਹੌ

and so on in the same way for the other consonants.

26.5 As in English, there is some difference between the printed and the written forms of the letters. The general rule is that each letter is written with a fresh stroke, beginning at the top left-hand corner, although joined on to the previous letter. When writing on lined paper, the *tops* of the letters are written on the line.

ਗ ਨ ਥ ਲ are usually written as 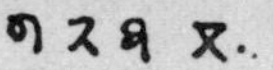. The other letters are written more or less as printed.

Exercise 26A

(1) Write these words in Gurmukhi script: **/dəs/**, **/vyc/**, **/hwn̩/**, **/hwn̩e/**, **/gylās/**, **/k͟h͟wṣ/**, **/jan̩na/**, **/choṭi/**, **/koi/**, **/əktūbər/**, **/wmēd/**, **/əytvar/**.

(2) Write these words in Roman script: ਦੇ, ਦਾ, ਨੇ, ਜਾਣਾ, ਬੋਤਲ, ਵੀਰਵਾਰ, ਕਰੋੜ, ਸੂਰਜ, ਟਿਕਟ, ਵੇਲੇ, ਉਠ, ਔਖਾ, ਸ਼ਾਮ, ਅਖ਼ਬਾਰ, ਹਜ਼ਾਰ.

(3) Arrange the words in (2) in alphabetical order.

26.6 Three additional signs are used, all written above the line of writing. (These do not affect the alphabetical order of words.)

Sign	*Written with* ਕ	*Name*
˘	ਕੱ	**/əddək/**
ੰ	ਕੰ	**/ṭyppi/**
·	ਕਾਂ	**/byndi/**

/əddək/ doubles the following consonant, *e.g.*

ਵੱਡਾ **/vəḍḍa/** ਰੱਖੋ **/rəkkho/** ਅੱਖ **/ək(k)h/**

/ṭyppi/ and **/byndi/** have the following values:

(i) At the end of a word, they indicate a nasalized vowel: ਹੱਥਾਂ **/hətthaŋ/**.

(ii) In the middle of a word, they indicate nasal consonants before a consonant of the same class (*cf.* the consonant table on p. 5), so they are used for

/ṅ/ before /k/, /kh/ and /g/	ਚੰਗਾ	/cəṅga/
/ñ/ before /c/, /ch/ and /j/	ਪੰਜਾਬੀ	/pəñjābi/
/ṇ/ before /t/, /ṭh/ and /ḍ/	ਪਿੰਡ	/pyṇḍ/
/n/ before /t/, /th/, /d/ and /n/	ਜਾਂਦਾ	/janda/
/m/ before /p/, /ph/, /b/ and /m/	ਕੰਮਾ	/kəmmaṇ/

Note that the nasal letters ਙ, ਞ, ਣ, ਨ, ਮ are not used in such a position, but only when the nasal is of a different class from the following letter, *e.g.*

	ਬਣਦਾ	/bəṇda/	becoming
but	ਬੰਦਾ	/bənda/	man

(iii) Some vowel-signs have /typpi/, others /byndi/, depending on whether the signs are used with vowel-bearers or not. In the following table those which take /typpi/ are asterisked :

Vowel	With consonant	With bearer
/ə/	ਕੰ*	ਅੰ*
/a/	ਕਾਂ	ਆਂ
/y/	ਕਿੰ*	ਇੰ*
/i/	ਕੀਂ	ਈਂ
/w/	ਕੁੰ*	ਉੰ*
/u/	ਕੂੰ*	ਊੰ*
/e/	ਕੇਂ	ਏਂ
/əy/	ਕੈਂ	ਐਂ
/o/	ਕੋਂ	ਓਂ
/əw/	ਕੌਂ	ਔਂ

Exercise 26B

(1) Write these words in Gurmukhi script : /pəkka/,
/tyn(n)/, /tynnaŋ/, /boleŋ/, /jaṇḍa/, /pycchoŋ/,
/kəyñci/, /nuŋ/, /pəwṇḍ/, /yṅgləÿṇḍ/, /hətthiŋ/,
/rəkkhaṅgiaŋ/.

(2) Arrange the words in (1) in alphabetical order.

26.7 Three letters have special subscript forms, written
beneath the letter which they follow :

	Full form	*Subscript form*	*Example*	
(*a*)	ਰ	ৢ	ਤ੍ਰੈ	/trəy/
(*b*)	ਵ	౼	ਸ੍ਵੈਂ	/svəy/
(*c*)	ਹ	ৢ		

Note that /ə/ is not pronounced before the subscript
letter. (*a*) is used quite commonly under the first letter
of words ; (*b*) is seldom written. For the use of (*c*),
see 26.9.

26.8 At the beginning of a word, the letter ਹ is pronounced as /h/, *e.g.*

          ਹੱਖ   /hət(t)h/   ਹਰਾ   /həra/

In all other cases, ਹ is not pronounced, but affects the
tone of the adjacent vowels :

(i) Final ਹ indicates high tone on the preceding
vowel, *e.g.*

          ਜਾਹ   (spelt /jah/)   pronounced /já/
          ਮੀਂਹ   (spelt /miŋh/)   pronounced /mín/

(ii) ਹ between two long vowels indicates high tone on
the preceding vowel, *e.g.*

| ਲਾਹੀ | (spelt /lahi/) | pronounced /láì/ |
| ਬੂਹਾ | (spelt /buha/) | pronounced /búa/ |

(iii) ਹ after a short vowel and before a long vowel indicates low tone on the following vowel, or a diphthong with low tone, *e.g.*

| ਕਹਾਣੀ | (spelt /kəhaṇi/) | pronounced /kàṇi/ |
| ਤੁਹਾੜਾ | (spelt /twhaḍa/) | pronounced /twàḍa/ |

(iv) /é/, /əý/, /ó/ and /əẃ/ are usually spelt in the following ways :

	ਇਹ	(spelt /yh/)	pronounced /é/
	ਕਹਿ	(spelt /kəhy/)	pronounced /kəý/
or	ਕਹ	(spelt /kəh/)	
	ਉਹ	(spelt /wh/)	pronounced /ó/
	ਬਹੁਤ	(spelt /bəhwt/)	pronounced /bəẃt/

Exercise 26C

Write these words in Gurmukhi script : /cá/, /ví/, /núṇ/, /kýa/, /ṣəýr/, /éo jýa/, /vəẃṭi/, /kéṛa/, /pəýlaŋ/, /rýa/, /réiaŋ/, /néiŋ/.

26.9 The tones are also written with five letters of the alphabet, and five other letters written with the sub-script ਹ (26.7) :

Letter		*Letter with subscript* ਹ	
ਘ	(spelt as /gh/)	ਨ੍	(spelt as /nh/)
ਝ	(spelt as /jh/)	ਮੁ	(spelt as /mh/)
ਢ	(spelt as /ḍh/)	ਰੁ	(spelt as /rh/)
ਧ	(spelt as /dh/)	ਲੁ	(spelt as /lh/)
ਭ	(spelt as /bh/)	ੜੁ	(spelt as /ṛh/)

In all cases, the /h/ in these letters is not pronounced ;
instead they affect the tone of the adjacent vowels :

(i) When final these letters indicate high tone on the
preceding vowel, *e.g.*

| ਕੁਝ | (spelt /kwjh/) | pronounced as /kẃj/ |
| ਪੜ੍ਹ | (spelt /peṛh/) | pronounced as /péṛ/ |

(ii) When between two long vowels, or when double
after a short vowel and before a long vowel, these letters
indicate high tone on the preceding vowel, *e.g.*

| ਮਾਝੀ | (spelt /majhi/) | pronounced as /máji/ |
| ਕੱਢੇ | (spelt /kéḍḍhe/) | pronounced as /kéḍḍe/ |

Note that ੜ and ਝ may be written with /éddək/ to show
high tone on the preceding vowel, even though they are
not pronounced double, *e.g.*

| ਵੱਗੁ | (spelt /verrha/) | pronounced as /véra/ |
| ਪੱੜ੍ਹਿਆ | (spelt /peṛṛhya/) | pronounced as /péṛya/ |

(iii) When after a short vowel and before a long vowel
(and when *not* doubled), these letters indicate low tone
on the following vowel, *e.g.*

| ਸਭਾ | (spelt /sebha/) | pronounced as /sebà/ |
| ਪੜ੍ਹਾਈ | (spelt /peṛhai/) | pronounced as /peṛài/ |

(iv) When initial, these letters indicate low tone on the
following vowel : in this position, the first five letters
are ' de-voiced ' and pronounced as /k/, /c/, /t/, /t/ and /p/
respectively :

ਘਰ	(spelt /ghər/)	pronounced as /kòr/
ਧੋਬੀ	(spelt /dhobi/)	pronounced as /tòbi/
ਭਾਈ	(spelt /bhai/)	pronounced as /pài/
ਨ੍ਹਾਤਾ	(spelt /nhata/)	pronounced as /nàta/

Exercise 26D

Write these words in Gurmukhi script : /bẃd(d)/,
/bẃdvar/, /baraŋ/, /bárvaŋ/, /t̪ài/, /t̪ì/, /kòṛyaŋ/, /khólṇa/,
/pəỳŋ/, /cèt̪pət̪/, /céṛya/, /cəṛàya/.

26.10 Some additional minor points about Gurmukhi
spelling should be noted :

(i) In those forms of verbal roots in /-a/ which have
/əw/, this is written as /aw/, *e.g.*

| ਆਉਣਾ | (spelt /awṇa/) | pronounced as /əwṇa/ |
| ਆਉਂਦਾ | (spelt /awnda/) | pronounced as /əwnda/ |

(ii) Final /-o/ is often written as /-w/, *e.g.*

| ਪਿਊ | (spelt /pyw/) | pronounced as /pyo/ |
| ਜਾਹੁ | (spelt /jahw/) | pronounced as /jáo/ |

(iii) Pronouns and pronominal adverbs beginning with
/e-/ or /o-/ are usually spelt with initial /y-/ or /w-/, *e.g.*

ਉਸ	(spelt /ws/)	pronounced as /os/
ਇਨ੍ਹਾਂ	(spelt /ynhaŋ/)	pronounced as /énaŋ/
ਇੱਥੇ	(spelt /ytthe/)	pronounced as /éthe/
ਉੱਧਰ	(spelt /wddhər/)	pronounced as /óder/

(iv) A few words are spelt in slightly irregular ways,
e.g.

| ਕੀ | (spelt /ki/) | pronounced as /kí/ |
| ਸਿੰਘ | (spelt /syṅgh/) | pronounced as /sýṅ/ |

Punjabi spelling is generally less standardized than
English, and alternative spellings are commonly met
with. In particular, /ə́ddək/ is often omitted, especially

before a final consonant, which is never pronounced double ; and the tones are spelt in more than one way, *i.e.* either with ਹ (26.8) or with one of the letters dealt with in 26.9.

26.11 A special set of numerals is used with the Gurmukhi script :

੧	੨	੩	੪	੫	੬	੭	੮	੯	੦
1	2	3	4	5	6	7	8	9	0

26.12 At the end of sentences an upright stroke ।
(/dəndi/) is used. Apart from the full-stop, English
punctuation marks may be used, although generally
rather irregularly.

26.13 The apostrophe is used to mark initial abbreviations, as in English, *e.g.*

'ਚ   /yc/, /cə/   (for /vyc/)
'ਤੇ   /te/   (for /wtte/)

For abbreviations of titles, the sign : is used, *e.g.*

ਸ: = ਸਰਦਾਰ /sərdar/   ' Mr.' (used only with
                           Sikh names)

ਭਾ: = ਭਾਈ /pài/   Brother (Sikh religious
                           title)

ਡਾ: = ਡਾਕਟਰ /dak?ər/   Dr.

ਪ੍ਰੋ: = ਪ੍ਰੋਫ਼ੈਸਰ /profəysər/ Prof.

cf. also ਸ: ੧੯੬੮ /sən wnni səw əthàth/   1968.

For initials in someone's name, the names of the
English letters are written out phonetically, *e.g.*

ਜੀ. ਐਸ. ਪਾਲ   /ji. əys. pal/   G. S. Pal

Exercise 26E

Write the sentences in Exercise 24A in Gurmukhi script.

Exercise 26F

Translate the following two short passages written in the Gurmukhi script into English, using the vocabularies given :

ਮੈਨੂੰ ਹੈਰਾਨੀ ਹੋਈ ਹੈ ਕਿ ਟਰਾਂਸਪੋਰਟ ਕਮੇਟੀ ਨੇ ਸਿੱਖਾਂ ਦੀ ਪੱਗ ਤੇ ਪਾਬੰਦੀ ਲਾ ਦਿੱਤੀ। ਖ਼ਾਸ ਤੌਰ ਤੇ ਜਦੋਂ ਉਸ ਦੇ ਦੂਜੇ ਕੰਡਕਟਰਾਂ ਤੇ ਡਰਾਇਵਰਾਂ ਨੂੰ ਚੰਗੀ ਤਰ੍ਹਾਂ ਵਰਦੀ ਪਾਉਣ ਲਈ ਮਜਬੂਰ ਨਹੀਂ ਕਰਦੀ। ਸਾਨੂੰ ਦੱਸਿਆ ਗਿਆ ਕਿ ਵਰਦੀ ਨਾਲ ਟੋਪੀ ਉਦੋਂ ਤਕ ਨਹੀਂ ਦਿੱਤੀ ਜਾਂਦੀ ਜਦੋਂ ਤਕ ਕਿ ਕੋਈ ਮੰਗ ਹੀ ਨਾ ਕਰੇ। ਨੌਕਰੀ ਕਰਨ ਵਾਲਿਆਂ ਨੂੰ ਡਿਊਟੀ ਤੇ ਪੂਰੀ ਵਰਦੀ ਪਾਉਣੀ ਚਾਹੀਦੀ ਹੈ। ਉਨ੍ਹਾਂ ਨੂੰ ਆਪਣੀ ਨੌਕਰੀ ਤੇ ਫ਼ਖਰ ਕਰਨਾ ਚਾਹੀਦਾ ਹੈ ਜਦੋਂ ਕਿ ਉਹ ਆਪਣੀ ਮਰਜ਼ੀ ਨਾਲ ਲਗਾਵੇ ਹੋਣ। ਜਦੋਂ ਫ਼ੌਜ ਵਰਦੀ ਨਾਲ ਪੱਗ ਨੂੰ ਮੰਨਦੀ ਹੈ ਤਾਂ ਟਰਾਂਸਪੋਰਟ ਕਿਉਂ ਨਹੀਂ।

Vocabulary

(English loan-words : ਟਰਾਂਸਪੋਰਟ, ਕਮੇਟੀ, ਕੰਡਕਟਰ, ਡਰਾਇਵਰ, ਡਿਊਟੀ.)

ਹੈਰਾਨੀ F.	amazement, surprise	ਫ਼ਖਰ M.	pride
ਖ਼ਾਸ ਤੌਰ ਤੇ	especially	ਫ਼ੌਜ F.	army
ਜਦੋਂ ਕਿ	when	ਮੰਗ ਕਰਨਾ	ask for, request
(= ਜਦੋਂ)		ਮਜਬੂਰ ਕਰਨਾ	force, compel
ਟੋਪੀ F.	hat, cap	ਮਰਜ਼ੀ F.	pleasure, ' freewill '
ਪੱਗ F.	turban	ਵਰਦੀ F.	uniform
ਪਾਬੰਦੀ F.	restriction, ban		

ਸਿੱਖ ਆਪਣੇ ਕੇਸ ਨਹੀਂ ਕੱਟਦੇ । ਕਈਆਂ ਦੇ ਗੋਡਿਆਂ ਤਕ ਲੰਮੇ ਹੁੰਦੇ ਹਨ ।
ਇਸ ਕਰਕੇ ਤੁਸੀਂ ਅੰਦਾਜ਼ਾ ਲਾ ਸਕਦੇ ਹੋ ਕਿ ਕਿੰਨੇ ਹਾਸੋ ਹੀਣ ਹੋਣਗੇ ਜਵੇਂ
ਟੋਪੀ ਪਾਉਣਗੇ । ਮੈਨੂੰ ਤਾਂ ਕੋਈ ਨੁਕਸ ਨਜ਼ਰ ਨਹੀਂ ਆਉਂਦਾ ਜੇ ਇਹ ਪੱਗ
ਨਾਲ ਨੌਕਰੀ ਕਰਨਗੇ । ਮੈਂ ਇਨ੍ਹਾਂ ਨੂੰ ਬਹੁਤ ਭਰੋਸੇ ਜੋਗ ਤੇ ਬੜੇ ਹੁਸ਼ਿਆਰ
ਵੇਖਿਆ ਹੈ । ਅਜ ਕਲ ਤਾਂ ਵਾਲ ਕੱਟਣ ਨਾਲ ਇਸਤ੍ਰੀ ਤੇ ਮਰਦ ਦੀ
ਪਛਾਣ ਔਖੀ ਹੋ ਗਈ ਹੈ । ਬੋਲਣ ਤੋਂ ਪਤਾ ਲਗਾਦਾ ਹੈ ।

Vocabulary

ਅੰਦਾਜ਼ਾ	judge,	ਗੋਡਾ M.	knee
ਲਾਉਣਾ	reckon	ਨਜ਼ਰ ਆਉਣਾ	appear (*cf.*
ਇਸਤ੍ਰੀ F.	woman		16.8)
ਹਾਸੋ ਹੀਣ	ridiculous	ਨੁਕਸ M.	harm
ਹੁਸ਼ਿਆਰ	sensible	ਭਰੋਸੇ ਜੋਗ	trustworthy
ਕੱਟਣਾ	cut	ਮਰਦ M.	man
ਕੇਸ M.Pl.	Sikhs' long, uncut hair		

Grammatical Tables

These tables are not exhaustive, but it is hoped that they will prove useful to the student as a guide and a reference. They may also be used as an index by referring to the numbers of the paragraphs where grammatical points are more fully dealt with.

Nouns

Gender (3.1) :

> Males and most nouns in /-a/ are masculine.
> Females and most nouns in /-i/ are feminine.

Formation of feminine from masculine nouns (24.9).

Declension (4.1) :

I   Masculine nouns in /-a/ of more than one syllable.
II   Other masculine nouns.
III   Feminine nouns.

Case-endings :	I	II	III
S.Dir. (4.1)	/-a/	—	—
Obl. (7.1)	/-e/	—	—
Voc. (14.4)	/-ya/	/-a/	/-e/
Abl. (17.5)	/-yoŋ/	/-oŋ/	/-oŋ/
Loc. (22.6)	(/-e/)	(/-e/)	(/-e/)
P.Dir. (4.1)	/-e/	—	/-aŋ/
Obl. (8.1)	/-yaŋ/	/-aŋ/	/-aŋ/
Voc. (14.4)	/-yo/	/-o/	/-o/
Loc. (22.4)	/-iŋ/	/-iŋ/	/-iŋ/

For the changes undergone by some nouns of Declensions II and III in the plural, see 4.2 and 8.2.

Adjectives

' Red ' adjectives indeclinable (3.2).

' Black ' adjectives with masculine singular in /-a/ :
masculine as Declension I, feminine as Declension III :

		M.	F.
S.Dir. (3.2)		/-a/	/-i/
Obl. (7.2)		/-e/	/-i/
P.Dir. (4.3)		/-e/	/-iaṇ/
Obl. (8.3)		/-e/ (/-yaṇ/)	/-iaṇ/

' Black ' adjectives in /-aṇ/ are nasalized throughout (9.1).
The adjective is generally in the oblique when used
with nouns in the vocative (14.4), the ablative singular
(17.5) and the locative plural (22.5).

Numerals

/yk/, *one,* indeclinable : other cardinals as :

Dir.	—
Obl. (20.2)	/-aṇ/
Loc. (22.5)	/-iṇ/

For other numerals see Lesson 20.

Pronouns

1. Personal Pronouns

Dir. (1.1)	/məyṇ/	/tuṇ/	/əsiṇ/	/twsiṇ/
Agent (17.3)	/məyṇ/	/tuṇ/	/əsaṇ/	/twsaṇ/
Dat. (Acc.) (9.5)	/məynuṇ/	/təynuṇ/	/sanuṇ/	/tẁanuṇ/
Abl. (11.1)	/məythoṇ/	/təythoṇ/	/sathoṇ/	/tẁathoṇ/
Poss.	/mera/	/tera/	/saḍa/	/tẁaḍa/

The possessives are declined like ' black ' adjectives.

2. Demonstratives

S.Dir. (1.3)	/ó/		/é/	
Obl. (7.3, 11.1, 25.3, 26.10)	/ó/	/os/	/é/	/es/

P.Dir. (1.3) /ó/ /ế/
  Obl. (8.4) /ónaŋ/ /énaŋ/
  Loc. (22.5) /óniŋ/ /éniŋ/

3. Emphatic Demonstratives (22.7)

S.Dir. /ói/ /éi/
  Obl. /ose/ /ese/
P.Dir. /ói/ /éi/
  Obl. /ónaŋ hi/ /énaŋ hi/

4. Interrogatives and Relatives

(a) /kéɽa/ (7.4) and /jéɽa/ (20.7), declined like ' black '
adjectives.

(b) S.Dir. (1.7) /kəwn̩/ /kí/ (20.7) /jo/
     Obl. (7.5) /kys/ /jys/
     P.Dir. (/kəwn̩/) /jo/
     Obl. (/kýnaŋ/) /jýnaŋ/

The oblique singular has an alternative form, more
common in speech than writing—/ké/ and /jé/, e.g.
/jénuŋ/ for /jys nuŋ/. /kí/ has an oblique singular form
/ká/, common only in the expression /káde ləi/, what for ?,
why ?

5. Indefinite Pronouns

S.Dir. (12.6) /koi/ /kẃj/
  Obl. (12.7) /kyse/

6. Reflexive Pronoun (18.4)

Dir. /ap/
Obl. /ap/
Dat. (Acc.) /apṇe ap nuŋ/
Loc. /apo vyc/
Poss. (12.5) /apṇa/

7. Other Pronouns (15.8)

S./P.Dir.	/hor/	/sə́b(b)/	/lokiŋ/
P.Obl.	/hornaŋ/	/sə́bnaŋ/	/lokaŋ/
P.Loc.	/horniŋ/	/sə́bniŋ/	—

Correlatives

There are many sets of four words, comprising two demonstratives, a relative and an interrogative : these may be pronouns, pronominal adjectives or adverbs:

	Near Demonstrative	Far Demonstrative	Relative	Interrogative
1.	/é/	/ó/	/jo/ /jéɾa/	/kəwŋ/, /kí/ /kéɾa/
2.	/enaŋ/	/onaŋ/	/jynnaŋ/	/kynnaŋ/
3.	/éo jýa/	/óo jýa/	/jýo jýa/	/kýo jýa/
4.	/éthe/	/óthe/	/jýtthe/	/kýtthe/
5.	/éthoŋ/	/óthoŋ/	/jýtthoŋ/	/kýtthoŋ/
6.	/édər/	/ódər/	/jýddər/	/kýddər/
7.	(/hwŋ/)	/odoŋ/	/jədoŋ/, /jəd/	/kədoŋ/, /kəd/
8.	/eveŋ/	/oveŋ/	/jyveŋ/	/kyveŋ/

Other sets may be made with oblique pronouns and nouns, *e.g.*

9.	/es veḷe/	/os veḷe/	/jys veḷe/	/kys veḷe/
10.	/es təràŋ/	/os təràŋ/	/jys təràŋ/	/kys təràŋ/

Postpositions

There are four types :

1. Those immediately following a noun in the oblique case, and having special forms when used with a personal pronoun (11.2, 17.1) :

/da/   /nuŋ/   /toŋ/   /ne/

2. Those following a noun in the oblique with /toŋ/, or a noun in the ablative singular, or a personal pronoun in the ablative case (15.6) :

/pəýlaŋ/   /bad/   /məgər/   /bár/   /chwṭ/   /bynāŋ/

and postpositions with meanings similar to these.

3. Those following a noun in the oblique with or without /di/, or a personal pronoun in the feminine possessive form :

/thaŋ/   /ráiŋ/   (and one or two others).

4. Those following a noun in the oblique with or without /de/, or a personal pronoun in the masculine possessive oblique form :

   all other postpositions (occasionally even including those given in 2 above).

Note that the demonstratives are treated like nouns, and the reflexive pronoun like the personal pronouns, when used with postpositions.

For ' ablative ' postpositions in /-oŋ/, see 17.6.

Verbs
Auxiliary :

	Present		Past (2.1)
	Spoken form (1.4)	*Written form* (25.3)	
S.1.	/aŋ/	/haŋ/	/saŋ/
2.	/eŋ/	/həyŋ/	/səyŋ/
3.	/e/	/həy/	/si/
P.1.	/aŋ/	/haŋ/	/saŋ/
2.	/o/	/ho/	/səw/
3.	/ne/	/hən/	/sən/

For the negative, see 2.2.
For emphatic forms of the third person, see 22.8.

Regular Verb:

1. Infinitives and Participles (indeclinable forms are asterisked)

Infinitive (16.4)	/-ŋa/
Oblique Infinitive (18.1)	/-(ə)ŋ/*
Verbal Agent (19.3)	/-(ə)ŋ vaḷa/
Conjunctive Participle (19.1)	/-ke/*
Present Participle (5.2)	/-da/
	vowel-roots :
	/-nda/
Present Adverbial Participle (24.5)	/-dyaŋ/* (/-de/*)
	vowel-roots :
	/-ndyaŋ/*
	(/-nde/*)
Present Participle Passive (24.3)	/-ida/
Past Participle (15.1)	/-ya/
Past Adverbial Participle (24.6)	/-yaŋ/* (/-e/*)
Gerund (23.5)	/-ya/*

2. Tenses formed directly from the root

	Imperative (14.1)	*Future* (*polite*) *Imperative* (14.3)
Sing.	—	/-iŋ/
Plur.	/-o/	/-yo/

Negative with /na/ (14.2).

	Present Subjunctive (23.1)	*Future* (12.1) *Masculine*	*Feminine*
S.1.	/-aŋ/	/-aṅga/	/-aṅgi/
2.	/-eŋ/	/-eṅga/	/-eṅgi/
3.	/-e/	/-ega/	/-egi/
P.1.	/-ie/	/-aṅge/	(/-aṅgiaŋ/)
2.	/-o/	/-oge/	(/-ogiaŋ/)
3.	/-(ə)ŋ/	/-(ə)ŋge/	/-(ə)ŋgiaŋ/

Negative with /na/ (23.1). Negative with /nə́iŋ/ (12.2).
The first person singular of the Future sometimes has
the ending /-uṅga/ (or /-uṅgi/). There is also a colloquial
short form of the Future, only used in the 1S. (/-uŋ/),
and the 3S. (/-u/).

Present Continuous (9.2)	root—/rýa/—pres. aux.
Past Continuous (10.1)	root—/rýa/—past aux.

Neither of these tenses is used in the negative (10.2).

3. Tenses formed with the Present Participle

Present (5.3)	pres. part.—pres. aux.
Negative (6.2)	/nə́iŋ/—pres. part.—(pres. aux.)
Present II (24.4)	pres. part. in /-na/—pres. aux.
Imperfect (6.1)	pres. part.—past aux.
Negative (6.2)	/nə́iŋ/—past aux.—pres. part.
Past Subjunctive (24.1)	pres. part.
Negative (24.1)	/na/—pres. part.

4. Tenses formed with the Past Participle

Past (15.3)	past part.
Negative (15.4)	/nə́iŋ/ or /na/—past part.
Perfect (16.1)	past part.—pres. aux.
Negative (16.1)	/nə́iŋ/—past part.—(pres. aux.)
Pluperfect (16.2)	past part.—past aux.
Negative (16.2)	/nə́iŋ/—past aux.—past part.
Future Perfect (16.3)	past part.—fut. of /ho-/
Negative (16.3)	/nə́iŋ/—past part.—fut. of /ho-/

For the construction of transitive verbs in these
tenses, see 17.1 and 17.2.

Minor irregularities in certain classes of verbs :

(i) Roots ending in a double consonant simplify this, except before an ending which begins with a vowel (12.3).

(ii) Roots ending in /-ŋ/, /-r/ and /-ɽ/ change /ŋ/ to /n/ in the endings of the Infinitive, Oblique Infinitive, Verbal Agent, and the third person plural of the Present Subjunctive and the Future.

(iii) Roots ending in /-a/ (except /ja-/ and /kha-/) change this to /-əw/ in the Infinitive (16.4) and the Present Participle (5.2). (*cf.* also 26.10).

(iv) Vowel-roots have some minor irregularities in the Imperative (14.1) and the Future and Present Subjunctive (12.1).

Irregular Participles

1. Irregular Present Participles

/ho-/   /hwnda/   be

Some other verbs have both regular and irregular present participles : the latter are usually colloquial shortened forms, and it is always correct to use the regular forms :

/de-/	/denda/	(or /dynda/)	give
/vekh-/	/vekhda/	(or /vénda/)	see
/akh-/	/akhda/	(or /ánda/)	say

2. Irregular Past Participles

Some verbs have both regular and irregular past participles : those forms which are less commonly used are bracketed in the following lists, which include a few verbs not introduced in the lessons. Note that the gerund always has the form of a regular past participle (23.5).

(*a*) Past participles in /-a/

/lə́b(b)-/	(/lə́bbya/)	/lə́bba/	find, get
/ləg(g)-/		/ləgga/	begin, be attached to
/twt̩(t̩)-/	(/twt̩t̩ya/)	/twt̩t̩a/	break (*intrans.*)
/bəyt̩h-/		/bəyt̩ha/	sit

(*b*) Past participles in /-ta/

/pi-/		/pita/	drink
/syu-/		/sita/	sew
/nà-/	(/nàya/)	/nàta/	bathe, wash
/tò-/	/tòya/	(/tòta/)	wash
/khlo-/	(/khloya/)	/khlota/	stand
/pərō-/	(/pərōya/)	/pərōta/	thread, string
/gwac-/	/gwacya/	(/gwata/)	be lost
/jaŋ-/	(/janya/)	/jata/	know
/pəchā-/	(/pəchānya/)	/pəchāta/	recognize

(*c*) past participles in /-tta/

/de-/		/dytta/	give
/səwŋ-/	(/səwŋya/)	/swtta/	sleep
/jo-/		/jwtta/	yoke

(*d*) Monosyllabic past participles in /-ya/ (for declension see 15.2)

/ja-/		/gya/	go
/ləy-/		/lya/ (/lita/)	take
/pəy-/		/pya/	fall, lie
/tə̀ỳ-/		/t̀ỳa/ (/tə̀t̩t̩ha/)	fall down
/rəý-/		/rýa/	live
/kəý-/		/kýa/	say

(*e*) Other irregular past participles

/kər-/		/kita/	do
/kha-/		/kháda/	eat
/vekh-/	/vekhya/	(/ḍyṭṭha/)	see
/ləý-/		/ləttha/	come down
/mər-/		/moya/	die
/pí-/		/piṭha/	grind
/bén(n)-/		/bédda/	tie
/rẃj(j)-/	(/rẃjjya/)	/rẃdda/	be busy
/výn(n)-/	(/výnnya/)	/výdda/	prick
/phəs-/	(/phəsya/)	/phatha/	be entangled

Some other verbs have irregular past participles, but
these are less commonly met with.

Key to Exercises

1A

(1) The book is here. (2) Is that the station ? (3) This is a newspaper. (4) Where are you ? (5) They are Punjabi. (6) We are English. (7) Who is this Englishman ? (8) That is the bus. (9) Who are you ? (to a child, *etc.*) (10) The radio is here, but the book is there.

1B

(1) /twsiŋ kɏtthe o ʔ/ (2) /məyŋ éthe aŋ./ (3) /ó əṅgrēz e ʔ/ (4) /ó ki e ʔ/ (5) /ó əkhbār e./ (6) /kytāb óthe ve./ (7) /é kəwŋ e ʔ/ (8) /ó éthe ve ʔ/ (9) /ó kɏtthe ne ʔ/ (10) /əṅgrēz te pəñjābi óthe ne./

2A

(1) The girl was not there. (2) This bottle is empty. (3) Is this a book ? (4) No, it's not a book. (5) Where was the boy yesterday ? (6) Are you Punjabi ? (to a child, *etc.*) (7) Yes (sir), I'm Punjabi. (8) Who are they ? (9) They are English, and were there yesterday. (10) Why were you there at that time ?

2B

(1) /bəs lal e./ (2) /ó botəl khali e ʔ/ (3) /roṭi kɏtthe ve ʔ/ (4) /əj kwṛi éthe néiŋ./ (5) /pər kə́l ó éthe si./ (6) /os veḷe sṭeṣən óthe néiŋ si./ (7) /ó paṇi e ʔ/ (8) /néiŋ ji, botəl khali e./ (9) /redyo éthe kyoŋ e ʔ/ (10) /twsiŋ óthe kədoŋ səw ʔ/ (11) /mwṇḍa əṅgrēz si, pər kwṛi əṅgrēz néiŋ si./ (12) /hwṇ bəs khali e./

3A

(1) He (or ' this ') is a good man. (2) The book wasn't good. (3) Where was the woman yesterday ? (4) The big room was empty. (5) Is this bread good ? (6) Yes, it is. (7) The red book is small. (8) I was there, but where were you ? (9) Was that pen black or red ? (10) It was black. (11) The radio was good.

3B

(1) /é əkhbār vəḍḍa e./ (2) /ó cəṅga mwṇḍa kýtthe ve ?/
(3) /sṭeṣən vəḍḍa nə́iŋ si./ (4) /kə́l kəmra khali si ?/
(5) /nə́iŋ ji, khali nə́iŋ si./ (6) /ó vəḍḍa bənda əṅgrēz e./
(7) /kələm vəḍḍa e jaŋ choṭa ?/ (8) /é paṇi cəṅga nə́iŋ./
(9) /kə́l kytāb te əkhbār óthe sən./ (10) /tiviŋ choṭi si./

4A

(1) /mwṇḍe choṭe ne./ (2) /ṭəyksiaŋ tez sən./ (3) /é vəḍḍe kə̀r ne./ (4) /é tiviaŋ əṅgrēz ne./ (5) /əsiŋ choṭe bənde aŋ./
(6) /kələm kaḷe ne./ (7) /kə́l bəsaŋ khali sən./ (8) /meriaŋ kytābaŋ kaḷiaŋ nə́iŋ./

4B

(1) There are two men here now, the two men are here now, *etc.* (2) There were four books and a newspaper there. (3) Where is my room ? (4) Where is your mother ?
(5) Those bottles are empty. (6) These are my pens.
(7) These three boys are good. (8) Is this your radio ?
(9) Yes, it is.

4C

(1) /əj bəs tez e./ (2) /t̀wadiaŋ kytābaŋ kýtthe ne ?/
(3) /os veḷe kəmre khali sən./ (4) /ṭəyksiaŋ kaḷiaŋ ne, pər bəsaŋ lal ne./ (5) /car kytābaŋ, do əkhbār te yk kələm éthe sən./ (6) /é mwṇḍe əṅgrēz ne ?/ (7) /nə́iŋ ji, (é) əṅgrēz nə́iŋ./ (8) /é tẁaḍa kə̀r e./ (9) /tiviaŋ éthe kyoŋ sən ?/ (10) /é cəṅgi kytāb nə́iŋ./ (11) /kwṛiaŋ

óthe kədoŋ sən ?/ (12) /saḍi maŋ pəñjābi e, ṇər əsiŋ
əṅgrēz aŋ./

5A

(1) The boy goes to school every day. (2) Three women
work here. (3) This tea is strong. (4) Where does the
bus go ? (5) It goes to London. (6) Where do you eat ?
(7) This girl always drinks water. (8) We come to
London every day. (9) My office was not there. (10) The
taxis go to the station. (11) That Englishman sometimes
drinks coffee. (12) Are these bottles mine or yours ?

5B

(1) /twsiŋ roz kýddər jande o ?/ (2) /məyŋ ləŋḍən jandi
aŋ./ (3) /ó kwṛi kəde skul əwndi e./ (4) /bəsaŋ kýtthoŋ
əwndiaŋ ne ?/ (5) /ó éthe khaṇa khande ne ?/ (6) /twsiŋ
roz kə̀r kədoŋ jande o ?/ (7) /tera skul kýtthe ve ?/
(8) /tuŋ roz skul jandi eŋ ?/ (9) /é bənda səda sygrəṭ
pinda e./ (10) /é cá e, kafi nə́iṇ./ (11) /twsiŋ sygrəṭ
kyoŋ pinde o ?/ (12) /twsiŋ roz dəftər kyoŋ əwnde o,
te óthe kí kəm kərde o ?/ (13) /meri maŋ kade cá pindi e./

6A

(1) /mwṇḍa roz skul nə́iŋ janda./ (2) /mwṇḍa roz skul
nə́iŋ si janda./ (3) /tiviaŋ éthe kəm nə́iŋ kərdiaŋ./
(4) /ó sygrəṭ kəde nə́iŋ sən pinde./ (5) /əsiŋ roz ləŋḍən
nə́iŋ əwnde./ (6) /é saḍe kəmre nə́iṇ./ (7) /ó khaṇa
nə́iŋ si khandi./ (8) /məyŋ paṇi nə́iŋ saŋ pinda./

6B

(1) We used to go to the shops every day. (2) The bottle
and the glass(es) are on the table. (3) Where does this
train come from ? (4) It comes from the city. (5) Did
you go from the station by bus ? (6) No, I used not to
go by bus. (7) The workmen were always drinking tea.
(8) This girl lives in London. (9) He usually came by

taxi. (10) He never goes to the shops. (11) Did you
work in the city ? (12) The train was never empty.

6C

(1) /os veḷe twsiŋ kýtthe rəýnde səw ?/ (2) /əsiŋ ləŋḍən
yc rəýnde saŋ./ (3) /əsiŋ əksər bəzār jande saŋ./
(4) /(twsiŋ) bəs naḷ jande səw ?/ (5) /meri maŋ bəs naḷ
jandi si, pər məyŋ kəde ṭren naḷ janda saŋ./ (6) /twsiŋ
dəftər yc kəm kərde səw ?/ (7) /néiŋ ji, məyŋ məzdūr
saŋ./ (8) /tẁaḍa gylās kýtthe ve ?/ (9) /ó mez te si, pər
hwṇ óthe néiŋ./ (10) /ó cá pinda e ?/ (11) /ó kəde (cá)
pinda e, pər əksər kafi pinda e./ (12) /vəḍḍi kwrsi kýtthe
ve ?/ (13) /hwṇ kə̀r yc e./

7A

(1) /choṭa kəmra : choṭe kəmre yc/ (2) /ləmme bənde :
ləmme bənde toŋ/ (3) /pwrāṇa kə̀r : pwrāṇe kə̀r əndər/
(4) /kaḷiaŋ kytābaŋ : kaḷi kytāb yc/ (5) /tẁaḍi kar :
tẁaḍi kar te/ (6) /meri maŋ : meri maŋ naḷ/ (7) /ləmmi
cyṭṭhi : ləmmi cyṭṭhi yc/ (8) /vəḍḍe bəkəs : vaḍḍe bəkəs
toŋ/

7B

(1) Your letter was in the envelope. (2) The woman
lives in the old house. (3) Used you to live in this
village ? (4) No, I lived in the city. (5) There's a book,
not a letter, in the big envelope. (6) The boy used to
come in (' by ') a very old car. (7) On this long envelope
there are three stamps. (8) What is this (thing) ?
(9) It's a box, and in the box there is a pen. (10) Which
pen ? Ours. (11) Who's that tall girl ? (12) I used to
write a letter.

7C

(1) /mere ṭykəṭ kýtthe ne ?/ (2) /ó vəḍḍe lal lyfāfe yc ne./
(3) /ləŋḍən yṅgləȳŋḍ yc e, te bəẃt vəḍḍa ṣəýr e./ (4) /twsiŋ

óthe rəýnde e ?/ (5) /nɛ́iŋ ji, məyŋ os veḷe óthe rəýnda saŋ, pər hwɳ yk choḷe pyɳḍ yc rəýnda vaŋ./ (6) /é pəykəṭ yc car sygrṭaŋ ne, pər məyŋ sygrəṭ nɛ́iŋ pinda./ (7) /choṭi bəs kys veḷe əwndi e ?/ (8) /əksər jəldi əwndi e./ (9) /vəḍḍi mez te ki (ciz) e ?/ (10) /óthe do pəykəṭ ne: lal pəykəṭ yc cá e, te kaḷe (pəykəṭ) yc kafi e./ (11) /əksər twsiŋ kys veḷe cá pinde o ?/ (12) /hwɳ məyŋ cá kəde nɛ́iŋ pinda./

8A

(1) /duje kəmre: duje kəmryaŋ toŋ/   (2) /pwrãɳe ṣəýr əndər: pwrãɳe ṣəýraŋ əndər/   (3) /vəḍḍe kaləj: vəḍḍe kaljaŋ yc/   (4) /é lal bəsaŋ: énaŋ lal bəsaŋ te/   (5) /choṭa dəftər: choṭe dəftraŋ yc/   (6) /pəýle bənde: pəýle bəndyaŋ toŋ/   (7) /ləmme mwɳḍe naḷ: ləmme mwɳḍyaŋ naḷ/   (8) /vəḍḍe həth te: vəḍḍe hətthaŋ te/

8B

(1) The English speak English. (2) He's a teacher in the big city, and teaches English there. (3) I can't speak Punjabi. (4) What do these men do ? They are labourers. (5) What you say (' your matter ') is right : this is very good tea. (6) This Punjabi newspaper is for Sikhs. (7) Who used to live in those houses ? (8) The other glasses were on the table. (9) The girls cannot read this book. (10) Our letters were in the other envelopes. (11) Who was the first teacher at (in) your college ? (12) I can't eat this food : it's horrible (' very bad ').

8C

(1) /duje kəmryaŋ yc car kwrsiaŋ te do mezaŋ sən./ (2) /məyŋ əj a səkda vaŋ./   (3) /ki gəl e ? ó kaḷi kar khərāb e./ (4) /é wstād ónaŋ skulaŋ yc əṅgrēzi pəṛəẁnda si./ (5) /sykh sygrəṭ kəde nɛ́iŋ pinde./ (6) /os veḷe é mere pəýle kəm sən./ (7) /əkhbāraŋ yc əṅgrēzi gəḷt e./ (8) /é ṭren kýtthoŋ əwnda e ?/ (9) /ónaŋ ṣəýraŋ toŋ əwnda e./

(10) /məzdūr pwrāṇe kèraŋ yc rəýnde ne./ (11) /ó mwṇḍe
kéɾe kəmryaŋ yc rəýnde sən./ (12) /ó roz (yk) ləmmi
cyṭṭhi lykh səkdi si./

9A

(1) /ləmmi chwṭṭi yc : ləmmiaŋ chwṭṭiaŋ yc/ (2) /əwkhe
səbək : əwkhe səbkaŋ yc/ (3) /cəṅge pwttər nuŋ : cəṅge
pwtraŋ nuŋ/ (4) /choṭe pyṇḍ neɾe : choṭe pyṇḍaŋ neɾe/
(5) /nəveŋ bəkəs te : nəveŋ bəksaŋ te/ (6) /ləmmi tì
ləi : ləmmiaŋ tìaŋ/ (7) /ó vəḍḍe bənde nuŋ : ónaŋ
vəḍḍe bəndyaŋ nuŋ (ónaŋ vəḍḍyaŋ bəndyaŋ nuŋ)/

9B

(1) Where are you coming from ? (2) I am coming from
the college. (3) Where's that ? (4) It's near the new shop,
but our college is very old. (5) What do you do there ?
(6) I don't work in the college now, but my daughter
teaches the girls English there. (7) Where does she go
in the holidays ? (8) She usually goes to London. (9) He's
sending your mother a letter. (10) Is this bus gcing to
London ? (11) No, it's coming from there. (12) Where
used you to get your tea from ? (13) We used to get it
from the shops. (14) He's drinking your coffee.

9C

(1) /ó mwṇḍyaŋ nuŋ səbək de rýa e./ (2) /əsiŋ cyṭṭhi pèj
rée aŋ./ (3) /mera pwttar éthoŋ ṭykəṭ ləy rýa e./ (4) /ó
khaṇa kha réiaŋ ne./ (5) /tuŋ kí kəm kər rýa eŋ ?/
(6) /məyŋ məzdūr nuŋ sygrəṭ de rýa vaŋ./ (7) /meri tì óthoŋ
a réi e./ (8) /ó bənde əkhbār péɾ rée ne./

9D

(1) /tẁaḍa pwttər kýddər ja rýa e ?/ (2) /ó nəveŋ kaləj
ja rýa e./ (3) /óthe mwṇḍyaŋ nuŋ səbək denda e./
(4) /məyŋ chwṭṭiaŋ ləi tẁaḍe pyṇḍ a rýa vaŋ./ (5)/ ó
éthoŋ bəẁt dur néiŋ./ (6) /ó kwɾi éthe sygrəṭ kyoŋ pi
réi e ?/ (7) /məyŋ ónaŋ nuŋ pəykəṭ pèj rýa vaŋ./ (8) /é

nəvaŋ səbək e, te bəẃt əwkha e./ (9) /hwŋ əsiŋ kəm kər
rée aŋ, pər əj jəldi kə̀r ja rée aŋ./ (10) /vəḍḍa bənda
choṭe mwŋḍe nuŋ cyṭṭhi de rýa e./ (11) /ó sanuŋ kytābaŋ
de rýa e./ (12) /meri tì tẃanuŋ ṭykəṭ pèj réi e./

10A

(1) /kwṛi da həth: kwṛi de həth: kwṛiaŋ de həth:
kwṛiaŋ de hətthaŋ te/ (2) /mere pài da dəftər: mere
pàiaŋ da dəftər: mere pàiaŋ de dəftər/ (3) /óde kə̀r
əndər: ónaŋ de kə̀r əndər: ónaŋ de kə̀raŋ əndər: ónaŋ
kə̀raŋ əndər/ (4) /yṅgləẏŋḍ de şəýr: yṅgləyŋḍ de
şəýraŋ toŋ: yṅgləẏŋḍ de ónaŋ şəýraŋ toŋ/ (5) /é tiviŋ
da pyŋḍ: énaŋ tiviaŋ de pyŋḍ: énaŋ tiviaŋ de pyŋḍaŋ
yc/ (6) /ódi choṭi tì di kytāb: ódiaŋ choṭiaŋ tìaŋ diaŋ
kytābaŋ: ódiaŋ choṭiaŋ tìaŋ diaŋ kytābaŋ yc/ (7) /ləŋḍən
de nəveŋ kə̀r: ləŋḍən de nəveŋ kə̀raŋ ləi/ (8) /kaḷiaŋ
kytābaŋ da vəḍḍa bəkəs: kaḷiaŋ kytābaŋ de vəḍḍe bəkəs:
kaḷiaŋ kytābaŋ de vəḍḍe bəksaŋ yc/

10B

(1) What time is your sister coming ? (2) She is coming
to-night. (3) And where is she coming from ? (4) She is
coming from their father's house. (5) We were going to
their brother's house on Tuesday evening. (6) The train
was in that station of the city. (7) Are you eating here ?
(8) No, I am not eating, I'm having some tea. (9) This
boy works in my father's shop. (10) They were getting
(taking, buying) books from there on Monday afternoon.
(11) Certainly he usually goes to the office every day,
but he's going to our sister's school now. (12) That
girl's office is a long way ('far') from my mother's
house.

10C

(1) /somvar şam nuŋ ó dəftər toŋ kə̀r ja rýa si./ (2) /ó
bənde da pwttər mere pyo de skul yc kəm kərda si./

(3) /é pwrāɳe pyɳḍ da pəýla nəvaŋ kə̀r e./ (4) /wstād
di tì de kə̀r de é kəmre yc yk mez te car kwrsiaŋ sən./
(5) /kə́l səvēr nuŋ məyŋ ónaŋ de pài nuŋ səbək de rýa
saŋ./ (6) /hwŋ ó zərūr tẃaḍe pài naḷ a rýa e./ (7) /məyŋ
é bənde di həṭṭi toŋ sygrəṭ ləynda saŋ./ (8) /ónaŋ de
pevaŋ diaŋ karaŋ bár ne./ (9) /gylāsaŋ de bəkəs ódi
pə̀yŋ di həṭṭi yc sən./ (10) /əj səvēr nuŋ ó bəs naḷ bəzār
ja rə́i si./ (11) /ó sykh de pwttər mere choṭe pài naḷ skul
a rə́e sən./ (12) /məṅgəḷ ṣam nuŋ ó saḍiaŋ cyṭṭhiaŋ ləi
ṭykəṭ ləy rə́i si./ (13) /meriaŋ pə̀yŋaŋ roz kaləj jandiaŋ
sən, pər əj ṣam nuŋ ó lənḍən ja rə́iaŋ ne./ (14) /óde
pài di gəl gəḷṭ si : ó əytvar nuŋ cyṭṭhi kəde nə́iŋ lykhde.
(15) /ónaŋ diaŋ tìaŋ cá nə́iŋ pindiaŋ./

11A

(1) /kwṛi bəṛi (bəẃt) sóni e./ (2) /é kwṛi ónaŋ di pə̀yŋ
naḷoŋ (toŋ) sóni e./ (3) /ó skul di sə́b toŋ sóni kwṛi e./
(4) /é bəṛi (bəẃt) cəṅgi kytāb e./ (5) /é kytāb os toŋ
(naḷoŋ) bəṛi cəṅgi e./ (6) /é sə́b toŋ cəṅgiaŋ kytābaŋ ne./

11B

(1) The doctor's children are very clever. (2) Nowadays
their father lives in Lahore. (3) London is the biggest
city in our country. (4) The village school was smaller
than your brother's house. (5) The cleverest boy in the
school was going there. (6) What were you writing with
my pen ? (7) His eldest (' biggest ') daughter cannot
read Punjabi. (8) This little girl is very beautiful, but
she isn't cleverer than my sister. (9) These Sikhs' land
is near Amritsar. (10) Lahore is the biggest city of the
Punjab. (11) Our doctor comes less nowadays : he can
only come on Monday mornings. (12) Who is cleverer
than him ?

11C

(1) /é car mwnḍe bəẃt (bəṛe) syaɳe nə́iŋ./ (2) /əmrytsər

loẅr toŋ bǝẁt choṭa e./   (3) /ǝịkǝl twsiŋ édǝr kèṭ kyoŋ
ǝwnde o P/   (4) /ó bǝnde di zymīŋ kýtthe ve P/   (5) /mǝyŋ
ḍakṭǝr de pwttǝr naḷoŋ (toŋ) véd néịŋ pi sǝkda : ó mǝythoŋ
vǝḍḍa e./   (6) /lǝẅr ǝmrytsǝr toŋ dur néịŋ, par ó pakystan
yc e, te ǝmrytsǝr pàrǝt yc./   (7) /saḍa deṣ yngląẏŋḍ toŋ
(naḷoŋ) cǝnga te sóna e./   (8) /é sǝb kǝlǝm ó mwnḍe de
ne, par ó tẅaḍa e./   (9) /sǝb toŋ pwrāṇi kytāb kéṛi e P/
(10) /é kytāb os toŋ nǝviŋ e./   (11) /twsiŋ óthoŋ roṭi
kyoŋ lǝy rǝ́e sǝw P ó ṣǝẏr di sǝb toŋ pǝẏṛi hǝṭṭi e./

12A

(1) /kél kǝmra k̲h̲ali hovega./   (2) /é dẃd cǝnga néịŋ
hovega./   (3) /ó éthe khaṇa khaṇge./   (4) /ǝsiŋ lǝŋḍǝn
yc révaṅge./   (5) /mǝyŋ bǝs naḷ avaṅga./   (6) /ó bǝkǝs
pèjega./

12B

(1) His friend will come next Thursday. (2) I never take
(' drink ') milk in coffee. (3) Their daughter will bring
bread and sugar from the shops. (4) My wife was
coming from there last Saturday. (5) These men will
do this job the day after to-morrow with their children.
(6) I couldn't see anything there. (7) It will be Tuesday
the day after to-morrow. (8) Your friend is taller than
his father. (9) Where will the boy be able to put the
milk ? (10) We shall only stay (' live ') in our brother's
house until the day after to-morrow. (11) He was
reading somebody's newspaper. (12) There will only
be two men and three boys.

12C

(1) /ó cini apṇe pyo di hǝṭṭi toŋ lǝvegi./   (2) /wstād ǝgle
virvar ṣam nuŋ avega./   (3) /pǝrsoŋ koi roṭi lyavega./
(4) /kél ṣǝnychǝr si, te pǝrsoŋ ṣwkkǝrvar si./   (5) /kél
kéṛa dyn hovega P kǝl somvar hovega./   (6) /tẅaḍe
pài de kǝmre yc mǝyŋ mez te kẃj vekh sakda vaŋ./

(7) /kwɽiaŋ kèr kədoŋ jaŋgiaŋ ?/ (8) /pychle bẃd nuŋ
koi éthe si./ (9) /ó kél taiŋ kẃj néiŋ kər səkda./ (10) /koi
kél da əkhbār néiŋ si pérda./ (11) /ó dẃd néiŋ piega./
(12) /ódi vəẃṭi syaṇi tiviŋ zərūr hovegi./ (13) /hwŋ əsiŋ
ləẁr kèṭ ja səkaṅge./

13A

(1) /saḍe do pài ne./ (2) /ónaŋ de koḷ pəñj bəkəs ne./
(3) /tẁaḍiaŋ do həṭṭiaŋ ne./ (4) /kwɽi nuŋ é bəɽi wmēd si./
(5) /bẃḍḍe di kẃj zymīŋ e./ (6) /mere koḷ yk kaḷi
kytāb si./

13B

(1) I think that our next lesson will be very difficult.
(2) To-morrow I will cook you potatoes. (3) How many
pens have you ? (4) I haven't got any pens, only this
old letter. (5) This potato is bigger than the head of the
poor man's child. (6) That country's rivers aren't very
big (as a rule). (7) I know they had no servant. (8) Our
elder brother's friend was working under the table.
(9) The fourth day in the week is Wednesday. (10) This
old man will never have any desire. (11) There were
many thoughts in the clever boy's head. (12) The old
Sikh's daughter was writing her address.

13C

(1) /həfte yc kynneŋ dyn hwnde ne ?/ (2) /həfte da
pəẏla dyn əytvar hwnda e jaŋ somvar ?/ (3) /mera
khyal e ky əytvar həfte da pəẏla dyn hwnda e./ (4) /tẁaḍe
koḷ (kẃj) cá e ?/ (5) /é sóŋe kèr yc kəi bənde rəẏnde
sən./ (6) /əjkəl (ó) bẃdda kèṭ gərīb e : óde che nəwkər ne./
(7) /ó apṇi cyṭṭhi tẁaḍe bəksaŋ heṭh rəkh rẏa si./ (8) /əgli
bəs pərsoŋ səvēr nuŋ pyṇḍ avegi./ (9) /koi énaŋ pəẏɽe
mwṇḍyaŋ nuŋ kẃj néiŋ pəɽá səkda./ (10) /məynuŋ
wmēd e ky koi é naveŋ alu néiŋ khavega./ (11) /ó nədi
koḷ mere pyo de nəwkər da (yk) kèr si./ (12) /ó səda

ṣwkkərvar nuŋ əwnda e, pər məynuŋ pəta e ky ó əgle
həfte (nuŋ) nə́iŋ a səkega./

14A

(1) /kẃj khá(-o) !/   (2) /zymīndar nuŋ myl(-o) !/
(3) /sygrəṭ pi(-o) !/ (4) /zəra ónaŋ nuŋ pwch (pwccho) !/
(5) dəs vəje já(-o) !/ (6) /es əkẖbār nuŋ ləý (ləẃ) !/

14B

(1) There is not much (less) rain here in the summer.
(2) We'll wait for you under that big tree. (3) Boy,
clean this room ! (4) There are four weeks in the second
month of the year. (5) Our dear friend is ill, so we shall
not come next month. (6) All these fields can't belong to
that poor farmer. (7) Generally more snow falls in winter.
(8) The man was waiting for the girl near the station until
eleven o'clock. (9) What Englishman is not happy in
the sun(shine) ? (10) In that field ten Sikhs were working
with their (own) hands. (11) This is my favourite
(dearest) daughter : please meet her. (12) This is a very
special book : only clever women can read it.

14C

(1) /ó pwrāṇe rwkh de pəttər gərmiaŋ yc həre hwnde ne,
(pər) syaḷ yc nə́iŋ./ (2) /cəwtha khet ó bẃḍḍe zymīndar
da e./ (3) /məynuŋ wmēd e ky əgle vére bərf éthe nə́iŋ
pəvegi./ (4) /məynuŋ pəta nə́iŋ : es kərke məyŋ tẁaḍi
maŋ nuŋ pwch rýa vaŋ./ (5) /ó vəḍḍi nili kytāb nuŋ ləẃ,
pər óde vyc kẃj na lykho !/ (6) /əjkəl ó kafi kèṭ pinda e,
kẖas kərke rat nuŋ./ (7) /məyŋ nəwŋ vəje taiŋ tẁanuŋ
bár wḍīkanga./ (8) /es deṣ yc tẁp syaḷ yc véd pəyndi
e; gərmiaŋ yc míŋ kərke kèṭ pəyndi e. (9) /ó énuŋ mere
kəmre vyc rəkh səkda e./ (10) /məyŋ kẖas kərke tẁaḍe
dost ləi (kẃj) cini lyavaṅga./ (11) /é əṭh gylās tẁaḍe ne :
énaŋ nuŋ jəldi saf kəro./ (12) /mera kẖyal e ky kwṟiaŋ
ṣənychər ṣam nuŋ sət vəje a(və)ŋgiaŋ./

15A

(1) /os toŋ chwṭ./   (2) /óde koḷ./   (3) /kə̀r (de) əndər./
(4) /kə̀r toŋ bár./   (5) /ṣam toŋ pəẏlaŋ./   (6) /hor kyse
kwṛi toŋ bynāŋ./ Or /bynāŋ hor kyse kwṛi toŋ./

15B

(1) We went to your friend's house on Sunday evening.
(2) Why did they forget ?   (3) Our daughter got up
before 7 o'clock yesterday. (4) He is opening the window,
and then he will close the door. (5) The farmer came
with his dogs. (6) After the rain all the windows in our
house have got very dirty. (7) Besides this, everything
seems alright. (8) Why did you live there without those
people ? (9) His dog sleeps every day until midday.
(10) I don't understand : what you say is very difficult.
(11) The woman brought them butter and sugar.
(12) Where could the boy go after midnight ?

15C

(1) /kə́l rat nuŋ kwṛiaŋ der naḷ kə̀r aiaŋ, pər əj səvə̀r
nuŋ jəldi wṭṭhiaŋ./   (2) /bẃḍḍa bəṛa təgra japda si,
pər fer bəmār ho gya./ (3) /es gəl nuŋ syaṇe lokiŋ kəde
nə́iŋ səmj səkəŋge./   (4) /bari maro, te búa na láo !/
(5) /pyŋḍ toŋ bár zymīndar da yk hor khet si./ (6) /məynuŋ
wmēd e ky wstād ó pəẏ̀ṛe mwŋḍe nuŋ marega./ (7) /ó
dəftər əṭh vəje jandi si, pər kə́l nəwŋ vəje toŋ bad gəi./
(8) /mera khyal e ky virvar rat nuŋ hor koi tẁaḍe kəmre
yc swtta./ (9) /nədi da paṇi bəẁt gənda japda si, es
kərke ó ódər nə́iŋ gya./ (10) /mere pyo da nəwkər hor
sə́b kẃj pẁl gya./ (11) /əj səvə̀r nuŋ bərf pəi, es kərke
bẃḍḍi apṇe kə̀r toŋ bár nə́iŋ ja səki./ (12) /tẁaḍe sykh
dost mere naḷ pəñjābi kyoŋ nə́iŋ bole ?/

16A

(1) That woman doesn't know how to cook (food).
(2) Write (your) name and address here. (3) The boy

will have washed in the other bathroom. (4) That is
quite true. (5) Suddenly all the birds begin to fly in
the sky. (6) I never want to listen to the radio : they
always tell lies on it. (7) Why didn't your friend come
by plane ? (8) How did they get this beautiful book ?
(9) That clever girl wanted to learn English well.
(10) To-morrow my wife will begin to wash the clothes.
(11) It seems as if (' this way, that ') they didn't remember their brother's address. (12) Just listen to me (' to
what I have to say ') : our old teacher has gone to
London. (13) He didn't catch the bus, so he was walking
along the broad village street. (14) He wanted to go
there with us, but suddenly he fell ill. (15) The girl
certainly went there, but she didn't get the farmer's
address ; so she didn't meet him.

16B

(1) /nile əsmān yc həvāi jàz pəñchi vang wǫ réi si./
(2) /məyŋ təynuŋ mənŋa cə́wnda vaŋ, pər mera khyal
e ky tuŋ cùṭh bol rýa eŋ./   (3) /bylkwl sɘcci gəl e ky
bẃḍḍa ódər kəde néiŋ si gya./   (4) /tẁanuŋ é sóŋa kəpṛa
kýtthoŋ mylya (lébba) ?/   (5) /kél səvēr nuŋ pwrāŋe
bəzār yc mylya (lébba)./   (6) /meri choṭi tì tòbi vang
kəpṛe tòŋe ṣwru kər réi e./   (7) /gwsəlkhana bəẃt gənda
ho gya e : ónuŋ (əj) ṣam nuŋ saf kəro (kərna)./
(8) /məynuŋ wmēd e ky hwŋ ónuŋ sərək da naŋ yad
aya e./   (9) /paṇi toŋ bynāŋ nəẁŋa əwkha (hwnda) e./
(10) /sə́b toŋ syaŋe mwŋḍe kéṛe kalyj yc pə́ṛna cə́wnde
ne ?/   (11) /gərīb nuŋ əkhbār di koi gəl néiŋ si sémj ai
(a réi)./   (12) /es təràŋ bolŋa gəḷt e, pər mwŋḍe nuŋ
əŋgrēzi néiŋ əwndi./   (13) /es toŋ bynāŋ ó kys təràŋ kəm
kərna ṣwru kər səkəŋge ?/   (14) /sanuŋ pəta néiŋ, pər
əsiŋ tẁaḍi pəỳŋ nuŋ pwchŋa cə́wnde aŋ./   (15) /choṭe
kəmre yc səmān rəkhŋa bəṛa əwkha ho gya e./

17A

(1) /məyŋ mwŋḍa vekhya./   (2) /məyŋ mwŋḍa vekh

səkya./ (3) /tòbi ne kəpɽe ləe./ (4) /tòbi kəpɽe lyaya./
(5) /twsaŋ kafi piti ?/ (6) /óne məynuŋ pəyse dytte./
(7) /əsaŋ é mez nuŋ bənāya./ (8) /bənde ne khaɳa kháda./
(9) /mwŋɖe ne kwɽi nuŋ kýa./ (10) /mwŋɖa pəñjābi
bolya./ (11) /ónaŋ ne əṅgrēzi pəɽài./ (12) /tuŋ mere dost
nuŋ mylya./

17B

(1) How much money did the rich man give you ?
(2) He still hasn't done this job. (3) Where did you put
your purse ? (4) I must wait for them right in front of
the door. (5) The rich don't need money. (6) My servant
will have to give (them) more money. (Or ' (He) will
have to give my servant more money.') (7) The woman
will have told her friends the *whole* story of the film.
(8) They shut the door, but now I must open the window.
(9) Then the teacher told the boy a lot more words.
(10) He began to make a chair. (11) We didn't believe
what they said. (12) Our father wanted to come by
plane, but he couldn't (didn't) get the money.

17C

(1) /tẁanuŋ é sare pəyse apɳi thəyli vyc rəkhɳe cáide ne./
(2) /mera khyal e ky tẁaɖi boli saɖi naɭoŋ bəɽi myʈʈhi e./
(3) /məynuŋ pəñjābi jəldi sykhɳi pəi, pər hwŋ cəṅgi
təràŋ əwndi e./ (4) /syaɳi kwɽi nuŋ vi pəta néiŋ si : es
kərke, ónaŋ sariaŋ ne wstād nuŋ pwcchya./ (5) /bẃɖɖe
zymīndar ne sanuŋ (kẃj) roʈi dytti si./ (6) /mwŋɖa
(apɳe) pyŋɖoŋ tẁaɖe ləi hor məkkhəŋ lyaya e./ (7) /é
kəpɽe bəẃt hi pwrāɳe ne. twànuŋ gərībaŋ nuŋ deɳe
néiŋ cáide./ (8) /óne məynuŋ dəssya si ky é ləmmi
kàɳi bylkwl səcci e./ (9) /ó bəmār ho gya (pya), pər əje
vi óne mwŋɖyaŋ nuŋ əṅgrēzi pəɽài./ (10) /óne meri
thəyli vyccoŋ bəẃt sare pəyse ləe ne./ (11) /ónaŋ ne
apɳi boli bolɳi ṣwru kiti./ (12) /óne kýa ky pəñjābi
əṅgrēzi naɭoŋ bəẃt hi səwkhi e./

18A

(1) My mother-in-law told me to wait. (2) I let him marry my daughter. (3) The man tried to light the fire, but couldn't. (4) The woman wanted to sit down, but she didn't get a seat. (5) He stood up, and started to make tea. (6) What date are you going ? (7) Your friend will try to come on 9th December, but it may be that he won't be able to come because of the snow (or ' ice '). (8) You just sit down, and we will get the room ready ourselves. (9) His mother and mother-in-law were talking to some other woman. (10) They made great efforts to earn more money. (11) Hoping to become warm, she shut the door, and then sat down right in front of the fire. (12) We'll tell the servant to bring two glasses of milk. (13) Those men earn little (money) : so people consider them poor. (14) The cat didn't want to go out of the house, but suddenly your son put it out. (15) We want cold milk, but he only let us drink warm water.

18B

(1) /ó apṇe jwāi naḷ gəllaŋ kərən ləgga./ Or /óne apṇe jwāi naḷ gəllaŋ kərniaŋ ṣwru kitiaŋ./ (2) /kwṛi pəýli jun nuŋ əwṇ di koṣyṣ kiti./ (3) /tyn pəwṇḍ məkkhən khaŋ toŋ (khaṇoŋ) bad bəcca bəmār ho gya./ (4) /məyŋ ónuŋ óthe bəythən ləi kýa, pər óne khloṇa cáya./ (5) /mwṇḍe nuŋ apṇi kytāb óthe chəḍḍən di wmēd si./ (6) /vyá kərən toŋ (kərnoŋ) bad ó (apṇe) səẃre nuŋ pəýli vari mylya./ (7) /syaṇi bəcci apṇe ap nuŋ jaŋ ḷai tyar ho gəi./ (8) /ó gərīb apṇe des nuŋ chəḍṇa cəẃnda si, te yŋgləýṇḍ əwṇ di koṣyṣ kiti./ (9) /óne apṇi tì nuŋ əg jələ̄ẉn néiŋ si dytta./ (10) /os toŋ chwṭ óne saḍe koḷoŋ kẃj néiŋ lya./ (11) /yaraŋ əgəst nuŋ ónuŋ do vari duje pyṇḍ jaṇa pya./ (Or : /óne . . . jaṇa si./) (12) /əktūbər (de mèine) yc kynneŋ dyn hwnde ne ?/ (13) /bənda ap sanuŋ yk pyala cá lyaya./ (14) /ó apṇe ap nuŋ syaṇe

səmjde ne, pər ónaŋ ne sanuŋ kýa (dəssya) ky əg ţhəŋḍi
hwndi e, te bərf gərəm (hwndi e)./ (15) /ónuŋ pwcchəŋ
toŋ pəýlaŋ ódi núŋ ne bẃḍḍə nal̬ gəllaŋ kərən di koşyş
kiti./ (16) /der hoŋ kərke zymĭndar apŋe khetaŋ vəl jəldi
ţwr rýa si./

19A

(1) /səva ɣaraŋ vəje./ (2) /pəwŋe tyn vəje./ (3) /sáḍe
baraŋ vəje./ (4) /pəwŋe dəs vəje./ (5) /ḍéɽ vəja./
(6) /pəwŋe do pəwnḍ./ (7) /sáḍe tyn pəwnḍ./ (8) /ţài
pəwnḍ./ (9) /pəwŋe pəñj./ (10) /səva (yk)./ (11) /śdda
gylās dẃd./ (12) /ḍéɽ gylās dẃd./ (13) /lokaŋ da cəwtha
hyssa./

19B

(1) He came to the garden and met his daughter-in-law,
and then they went off to the station together. (2) We
went up the stairs and entered a rather small room.
(3) Just give me the two and a half rupee one. (4) We saw
two blue-ish birds on the roof of that tall house. (5) Those
workmen will begin work in the garden at 7.30 a.m.
(6) He will have got this sort of paper from some other
shopkeeper. (7) Our college shuts at 7.45. (8) Did you
put your luggage on my foot on purpose ? (9) The
little boy cried and began to tell a rather long story.
(10) The woman who was washing (washes) clothes
didn't ask him for anything. (11) We hoped to go
together, but my friend had to go to (see) the bread-man.
(12) That aside, everything else seems clean. (13) In this
garden it is forbidden to set foot on the grass. (14) The
bus was *just* about to go, but then it stayed in the
station until 1.15. (15) He was laughing and talking with
the men who were building the wall.

19C

(1) /məyŋ ónuŋ kəl pəwŋe do vəje əwŋ ləi kýa./ (2) /twsiŋ
kýo jəe kər yc rəýŋa cəẃnde o ? yk həri chət val̬e yc./

(3) /ləŋdən de rəýnvaļe é roz kərde ne./ (4) /bəmãr əj
səvēr wţh ke pəwŗiaŋ toŋ ləttha./ (5) /óne vaļ tòŋ ləi
saḍe koloŋ paṇi məṅgya./ (6) /óne həs ke sanuŋ dəssya
ky kà te bəyţhṇa məna e./ (7) /ó həţţi bənd kər ke sáḍe
peñj vəje kèr gya./ (8) /məynuŋ pəwŗi cáidi e, kyoṅky
chət te cə́ŗna e./ (9) /sóniaŋ əkkhaŋ vaļi kwŗi niveŋ kə́nd
te bəyţh gəi./ (10) /óne apṇi thəyli khól ke gərīb nuŋ
ḍéŗ rwpya dytta si./ (11) /óda pwttər te mera jwãi ykko
jáe ne./ (12) /əsiŋ os rwkkhaŋ vaļe bag nuŋ bəŗa sóṇa
sə́mjde aŋ./ (13) /yk ləmma jýa bənda vəḍḍe kèraŋ vaļi
səŗək te ţwr rýa si./ (14) /múŋ te həth rəkh ke, ó roŋ
ləgga./ (15) /kwrsi bəṇəw̄nvaļe ne ḍéŗ vəje kèr pəwñc ke
dopəýr da khaṇa məṅgya./

20A

(1) /sáḍe peñj həzãr./ (2) /baraŋ həzãr əţh səw sətāi./
(3) /səva səw./ (4) /pəwṇe tyn həzãr./ (5) /əţhãnveŋ
kərōŗ chyèttər ləkh cwrōñja həzãr tyn səw ykki./ (6) /ţài
ləkh./ (7) /dəs pynḍ./ (8) /dəsaŋ pynḍaŋ yc./ (9) /care
pynḍ./ (10) /ykkoi pynḍ yc./ (11) /tərveŋ dyn nuŋ./
(12) /teraŋ fərvəri nuŋ./

20B

(1) The cloth which you were cutting with the scissors
was mine. (2) The servant put 35 spoons, 39 forks and
62 knives on the big table. (3) In one hour there are
60 minutes and 3,600 seconds. (4) Amritsar is about
30 miles from Lahore, but both cities are in the Punjab.
(5) We can only recognize those Sikhs who have a beard
and turban. (6) On the 20th I ordered 18 eggs from the
milkman, not even one of which was fresh. (7) On
Sundays those seven workmen get double pay. (8) Beyond
the low wall all three children were playing. (9) Why
do you want to go where I'm going ? (10) We didn't
really know if they had had breakfast or not. (11) My
mother-in-law was waiting for me at the station to

which the train was going. (12) In India people eat
with their fingers, and seldom use forks. (13) The paper
which you got in the market will come in useful (be
useful) some day.

20C

(1) /məyŋ ap ónuŋ kýa ky əsiŋ páñji nuŋ zərūr avaṅge./
(2) /jo koṭ óne əj paya e, ónuŋ nykki həṭṭi vaḷe dərzi ne
sita./　(3) /naṣta kərən toŋ bad bẃḍḍi fer ləmmi pəi,
kyoṅky ó bəmār si./　(4) /yk pəwnḍ yc səw pəyniaŋ
hwndiaŋ ne./　(5) /syaḷ de ṣwru toŋ pəýlaŋ hi pəttər
rwkkhaŋ toŋ ḍygge sən./　(6) /kwtta, bylli te kòṛa sáb
caraŋ peyraŋ vaḷe janvər (hwnde) ne./　(7) /jéṛi cyṭṭhi
twsaŋ baraŋ nuŋ lykhi si, ó ykki nuŋ ai./　(8) /ádde
kəẏṇṭe toŋ bad ó ap tazi roṭi ləyŋ gəi./　(9) /jədoŋ məyŋ
ónuŋ kàṇi swnəw̄ŋ ləgga, odoŋ óne cə̀ṭpəṭ kýa ky məyŋ
ne (óne) pəýlaŋ swṇi e./　(10) /ó roṭi os chwri naḷ váḍḍən
di koṣyṣ kər rýa si, jéṛi tẁaḍe pyo ne məynuŋ dytti./
(11) /gərīb ne thoṛi cini cá vyc pa ke béi roṭi khaṇi
ṣwru kiti./　(12) /məyŋ ónuŋ pwcchya ky tẁanuŋ (ónuŋ)
ó ṭ̀ài səw pəwnḍ kys təràŋ myle./　(13) /doveŋ pài apṇiaŋ
chevaŋ pəẏ̀ŋaŋ naḷ rəl ke pwrāṇi fyləm vekhən ae./
(14) /ləṇḍən yc rəẏ́ŋvaḷa pài (jéṛa pài ləṇḍən yc rəýnda e)
sanuŋ dəssya ky məyŋ (óne) é fyləm che vari vekhi e./

21A

(1) /jagna, jəgəw̄ṇa, jəgvəw̄ṇa./　(2) /pəkṇa, pəkəw̄ṇa,
pəkvəw̄ṇa./　(3) /mwṛna, moṛna, mwṛəw̄ṇa./　(4) /swṇna,
swṇəw̄ṇa,　swṇvəw̄ṇa./　　(5) /lykhṇa, lykhəw̄ṇa,
lykhvəw̄ṇa./

21B

(1) How old is your daughter ? I should think she
would be scarcely 14 (years old). (2) What is this fruit
called in Punjabi ? (' What do they say to this fruit ? ')
It is called an apple. (3) The farmer was harvesting the

wheat together with his sons. (4) I got him to write this
letter and to put it in the envelope. (5) Last night he
woke up his sleeping wife three times. (6) We went
into the dining room and shut the open window. (7) In
the market to-day no one got (either) sugar or butter.
(8) It seemed as if he wanted to show us his new book.
(9) Suddenly two men came running from the direction
of (' from towards ') the field. (10) People who have a
lot of money are called rich. (11) Why are you getting
those workmen to build this high wall ? I just *am*!
(12) The landlord has sold the house which our friends
lived in for a long time. (13) This is not our own house :
we have to pay the landlord rent.

21C

(1) /cè̤ʈpət ó pẏjji hoi kà te bəyʈh gya./ (2) /é sóɳe phwl
nuŋ kí akhde (kəýnde) ne ? énuŋ gwlāb akhde ne.
(é gwlāb əkhvəw̄nda e.)/ (3) /məyŋ kwɾi koloŋ twànuŋ
ó caraŋ pəñchiaŋ vaḷi kàɳi swŋvāvaṅga./ (4) /ó pàɳɖa na
kevəl pwrāɳa, səgoŋ ʈwʈʈa hoya vi e./ (5) /sanuŋ vəkhāo
ky khyddo kyveŋ (kys təràŋ) swʈɳa cáida e./ (6) /ó na hi
bẃɖɖa e na hi bəmār, pər é choʈe bəkəs nuŋ nóiŋ cwk
səkya./ (7) /óne akhya (kýa) ky mere koḷ tí pèriaŋ
hoiaŋ botlaŋ ne, (te) hor nóiŋ cáidiaŋ./ (8) /os veḷe ódi
núŋ di wmər pəynti kw véryaŋ di si./ (9) /əg jələn toŋ
pycchoŋ (bad) ónaŋ de kəpɾe jəldi swkke ho gəe./
(10) /éthe kəŋkaŋ am kərke sətə̄mbər yc véɖɖiaŋ jandiaŋ
ne./ (11) /ónaŋ ne həs ke sanuŋ kýa (akhya) ky pyɳɖ
yc koi əkhbār nóiŋ vykda./ (12) /é maḷʈe os mwɳɖe ne
mez te rəkkhe sən, jys ṅuŋ twsiŋ sə́b toŋ pyara sə́mjde o./

22A

(1) He took away your books under his arm this afternoon. (2) He had taken off his shoes and was going
around barefoot. (3) He got a good job in the same
factory through my father-in-law. (4) Recently (' in

the last days ') their youngest daughter died. (5) Do up
your luggage and call a porter. No, leave it just here.
(6) All the five Muslim boys began to quarrel amongst
themselves. (7) He came home at noon and ate his
meal. (8) They will get the servant to put their clothes
in the cupboard. (9) Then, retracing his footsteps
(' going back in those feet '), the policeman reached the
same village. (10) With his left hand, he picked up all
his things from the ground. (11) We didn't see you there :
why ? I had to go to the office. (12) When the wind
began to blow we all went off inside. (13) Being an
employee, I can't tell you anything else. (14) The
man who had the new shop built is coming from the
right(-hand side).

22B

(1) /pwls ne ónaŋ nuŋ pwch lya ky nykke mwŋḍe nuŋ
kys ne mar swṭṭya./ (2) /kwrsi te bəyṭha hoya bẃḍḍa
ḍúŋgi sociŋ pya si./ (3) /ó pakystani te həy ve (həyga),
es kərke mwsəlman zərūr hovega./ (4) /hər koi apŋe
pwrāŋe dostaŋ naḷ gəllaŋ kər ke khwṣ hoya./ (5) /məyŋ
te ódi cyṭṭhi kə́l pə́ṛ ləi : hwŋ tẃanuŋ pə́ṛ dyaṅga./
(6) /sanuŋ ykko jə́i kwrsi kevəl səṭṭhiŋ rwpəiŋ myli./
(7) /ónaŋ ne kə́ý dytta si ky kə́l ṣam nuŋ əsiŋ bari nuŋ
ṭhik kərā dyaṅge./ (8) /jo karkhana əmīr ne nədi pəre
bəŋvā lya si, óthe sáḍe tyn səw kərəmcari ne./ (9) /jə́ṛa
əkhbār twsaŋ məṅg lya é, ó pərsoŋ gwac gya./ (10) /óne
doviŋ hətthiŋ vəḍḍe bəkəs nuŋ cwkkən di koṣyṣ kər
dytti./ (11) /óne akhya ky ói gəl e, pər hwŋ eveŋ japda
e jyveŋ bylkwl vəkhri gəl həygi./ (12) /óne rondi hoi
tiviŋ nuŋ cá pya dytti./ (13) /məyŋ ó bẃḍḍe sykh nuŋ
pəchāŋ lya, jə́ṛa pwls vaḷe naḷ gəlliŋ pya si./ (14) /ó səva
dəs vəje kə̀roŋ nykəl gya, te əje vapəs nə́iŋ aya./

23A

(1) People used to call his father Ram Singh. (2) Give

Mother whatever there is (may be) in the cupboard.
(3) Although I wasn't hungry, I still wanted to eat with
them. (4) We were afraid he might hit the boy. (5) A
notice was put up on the wall of the gurdwara, so that
all the Sikhs in the city might know about it. (6) Whether
it was winter or summer, he never wore anything on his
feet. (7) Because of the sun(shine) in the garden, all the
guests were feeling hot. (8) His neighbours used to keep
talking among themselves. (9) In the other cinema the
very same film is on, which we saw in 1958. (10) I certainly *do* want to meet them. Right then, let's go!
(11) If you come with me, she will certainly give us a meal.
(12) However long it takes, I will sit here. (13) I didn't
like the book so much last time. (14) Perhaps Father
will be angry when he hears this.

23B

(1) /ónaŋ ne kýa ky é kwñji gwsəlk̲h̲ane de búe de taḷe yc
néiŋ ləgdi./   (2) /ó sanuŋ vekh ke kýdre wdās na hove./
(3) /jéṛa ḍres meri pəẏŋ ne paya si, ó məynuŋ enaŋ
cəṅga néiŋ si ləgga./   (4) /ónaŋ ne apṇe ap nuŋ məynuŋ
dəssya ky gwrdwara sən əṭhāraŋ səw cwrāsi vyc bəṇāya
gya./   (5) /ónaŋ nuŋ akhyo ky əgle əktūbər tək aya
kərən./ (Or /. . . aya kərən ləi akhyo./) (6) /óne ónuŋ razi
kərən di koṣyṣ kiti, pər ó rondi rəẏndi si./   (7) /pànveŋ
tẅaḍa dost kynnaŋ cyr lae, taŋ vi məyŋ éthe wḍīkṇa e./
(8) /pyṇḍ de sare lokiŋ ónuŋ mata kərke sədde sən./
(9) /je tẅanuŋ tré ləgdi e, taŋ məyŋ cá pya dyaṅga./
(10) /tẅanuŋ cəṅga ləgge na ləgge (tẅanuŋ pàveŋ
cəṅga ləgge, pàveŋ na ləgge), é óda sèb toŋ sóṇa ḍres e./
(11) /jo pərəẅṇa ónaŋ ne səd dytta, ó kyte nəzriŋ néiŋ
si pya./   (12) /məyŋ əj ṣam nuŋ jaṇa cəẃnda saŋ (ji kərda
ky məyŋ əj ṣam nuŋ javaŋ), pər ónaŋ ne akhya ky ḍéṛ
kəẏṇṭa ləggega./   (13) /ó ḍərdi si ky gwáṇḍi é gəl na
mənnəŋ./   (14) /je ó tí nuŋ a jave, taŋ ónuŋ pwch ləẃ
ky ó kwṛi nuŋ mylya e jaŋ néiŋ./

24A

(1) Those things cost four rupees each, but I will give
you this for nothing. (2) He saw his grand-daughters
playing in the garden. (3) It is seven months since his
sister-in-law's marriage. (4) While he was living in those
large cities, he wanted to return to his own country.
(5) If my grandfather had not been quite alone, he would
not have employed the maid. (6) Sorry, I don't want any
food to-day. (7) If he hadn't had the chance of going
to England, he would have been quite different now.
(8) Without speaking he went slowly off to the mosque.
(9) I tell them every day that there is no immediate
need of that. (10) Famous doctors have prescribed the
same medicine for sick people. (11) When her sixth child
was born, the carpenter's wife had no free time off from
the various little household tasks. (12) He broke the
stick and ran away, and tried to hide behind the trees.
(13) He will have been reading the book for at least
two and a half hours. (14) As soon as the story came to
an end, my grandson went to sleep.

24B

(1) /məyŋ óde cace (mame) nuŋ vekhdyaŋ hi pəchāŋ lya./
(2) /mali te maləŋ ne bag de sare kəmmaŋ nuŋ sámb lya,
néiŋ taŋ əsiŋ os vəḍḍe kèr yc na rəýnde./ (3) /je ó tẃanuŋ
na dəsdi, taŋ məyŋ ap jwab denda./ (4) /məynuŋ uṭh
vekhyaŋ cəwdaŋ kw vére ho gəe hoŋge./ (5) /əjkəl
ó bəɽe bəɽe kəmmaŋ vyc ləgga hoya e, pər hər kyse nuŋ
vél di loɽ hwndi e./ (6) /óne tərkhāŋ koloŋ ónaŋ ləi
yk yk kwrsi bəŋvā dytti./ (7) /pyŋḍ tək pəẃñc ke, məyŋ
zymīndar nuŋ khetiŋ kəm kərdyaŋ vekhya./ (8) /sən
(wnni səw) cwtāḷi yc ó lwk chyp ke pàrət de bəẃt sare
ṣəýraŋ yc phyrda si./ (9) /é dwkh vali kàṇi swndyaŋ hi
ódi dadi (nani) mər gəi./ (10) /é kytāb soc soc ke péɽ
ləẃ, néiŋ taŋ kyse kəm néiŋ avegi./ (11) /bynāŋ kyse nuŋ
kẃj dəssyaŋ mere potre (dótre) ne chwri nuŋ əlmāri vyc

lwkā dytti./   (12) /apṇe potryaṇ dótryaṇ nuṇ eniaṇ
ləmmiaṇ kàṇiaṇ swṇā swṇā ke, ó thəki hoi si./   (13) /ódi
caci (mami) da jənəm sən (wnni səw) wnātti yc hoya, te
ó pychli məi yc mər gəi./   (14) /pàṇveṇ ó do bənde mylde
jwlde ne (ykko jáe ne), taṇ vi ó pài nái̇ṇ./

26A

(1) ਦਸ, ਵਿਚ, ਹੁਣ, ਹੁਣੇ, ਗਿਲਾਸ, ਖ਼ੁਸ, ਜਾਣਨਾ, ਛੋਟੀ, ਕੋਈ,
ਅਕਤੂਬਰ, ਉਮੇਦ, ਐਤਵਾਰ.

(2) /do/, /da/, /ne/, /jaṇa/, /botəl/, /virvar/, /kərōṛ/,
/surəj/, /tykəṭ/, /veḷe/, /uṭh/, /əwkha/, /ṣam/,
/əkhbār/, /həzār/.

(3) ਉਠ, ਅਖ਼ਬਾਰ, ਔਖਾ, ਸ਼ਾਮ, ਸੂਰਜ, ਹਜ਼ਾਰ, ਕਰੋੜ, ਜਾਣਾ, ਟਿਕਟ,
ਦਾ, ਵੇ, ਨੇ, ਬੋਤਲ, ਵੀਰਵਾਰ, ਵੇਲੇ.

26B

(1) ਪੱਕਾ, ਤਿਨ, ਤਿੰਨਾਂ, ਬੋਲੇਂ, ਜਾਣਦਾ, ਪਿੱਛੋਂ, ਕੈਂਚੀ, ਨੂੰ, ਪੌਂਡ,
ਇੰਗਲੈਂਡ, ਹੱਥੀਂ, ਰੱਖਾਂਗੀਆਂ.

(2) ਇੰਗਲੈਂਡ, ਹੱਥੀਂ, ਕੈਂਚੀ, ਜਾਣਦਾ, ਤਿੰਨ, ਤਿੰਨਾਂ, ਨੂੰ, ਪੱਕਾ, ਪਿੱਛੋਂ,
ਪੌਂਡ, ਬੋਲੇਂ, ਰੱਖਾਂਗੀਆਂ.

26C

ਰਾਹ, ਵੀਹ, ਨੂੰਹ, ਕਿਹਾ, ਸਹਿਰ, ਇਹੋ ਜਿਹਾ, ਵਹੁਟੀ, ਕਿਹੜਾ,
ਪਹਿਲਾਂ, ਰਿਹਾ, ਰਹੀਆਂ, ਨਹੀਂ.

26D

ਬੁੱਧ, ਬੁੱਧਵਾਰ, ਬਾਰਾਂ, ਬਾਰੁਵਾਂ, ਫਾਈ, ਧੀ, ਘੋੜਿਆਂ, ਖੋਲ੍ਹਣਾ,
ਭੇਟ, ਝਟਪੱਟ, ਚੱੜ੍ਹਿਆ, ਰੜ੍ਹਾਇਆ.

26E

(੧) ਉਨ੍ਹਾਂ ਚੀਜ਼ਾਂ ਦਾ ਮੁੱਲ ਚਾਰ ਚਾਰ ਰੁਪਏ ਵੇ (ਹੈ), ਪਰ ਮੈਂ ਤੁਹਾਨੂੰ ਇਹ ਮੁਫ਼ਤ ਦੇ ਦਿਆਂਗਾ । (੨) ਉਹ ਨੇ ਪੋਤਰੀਆ ਦੋਹਤਰੀਆ ਨੂੰ ਬਾਜ਼ਾ 'ਚ (ਵਿਚ) ਖੇਡਦਿਆਂ ਵੇਖਿਆ । (੩) ਉਹ ਦੀ ਸਾਲੀ ਦੇ ਵਿਆਹ ਹੋਇਆ ਸੱਤ ਮਹੀਨੇ ਹੋ ਗਏ ਨੇ (ਹਨ) । (੪) ਬਿਨਾਂ ਵੱਡੇ ਵੱਡੇ ਸ਼ਹਿਰਾਂ 'ਚ ਰਹਿੰਦਿਆਂ ਉਹ ਦਾ ਜੀ ਕਰਦਾ ਸੀ ਕਿ ਉਹ ਆਪਣੇ ਦੇਸ਼ ਮੁੜ ਜਾਵੇ । (੫) ਜੇਕਰ ਮੇਰੇ ਦਾਦੇ ਕੋਲੇ ਮੁਕੱਲੇ ਨਾ ਹੁੰਦੇ, ਤਾਂ ਨੌਕਰਾਣੀ ਨੂੰ ਕੰਮ 'ਚ ਨਾ ਲਾਉਂਦੇ । (੬) ਮਾਫ਼ ਕਰੋ, ਅਜ ਰੋਟੀ ਸ਼ੋਟੀ ਨਹੀਂ ਚਾਹੀਦੀ । (੭) ਜੇ ਉਹ ਨੂੰ ਇੰਗਲੈਂਡ ਜਾਣ ਦਾ ਮੌਕਾ ਨਾ ਮਿਲਦਾ, ਤਾਂ ਇਸ ਵੇਲੇ ਹੋਰ ਦਾ ਹੋਰ ਹੀ ਹੁੰਦਾ । (੮) ਬਿਨਾ ਬੋਲਿਆ ਉਹ ਹੌਲੀ ਹੌਲੀ ਮਸੀਤ ਵਲ ਟਰ ਪਿਆ । (੯) ਹਰ ਰੋਜ਼ ਮੈਂ ਉਨ੍ਹਾਂ ਨੂੰ ਦਸਨੀ ਆਂ (ਦਸਦੀ ਹਾਂ) ਕਿ ਹੁਣੇ ਉਹ ਦੀ ਕੋਈ ਲੋੜ ਨਹੀਂ । (੧੦) ਮੰਨੇ ਪਰਮੰਨੇ ਡਾਕਟਰਾਂ ਨੇ ਬਮਾਰਾਂ ਉਹੀ ਦਵਾਈ ਪਿਆ ਦਿੱਤੀ ਏ (ਹੈ) । (੧੧) ਜਵੇਂ ਉਹ ਦੇ ਛੇਵੇਂ ਬੱਚੇ ਦਾ ਜਨਮ ਹੋਇਆ, ਤਾਂ ਤਰਖਾਣੀ ਨੂੰ ਘਰ ਦੇ ਛੋਟੇ ਛੋਟੇ ਕੰਮਾਂ ਤੋਂ ਵਿਹਲ (ਵੇਲ੍ਹ) ਨਹੀਂ ਸੀ ਲੱਭੀ । (੧੨) ਸੋਟੇ ਨੂੰ ਤੋੜ ਤਾੜ ਕੇ ਉਹ ਨੱਸ ਗਿਆ, ਤੇ ਬੂਟਿਆਂ ਪਿੱਛੇ ਲੁਕਣ ਦੀ ਕੋਸ਼ਿਸ਼ ਕੀਤੀ । (੧੩) ਉਹ ਨੂੰ ਇਹ ਕਿਤਾਬ ਪੜ੍ਹਦਿਆਂ ਘੱਟੋਘੱਟ ਢਾਈ ਘੰਟੇ ਹੋ ਗਏ ਹੋਣਗੇ । (੧੪) ਕਹਾਣੀ ਮੁਕਦਿਆਂ ਸਾਰ ਮੇਰਾ ਪੋਤ੍ਰਾ (ਪੋਤਰਾ) ਸੌਂ ਗਿਆ ।

26F

(1) I was amazed that the Transport Committee placed a ban on the Sikhs' turban ; especially when it does not compel its other conductors and drivers to wear uniform properly. We were told that the cap is not issued with the uniform until someone actually asks for it. Those who are employed ought to wear full uniform on duty. They should take pride in their job, when they are employed of their own free will. When the army agrees to the turban with uniform, why doesn't the Transport Committee ?

(2) Sikhs do not cut their hair. Many of them wear
it to knee-length. So you can judge how ridiculous
they will be when they wear a cap. I for one (/taŋ/) can
see no harm if they do their job with turbans on. I have
found (' seen ') them very trustworthy and most sensible.
Nowadays it has become difficult to recognize a man or
woman from the way their hair is cut. One finds out
from their voices (' speaking ').

Punjabi–English Vocabulary

This vocabulary includes all words used in this book, written in both the Gurmukhi and Roman scripts. The only exception is that numerals above 12 have not been included, a complete list of these having been given in 20.1. Note that verbs are given in the Infinitive, as is normal in dictionaries.

Order of words

Words are arranged in the order of the Gurmukhi alphabet. For those using the vocabulary before learning the Gurmukhi script, the order of initial letters is as follows : /w/, /u/, /o/, /ə/, /a/, /əy/, /əw/, /y/, /i/, /e/, /s/ or /ʂ/, /h/, /k/, /kh/ or /k͟h/, /g/, /k`/, /c/, /ch/, /j/ or /z/, /c`/, /t/, /th/, /ḍ/, /t`/, /t/, /th/, /d/, /t`/, /n/, /p/, /ph/ or /f/, /b/, /p`/, /m/, /y/, /r/, /l/, /v/. The order of vowels after initial letters is /ə/, /a/, /y/, /i/, /w/, /u/, /e/, /əy/, /o/, /əw/.

Note : Most words with tones and some others will be found in places slightly different from those that would be suggested by the above guide. In a list of this size, it should, however, be possible to find such words fairly easily.

ਉਸਤਾਦ	/wstād/ M.	teacher
ਉਸ ਵੇਲੇ	/os vele/	then
ਉਹ	/ó/	that, those : he, she, it, they
ਉਹੀ	/ói/	that very, the same
ਉਹੋ ਜਿਹਾ	/óo jýa/	that sort of
ਉਂਗਲ	/wṅgəl/ F.	finger
ਉੱਚਾ	/wcca/	high
ਉਠਟਾ	/wṭhna/	rise, get up
ਉੱਡਟਾ	/wḍna/	fly
ਉਡੀਕਟਾ	/wḍīkna/	wait for
ਉੱਤੇ	/wtte/	on
ਉੱਥੇ	/óthe/	there
ਉੱਥੋਂ	/óthoŋ/	from there
ਉਦਾਸ	/wdās/	sad
ਉਦੋਂ	/odoŋ/	then
ਉੱਧਰ	/ódər/	to there
ਉਨ੍ਹਾਂ	/onaŋ/	so much, so many
ਉਮਰ	/wmər/ F.	age
ਉਮੇਦ	/wmēd/ F.	hope
ਉਠ	/uṭh/ M.	camel
ਓਏ	/oe/	oh !
ਅਸਮਾਨ	/əsmān/ M.	sky
ਅਸਾਨ	/əsān/	easy
ਅਸੀਂ	/əsiŋ/	we
ਅਕਸਰ	/əksər/	often, usually
ਅਕਤੂਬਰ	/əktūbər/ M.	October
ਅੱਖ	/ək(k)h/	eye

ਅਖ਼ਬਾਰ	/əkhbār/ M.	newspaper
ਅੱਖਰ	/əkkhər/ M.	letter (of alphabet)
ਅਖਵਾਉਣਾ	/əkhvəw̄na/	be called
ਅੱਗ	/əg(g)/ F.	fire
ਅਗਸਤ	/əgəst/ M.	August
ਅਗਲਾ	/əgla/	next
ਅੰਗ੍ਰੇਜ਼	/əṅgrēz/	English, Englishman
ਅੰਗ੍ਰੇਜ਼ੀ	/əṅgrēzi/ F.	English (language)
ਅਚਨਚੇਤ	/əcəncet/	suddenly
ਅੱਛਾ	/əccha/	good
ਅੱਜ	/əj/	to-day
ਅਜਕਲ੍ਹ	/əjkəl/	nowadays
ਅਜਿਹਾ	/əjẏa/	such
ਅਜੇ	/əje/	still, yet
ਅੱਠ	/ət(t)h/	eight
ਅੱਠਵਾਂ	/əṭhvaṇ/	eighth
ਅੰਦਰ	/əndər/	inside
ਅੰਦਾਜ਼ਾ ਲਾਉਣਾ	/əndāza ləwṇa/	judge, reckon
ਅੱਧਾ	/ə́dda/	half
ਅੱਧੀ ਰਾਤ	/ə́ddi rat/ F.	midnight
ਅਨੁਵਾਦ	/ənvād/ M.	translation
ਅਪ੍ਰੈਲ	/əprəẏl/ M.	April
ਅੰਮ੍ਰਿਤਸਰ	/əmrytsər/	Amritsar
ਅਮੀਰ	/əmīr/	rich
ਅਲਮਾਰੀ	/əlmāri/ F.	cupboard
ਅਰੰਭ ਕਰਨਾ	/ərə́mb kərna/	begin
ਆਉਣਾ	/əwṇa/	come (and cf. 16.8)
ਆਹੋ	/aho/	yes, ' yeah '

ਆਖਣਾ	/akhṇa/	say
ਆਂਡਾ	/aṇḍa/ M.	egg
ਆਦਮੀ	/admi/ M.	man, person
ਆਪ	/ap/	self
ਆਪਣਾ	/apṇa/	' own '
ਆਪਾਂ	/apaṇ/	we (*dial.*)
ਆਮ	/am/	general
ਆਮ ਕਰਕੇ	/am kərke/	generally
ਆਲੂ	/alu/ M.	potato
ਐਤਵਾਰ	/əytvar/ M.	Sunday
ਔਖਾ	/əwkha/	difficult
ਇਸ ਕਰਕੇ	/es kərke/	so, therefore
ਇਸਤ੍ਰੀ	/ystri/ F.	woman
ਇਹ	/ɛ́/	this, these : he, she, it, they
ਇਹੀ	/ɛ́i/	this very, the same
ਇਹੋ ਜਿਹਾ	/ɛ́o jýa/	this sort of
ਇੱਕ	/yk/	one
ਇੱਕੋ ਜਿਹਾ	/ykko jýa/	the same sort of, alike
ਇੱਕੋਈ	/ykkoi/	just one
ਇੰਗਲੈਂਡ	/yṅgleÿṇḍ/	England
ਇੱਥੇ	/ɛ́the/	here
ਇੱਥੋਂ	/ɛ́thoṇ/	from here
ਇੱਧਰ	/ɛ́dər/	to here
ਇੰਨਾ	/enaṇ/	so much, so many
ਈ	/i/	indeed (*coll.*)
ਏਵੇਂ	/eveṇ/	thus : for no reason

188   PUNJABI

ਸ:	/sən/	year (with dates)
ਸੱਸ	/səs(s)/ F.	mother-in-law
ਸ਼ਹਿਰ	/şəẏr/ M.	city, town
ਸਹੁਰਾ	/səẇra/ M.	father-in-law
ਸਕਣਾ	/səkṇa/	be able to
ਸਕਿੰਟ	/skynṭ/ M.	second
ਸਕੂਲ	/skul/ M.	school
ਸਗੋਂ	/səgoŋ/	but (rather)
ਸੱਚਾ	/səcca/	true
ਸੱਜਾ	/səjja/	right (not left)
ਸਟੇਸ਼ਨ	/sṭeşən/ M.	station
ਸੱਤ	/sət(t)/	seven
ਸਤੰਬਰ	/sətəmbər/ M.	September
ਸੱਤਵਾਂ	/sətvaŋ/	seventh
ਸੱਦਣਾ	/sədṇa/	call, invite
ਸਦਾ	/səda/	always
ਸ਼ਨਿੱਛਰ (ਵਾਰ)	/şənychər(var)/ M.	Saturday
ਸਬਕ	/səbək/ M.	lesson
ਸ਼ਬਦ	/şəbəd/ M.	word
ਸੱਭ	/sə́b/	all
ਸਭਾ	/səbà/ F.	assembly
ਸਮਝ ਆਉਣਾ	/sə́mj əwṇa/	understand (cf. 16.8)
ਸਮਝਣਾ	/sə́mjṇa/	understand
ਸਮਾਨ	/səmān/ M.	luggage
ਸਰਦੀ	/sərdi/ F.	cold
ਸਰਦੀਆਂ	/sərdiaŋ/ F.Pl.	winter
ਸਵਾ	/səva/	$+\frac{1}{4}$: $1\frac{1}{4}$
ਸਵੇਰ	/səvēr/ F.	morning

ਸੜਕ	/səɽək/ F.	road, street
ਸਾਡਾ	/saḍa/	our
ਸਾਢੇ	/sáḍe/	$+\frac{1}{2}$: half past
ਸਾਫ਼	/saf/	clean
ਸਾਫ਼ ਕਰਨਾ	/saf kərna/	clean
ਸਾਂਭਣਾ	/sámbṇa/	take care of, look after
ਸ਼ਾਮ	/ṣam/ F.	afternoon, evening
ਸਾਰਾ	/sara/	all, whole
ਸਾਲਾ	/saḷa/ M.	brother-in-law (wife's brother)
ਸਾਲੀ	/saḷi/ F.	sister-in-law (wife's sister)
ਸਿਆਣਾ	/syaṇa/	clever
ਸਿਆਲ	/syaḷ/ M.	winter
ਸਿੱਖ	/syk(k)h/ M.	Sikh
ਸਿੱਖਣਾ	/sykhṇa/	learn
ਸਿਗ੍ਰਟ	/sygrət/ F.	cigarette
ਸਿਨੇਮਾ	/synema/ M.(II)	cinema
ਸਿਰ	/syr/ M.	head
ਸਿਰਫ਼	/syrəf/	only
ਸੀਊਣਾ	/syuṇa/	sew
ਸੀਟ	/siṭ/ F.	seat
ਸੁਹਣਾ	/sóṇa/	beautiful
ਸ਼ੁੱਕਰ(ਵਾਰ)	/ṣwkkər(var)/ M.	Friday
ਸੁੱਕਾ	/swkka/	dry
ਸੁੱਟਣਾ	/swṭṇa/	throw
ਸੁਣਨਾ	/swṇna/	hear, listen to
ਸੁਣਾਊਣਾ	/swṇəẃṇa/	tell (story, *etc.*)

ਸ਼ੁਰੂ	/ṣwru/ M.	beginning
ਸ਼ੁਰੂ ਕਰਨਾ	/ṣwru kərna/	begin
ਸੂਚਨਾ	/sucna/ F.	notice
ਸੇਬ	/seb/ M.	apple
ਸੋਚਣਾ	/socṇa/	think
ਸੋਚੀਂ ਪੈਣਾ	/sociŋ pəyna/	be thoughtful
ਸੋਟਾ	/soṭa/ M.	big stick
ਸੋਟੀ	/soṭi/ F.	little stick
ਸੋਮਵਾਰ	/somvar/ M.	Monday
ਸੌ	/səw/	hundred
ਸ਼ੌਕ	/ṣəwk/ M.	desire
ਸੌਖਾ	/səwkha/	easy
ਸੌਂਣਾ	/səwṇna/	sleep
ਹੱਸਣਾ	/həsṇa/	laugh
ਹਜ਼ਾਰ	/həzār/	thousand
ਹੱਟੀ	/həṭṭi/ F.	shop
ਹੱਥ	/hət(t)h/ M.	hand
ਹਫ਼ਤਾ	/həfta/ M.	week
ਹਰ	/hər/	every, each
ਹਰ ਕੋਈ	/hər koi/	everyone
ਹਰਾ	/həra/	green
ਹਵਾਈ ਜਹਾਜ਼	/həvāi jàz/ F.	aeroplane
ਹਾਂ	/haŋ/	yes
ਹਾਸੋਹੀਣ	/hasohiŋ/	ridiculous
ਹਿੱਸਾ	/hyssa/ M.	part
ਹੀ	/hi/	indeed, even (*emph.*)
ਹੁਸ਼ਿਆਰ	/hwṣyār/	sensible

ਹੁਣ	/hwṇ/	now
ਹੁਣੇ	/hwṇe/	right now, immediately
ਹੇਠ	/heṭh/	under
ਹੈਰਾਨੀ	/həyrāni/ F.	amazement, surprise
ਹੋ ਜਾਣਾ	/ho jaṇa/	become
ਹੋਣਾ	/hoṇa/	be
ਹੋਰ	/hor/	other, another, more
ਹੌਲੀ	/həwḷi/	softly, slowly
ਕਈ	/kəi/	many, several
ਕਹਾਣੀ	/kàṇi/ F.	story
ਕਹਿਣਾ	/kəýna/	say
ਕੱਚਾ	/kəcca/	raw, unripe
ਕੱਛੇ ਮਾਰਨਾ	/kəcche marna/	take under the arm
ਕੱਟਣਾ	/kəṭna/	cut
ਕਣਕ	/kəṇək/ F.	grain, wheat, corn
ਕਦ	/kəd/	when ?
ਕਦੇ	/kəde/	sometimes : (*with neg.*) never
ਕਦੋਂ	/kədoṇ/	when ?
ਕੰਧ	/kə́nd/ M.	wall
ਕਪੜਾ	/kəpṛa/ M.	cloth
ਕਪੜੇ	/kəpṛe/ M.Pl.	clothes
ਕੰਮ	/kəm(m)/ M.	work, job, task
ਕੰਮ ਵਿਚ ਲਾਉਣਾ	/kəm vyc ləwṇa/	employ
ਕਮਰਾ	/kəmra/ M.	room
ਕਮਾਉਣਾ	/kəməw̄ṇa/	earn
ਕਰਕੇ	/kərke/	because of, -ly

ਕਰਨਾ	/kərna/	do
ਕਰਮਚਾਰੀ	/kərəmcari/ M.	employee
ਕਰਾਇਆ	/kərāya/ M.	rent, fare
ਕਰੋੜ	/kərōṛ/	crore, ten million
ਕੱਲ੍ਹ	/kə́l/	yesterday, to-morrow
ਕਲਮ	/kələm/ M.	pen
ਕੱਲਾ	/kəlla/	alone
ਕਵਿਤਾ	/kəvyta/ F.	poetry
ਕਾਗਜ਼	/kagaz/ M.	paper
ਕਾਂਟਾ	/kanṭa/ M.	fork
ਕਾਫ਼ੀ	/kafī/ F.	coffee
ਕਾਰ	/kar/ F.	car
ਕਾਰਖ਼ਾਨਾ	/karkhana/ M.	factory
ਕਾਲਜ	/kaləj/ M.	college
ਕਾਲਾ	/kaḷa/	black
ਕਿ	/ky/	that (_conj._)
ਕਿਉਂ	/kyoŋ/	why ?
ਕਿਉਂਕਿ	/kyoṅky/	because
ਕਿਸ ਵੇਲੇ	/kys veḷe/	when ? at what time ?
ਕਿਹੜਾ	/kéṛa/	which ? who ?
ਕਿਹੋ ਜਿਹਾ	/kýo jýa/	what sort of ?
ਕਿਤਾਬ	/kytāb/ F.	book
ਕਿਤੇ	/kyte/	somewhere, any-where : (_with neg._) nowhere, perhaps
ਕਿੱਥੇ	/kýtthe/	where ?
ਕਿੱਥੋਂ	/kýtthoŋ/	where from ?

ਕਿੱਧਰ	/kýddər/	where to ?
ਕਿਧਰੇ	/kýdre/	somewhere, any-where : (*with neg.*) nowhere, perhaps
ਕਿੰਨਾ	/kynnaŋ/	how much ? how many ?
ਕਿੰਨਾ ਚਿਰ	/kynnaŋ cyr/	for a long time
ਕਿਵੇਂ	/kyveŋ/	how ?
ਕੀ (ਕੀਹ)	/kí/	what ?
ਕੁ	/kw/	about (with numbers)
ਕੁੰਜੀ	/kwñji/ F.	key
ਕੁੱਝ	/kẃj/	something, some : (*with neg.*) nothing, no, none
ਕੁੱਤਾ	/kwtta/ M.	dog
ਕੁਰਸੀ	/kwrsi/ F.	chair
ਕੁਲੀ	/kwli/ M.	porter
ਕੁੜੀ	/kwṛi/ F.	girl
ਕੇਸ	/kes/ M.Pl.	Sikh's long, uncut hair
ਕੇਵਲ	/kevəl/	only
ਕੈਂਚੀ	/kəyñci/ F.	scissors
ਕੋਈ	/koi/	someone, some : (*with neg.*), no one, no, none
ਕੋਸ਼ਿਸ਼	/koşyş/ F.	effort
ਕੋਸ਼ਿਸ਼ ਕਰਨਾ	/koşyş kərna/	try
ਕੋਟ	/koṭ/ M.	coat
ਕੋਲ	/kol/	beside : to (persons)

ਕੋਲੋਂ	/koḷoŋ/	from beside : from (persons)
ਕੌਣ	/kəwṇ/	who ?
ਖਬਰ	/khəbər/ F.	news
ਖੱਬਾ	/khəbba/	left
ਖਰਾਬ	/khərāb/	bad, broken
ਖਲੋਣਾ	/khloṇa/	stand
ਖਾਸ	/khas/	special
ਖਾਸ ਕਰਕੇ	/khas kərke/	especially
ਖਾਸ ਤੌਰ ਤੇ	/khas təwr te/	especially
ਖਾਣਾ	/khaṇa/	eat
ਖਾਣਾ	/khaṇa/ M.	food
ਖ਼ਾਲੀ	/khali/	empty
ਖਿਆਲ	/khyal/ M.	thought
ਖਿੱਦੋ	/khyddo/ M.	ball
ਖੁਸ਼	/khwṣ/	happy
ਖੁੱਲਣਾ	/khẃlṇa/	open (*intr.*)
ਖੇਡਣਾ	/kheḍṇa/	play
ਖੇਤ	/khet/ M.	field
ਖੋਲ੍ਹਣਾ	/khólṇa/	open (*trans.*)
ਗੱਡੀ	/gəḍḍi/ F.	train, vehicle
ਗੰਦਾ	/gənda/	dirty
ਗਰਮ	/gərəm/	hot, warm
ਗਰਮੀ	/gərmi/ F.	heat
ਗਰਮੀਆਂ	/gərmiaŋ/ F.Pl.	summer
ਗ਼ਰੀਬ	/gərīb/	poor
ਗੱਲ	/gəl(l)/ F.	matter, thing

ਗੱਲਾਂ ਕਰਨਾ	/gəllaŋ kərna/	talk
ਗੱਲੀਂ ਪੈਣਾ	/gəlliŋ pəyŋa/	start talking
ਗ਼ਲਤ	/gəlt/	wrong
ਗਿਲਾਸ	/gylās/ M.	glass
ਗੁਆਚਣਾ	/gwacŋa/	be lost
ਗੁਆਂਢੀ	/gwáɳḍi/ M.	neighbour
ਗ਼ਸਲਖ਼ਾਨਾ	/gwsalk̲h̲ana/ M.	bathroom
ਗ਼ੁੱਸਾ	/gwssa/ M.	anger
ਗ਼ੁੱਸੇ ਹੋਣਾ	/gwsse hoŋa/	be angry
ਗੁਰਦੁਆਰਾ	/gwrdwara/ M.	gurdwara, Sikh temple
ਗੁਲਾਬ	/gwlāb/ M.	rose
ਗੋਡਾ	/goḍa/ M.	knee
ਘੱਟ	/kə̀t/	less
ਘੰਟਾ	/kə̀ỳṇṭa/ M.	hour
ਘੱਟੋਘੱਟ	/kə̀ṭṭokə̀t/	at least
ਘਰ	/kə̀r/ M.	house, home
ਘਾਹ	/kà/ F.	grass
ਘੋੜਾ	/kòṛa/ M.	horse
'ਚ (=ਵਿਚ)	/yc/, /cə/	in
ਚੰਗਾ	/cəṅga/	good
ਚੰਮਚ	/cəmmɛc/ M.	spoon
ਚਲਾ ਜਾਣਾ	/cəla jaŋa/	go away, go off
ਚੜ੍ਹਨਾ	/cə́rna/	go up, rise, mount
ਚਾਹ	/cá/ F.	tea
ਚਾਹੀਦਾ ਹੈ	/cáida e/	it is necessary
ਚਾਹੁਣਾ	/cəẃŋa/	want

ਚਾਚਾ	/caca/	uncle (father's brother) : father
ਚਾਚੀ	/caci/	aunt (father's brother's wife)
ਚਾਰ	/car/	four
ਚਾਰੇ	/care/	all four
ਚਿੱਟਾ	/cyṭṭa/	white
ਚਿੱਠੀ	/cyṭṭhi/ F.	letter
ਚਿਰ	/cyr/ M.	time, delay
ਚੀਜ਼	/ciz/ F.	thing
ਚੀਨੀ	/cini/ F.	sugar
'ਚੋਂ (=ਵਿੱਚੋਂ)	/coŋ/	from in, among
ਚੌਥਾ	/cəwtha/	fourth
ਚੌੜਾ	/cəwṛa/	wide, broad
ਛੱਡਣਾ	/chədṇa/	leave
ਛੱਤ	/chət/ F.	roof, ceiling
ਛੁੱਟ	/chwṭ/	besides
ਛੁੱਟੀ	/chwṭṭi/ F.	holiday
ਛੁਰੀ	/chwri/ F.	knife
ਛੇ	/che/	six
ਛੇਵਾਂ	/chevaŋ/	sixth
ਛੋਟਾ	/choṭa/	small, little, short
ਜਗਾਉਣਾ	/jəgəw̃na/	wake up (trans.)
ਜਤਨ ਕਰਨਾ	/jətən kərna/	try
ਜਦ	/jəd/	when
ਜਦੋਂ	/jədoŋ/	when
ਜਨਮ	/jənəm/ M.	birth

ਸਨਵਰੀ	/jənvəri/ F.	January
ਜ਼ਰਾ	/zəra/	just
ਜ਼ਰੂਰ	/zərūr/	certainly, of course
ਜਲਣਾ	/jəlṇa/	burn (*intr.*)
ਜਲਦੀ	/jəldi/	quickly, early
ਜਲਾਉਣਾ	/jələw̄ṇa/	burn (*trans.*)
ਜਾਂ	/jaṇ/	or
ਜਾਗਣਾ	/jagṇa/	wake up (*intr.*)
ਜਾਣਨਾ	/jaṇna/	know
ਜਾਣਾ	/jaṇa/	go
ਜਾਨਵਰ	/janvər/ M.	animal
ਜਾਪਣਾ	/japṇa/	seem
ਜਿਹੜਾ	/jéṛa/	which, who
ਜਿਹਾ	/jýa/	rather, -ish
ਜਿੱਥੇ	/jýtthe/	where
ਜਿੱਥੋਂ	/jýtthoṇ/	from where
ਜਿੱਧਰ	/jýddər/	to where
ਜਿੰਨਾ	/jynnaṇ/	as much, as many
ਜ਼ਿਮੀਂ	/zymīṇ/ F.	earth, land, ground
ਜ਼ਿਮੀਂਵਾਰ	/zymīndar/ M.	farmer
ਜਿਵੇਂ	/jyveṇ/	as
ਜੀ	/ji/	(honorific, *cf.* 2.3)
ਜੀ	/ji/ M.	heart
ਜੀ ਕਰਨਾ	/ji kərna/	want
ਜੁਆਈ	/jwāi/ M.	son-in-law
ਜੁਆਬ	/jwab/ M.	answer
ਜੁਆਬ ਦੇਣਾ	/jwab deṇa/	answer, dismiss
ਜੁਲਾਈ	/jwlāi/ F.	July

ਜੂਨ	/jun/ M.	June
ਜੇ	/je/	if
ਜੇਕਰ	/jekər/	if
ਜੋ	/jo/	who, which, that
ਜੋ ਕੁੱਝ	/jo kẁj/	whatever
ਜੋ ਕੋਈ	/jo koi/	whoever
ਝੱਟਪੱਟ	/cə̀tpət/	immediately
ਝੂਠ	/cùṭh/ M.	lie
ਝੂਠ ਬੋਲਣਾ	/cùṭh bolṇa/	tell a lie, lie
ਟਰੇਨ	/ṭren/ M.	train
ਟਿਕਟ	/ṭykəṭ/ M.	ticket, postage-stamp
ਟੁੱਟਣਾ	/ṭwṭṇa/	break (intr.)
ਟੁਰਨਾ	/ṭwrna/	go along, walk
ਟੈਕਸੀ	/ṭəyksi/ F.	taxi
ਟੋਪੀ	/ṭopi/ F.	hat, cap
ਠੰਡਾ	/ṭhəṇḍa/	cold, cool
ਠੀਕ	/ṭhik/	right, correct
ਡਰਨਾ	/ḍərna/	fear, be afraid
ਡਰੇਸ	/ḍres/ M.	dress
ਡਾਕਟਰ	/ḍakṭər/ M.	doctor
ਡਿੱਗਣਾ	/ḍygṇa/	fall
ਡੂੰਘਾ	/ḍúnga/	deep
ਡੇਢ	/ḍéṛ/	1½

ਢਾਈ	/ṭài/	2½
ਤਕ	/tək/	until
ਤਗਾਰਾ	/təgra/	strong, fit
ਤਰਖਾਣ	/tərkhāṇ/ M.	carpenter
ਤਰ੍ਹਾਂ	/təràṇ/ F.	way, manner
ਤ੍ਰੈ	/trəy/	three (*dial.*)
ਤਰੀਖ਼	/tərīkh/ F.	date : history
ਤਰੇਹ	/tré/ F.	thirst
ਤਾਂ	/taṇ/	then
ਤਾਂ ਜੋ	/taṇ jo/	so that
ਤਾਈਂ	/taiṇ/	until
ਤਾਜ਼ਾ	/taza/	fresh
ਤਾਲਾ	/taḷa/ M.	lock
ਤਿਆਰ	/tyar/	ready
ਤਿੰਨ	/tyn(n)/	three
ਤਿੰਨੇ	/tynne/	all three
ਤੀਜਾ	/tija/	third
ਤੀਟਾ	/tiṭa/	triple
ਤੀਵੀਂ	/tiviṇ/ F.	woman
ਤੁਸੀਂ	/twsiṇ/	you (*plur. and polite*)
ਤੁਹਾਡਾ	/tẁaḍa/	your
ਤੂੰ	/tuṇ/	you (*sing.*)
ਤੇ	/te/	and
ਤੇ	/te/	well (*emph.*)
ਤੇ ('ਤੇ = ਉੱਤੇ)	/te/	on
ਤੇਜ਼	/tez/	quick : strong (tea *etc.*)

ਤੇਰਾ	/tera/	your (*sing.*)
ਤੋਂ	/toŋ/	from, than
ਤੋੜਨਾ	/toɾna/	break (*trans.*)
ਥੱਕਣਾ	/thəkna/	be tired
ਥਾਂ	/thaŋ/ F.	place : instead of
ਥੈਲੀ	/thəyli/ F.	bag, purse
ਥੋੜਾ	/thoɾa/	little, few
ਦਸ	/dəs/	ten
ਦੱਸਣਾ	/dəsna/	tell
ਦਸੰਬਰ	/dəsɔ̃mbər/ M.	December
ਦਸਵਾਂ	/dəsvaŋ/	tenth
ਦਫ਼ਤਰ	/dəftər/ M.	office
ਦਰਜ਼ੀ	/dərzi/ M.	tailor
ਦਾ	/da/	of
ਦਾਦਾ	/dada/ M.	grandfather (paternal)
ਦਾਦੀ	/dadi/ F.	grandmother (paternal)
ਦਾੜ੍ਹੀ	/dáɾi/ F.	beard
ਦਿਨ	/dyn/ M.	day
ਦੁਆਈ	/dwāi/ F.	medicine
ਦੋਹਤ੍ਰਾ	/dótra/ M.	grandson (daughter's son)
ਦੋਹਤ੍ਰੀ	/dótri/ F.	granddaughter (daughter's daughter)
ਦੁੱਖ	/dwk(k)h/ M.	pain, sorrow

ਵੱਧ	/dẃd(d)/ M.	milk
ਦੁਪਹਿਰ	/dwpəýr/ F.	noon, mid-day
ਦੂਜਾ	/duja/	second, (the) other
ਦੂਣਾ	/duṇa/	double
ਦੂਰ	/dur/	far
ਦੇਸ਼	/deṣ/ M.	country
ਦੇਣਾ	/deṇa/	give
ਦੇਰ	/der/ F.	time, delay, lateness
ਦੋ	/do/	two
ਦੋਸਤ	/dost/ M.	friend
ਦੋਵੇਂ	/doveṇ/	both
ਧੁੱਪ	/tẃp(p)/ F.	sunshine
ਧੀ	/tì/ F.	daughter
ਧੋਣਾ	/tòṇa/	wash
ਧੋਬੀ	/tòbi/ M.	washerman
ਨੱਸਣਾ	/nəsṇa/	run
ਨਹੀਂ	/náiṇ/	not, no
ਨਹੀਂ ਤਾਂ	/náiṇ taṇ/	otherwise
ਨੰਗਾ	/nənga/	bare, naked
ਨਜ਼ਰ	/nəzər/ F.	sight, look
ਨਜ਼ਰ ਆਉਣਾ	/nəzər əwṇa/	appear, be seen (cf. 16.8)
ਨਜ਼ਰੀਂ ਪੈਣਾ	/nəzriṇ pəyṇa/	appear, be seen
ਨਦੀ	/nədi/ F.	river
ਨਵੰਬਰ	/nəvəmbər/ M.	November
ਨਵਾਂ	/nəvaṇ/	new
ਨਾ (ਨ)	/na/	not, no

ਨਾ ... ਨਾ ...	/na ... na .../	neither ... nor ...
ਨਾਂ	/naŋ/ M.	name
ਨ੍ਹਾਉਣਾ	/nəẅna/	bathe, wash
ਨਾਸ਼ਤਾ	/naṣta/ M.	breakfast
ਨਾਨਾ	/nana/ M.	grandfather (maternal)
ਨਾਨੀ	/nani/ F.	grandmother (maternal)
ਨਾਲ	/naḷ/	with, by
ਨਾਲੋਂ	/naḷoŋ/	than
ਨਾਵਾਂ	/navaŋ/	ninth
ਨਿਕਲਣਾ	/nykəlna/	go out, come out
ਨਿੱਕਾ	/nykka/	small, little
ਨੀਲਾ	/nila/	blue
ਨੀਵਾਂ	/nivaŋ/	low
ਨਕਸ	/nwkəs/ M.	harm
ਨੂੰ	/nuŋ/	to
ਨੂੰਹ	/núŋ/ F.	daughter-in-law
ਨੇੜੇ	/neɽe/	near
ਨੌਂ	/nəwŋ/	nine
ਨੌਕਰ	/nəwkər/ M.	servant
ਨੌਕਰੀ	/nəwkri/ F.	employment, job
ਪਹਿਲਾ	/pəýla/	first
ਪਹਿਲਾਂ	/pəýlaŋ/	before
ਪਹਿਲੋਂ	/pəýloŋ/	before
ਪਹੁੰਚਣਾ	/pəẅñcna/	arrive, reach
ਪੱਕਣਾ	/pəkna/	cook (intr.), ripen
ਪੱਕਾ	/pəkka/	cooked, ripe

ਪਕਾਉਣਾ	/pəkəw̃na/	cook (*trans.*)
ਪੱਗ	/pəg(g)/ F.	turban
ਪਗੜੀ	/pəgṛi/ F.	turban
ਪਛਾਣਨਾ	/pəchāṇna/	recognize
ਪੰਛੀ	/pəñchi/ M.	bird
ਪੰਜ	/pəñj/	five
ਪੰਜਵਾਂ	/pəñjvaṇ/	fifth
ਪੰਜਾਬ	/pəñjāb/	Punjab
ਪੰਜਾਬੀ	/pəñjābi/	Punjabi
ਪੱਤਰ	/pəttər/ M.	leaf
ਪਤਾ	/pəta/ M.	address : clue
ਪਰ	/pər/	but
ਪਰਸੋਂ	/pərsoṇ/	day before yesterday/after to-morrow
ਪਰਾਹੁਣਾ	/pərəw̃na/ M.	guest
ਪਰੇ	/pəre/	beyond
ਪੱੜ੍ਹਨਾ	/pə́ṛna/	read : study
ਪੜ੍ਹਾਉਣਾ	/pəṛəw̃na/	teach
ਪਾਉਣਾ	/pəwna/	put in, put on, wear
ਪਾਸਾ	/pasa/ M.	side, direction
ਪਾਕਿਸਤਾਨ	/pakystan/	Pakistan
ਪਾਣੀ	/pani/ M.	water
ਪਾਬੰਦੀ	/pabəndi/ F.	restriction, ban
ਪਿਉ	/pyo/ M.	father
ਪਿਆਰਾ	/pyara/	dear, nice
ਪਿਆਲਾ	/pyala/ M.	cup
ਪਿਛਲਾ	/pychla/	last
ਪਿੱਛੇ	/pycche/	after

ਪਿੱਛੋਂ	/pycchoṇ/	after
ਪਿੰਡ	/pyṇḍ/ M.	village
ਪਿਤਾ	/pyta/ M. (II)	father (*respectful*)
ਪੀਣਾ	/piṇa/	drink : smoke
ਪੁੱਛਣਾ	/pwchṇa/	ask
ਪੁੱਤਰ	/pwttər/ M.	son
ਪੁਰਾਣਾ	/pwrāṇa/	old (of things)
ਪੁਲਸ	/pwls/ F.	police
ਪੈਸੇ	/pəyse/ M.Pl.	money
ਪੈਕਟ	/pəykəṭ/ M.	packet
ਪੈਣਾ	/pəyṇa/	fall
ਪੈਨੀ	/pəyni/ F.	penny
ਪੈਰ	/pəyr/ M.	foot
ਪੋਤਾ	/potra/ M.	grandson (son's son)
ਪੋਤੀ	/potri/ F.	granddaughter (son's daughter)
ਪੌਂਡ	/pəwṇḍ/ M.	pound
ਪੌਣੇ	/pəwṇe/	quarter less than : quarter to
ਪੌੜੀ	/pəwṛi/ F.	ladder, step, stair
ਫਖਰ	/fəkhər/ M.	pride
ਫਰਵਰੀ	/fərvəri/ F.	February
ਫਲ	/phal/ M.	fruit
ਫਿਰਨਾ	/phyrna/	turn : wander about
ਫਿਲਮ	/fyləm/ F.	film
ਫੁੱਲ	/phwl(l)/ M.	flower
ਫੇਰ	/fer/	again, then
ਫੌਜ	/fəwj/ F.	army

ਬਸ	/bəs/ F.	bus
ਬਸ	/bəs/	enough
ਬਹੁਤ	/bəẃt/	very
ਬਹੁਤ ਸਾਰਾ	/bəẃt sara/	many, a lot of
ਬਕਸ	/bəkəs/ M.	box
ਬੱਚਾ	/bəcca/ M.	child, boy
ਬੱਚੀ	/bəcci/ F.	child, girl
ਬਜ਼ਾਰ	/bəzār/ M.	market, ' shops '
ਬਣਨਾ	/bənna/	be made, become
ਬਟਾਉਣਾ	/bənəw̄na/	make, build
ਬੰਦ	/bənd/	shut
ਬੰਦ ਕਰਨਾ	/bənd kərna/	shut (trans.)
ਬੰਦਾ	/bənda/ M.	man
ਬੰਨ੍ਹਣਾ	/bénna/	tie
ਬਮਾਰ	/bəmār/	ill
ਬਰਫ਼	/bərf/ F.	snow, ice
ਬੜਾ	/bəɽa/	great : very
ਬਾਅਦ (ਬਾਦ)	/bad/	after
ਬਾਹਰ	/bár/	outside
ਬਾਗ਼	/bag/ M.	garden
ਬਾਰ੍ਹਵਾਂ	/bárvaŋ/	twelfth
ਬਾਰਾਂ	/baraŋ/	twelve
ਬਾਰੀ	/bari/ F.	window
ਬਾਰੇ ('ਚ)	/bare(yc)/	about, concerning
ਬਿਨਾਂ	/bynāŋ/	without
ਬਿਲਕੁਲ	/bylkwl/	quite, completely
ਬਿੱਲੀ	/bylli/ F.	cat
ਬੁੱਢਾ	/bẃḍḍa/	old (of people)

ਬੁੱਧ (ਵਾਰ)	/bẃd(var)/ M.	Wednesday
ਬੁਰਾ	/bwra/	bad
ਬੁਲਾਉਣਾ	/bwləẃṇa/	call, summon
ਬੂਹਾ	/búa/ M.	door
ਬੂਟ	/buṭ/ M.	boot, shoe
ਬੂਟਾ	/buṭa/ M.	tree
ਬੂਟੀ	/buṭi/ F.	shrub, plant
ਬੇਹਾ	/béa/	stale
ਬੈਠਣਾ	/bəythṇa/	sit
ਬੋਤਲ	/botəl/ F.	bottle
ਬੋਲਣਾ	/bolṇa/	speak
ਬੋਲੀ	/boli/ F.	language, speech
ਭਰਨਾ	/pèrna/	fill
ਭਰੋਸਾ	/pəròsa/ M.	trust
ਭਰੋਸੇ ਯੋਗ	/pəròse-yog/	trustworthy
ਭਾਈ	/pài/ M.	brother
ਭਾਗ	/pàg/ M.	part
ਭਾਂਡਾ	/pàṇḍa/ M.	pot, pan
ਭਾਰਤ	/pàrət/	India
ਭਾਵੇਂ	/pàṇveŋ/	although
ਭਾਵੇਂ... ਭਾਵੇਂ...	/pàṇveŋ ... pàṇveŋ .../	whether ... or ...
ਭਿੱਜਣਾ	/pỳjṇa/	be wet
ਭੁੱਖ	/pẃk(k)h/ F.	hunger
ਭੁੱਲ ਜਾਣਾ	/pẃl jaṇa/	forget
ਭੇਜਣਾ	/pèjṇa/	send
ਭੈਣ	/pəỳn/ F.	sister
ਭੈੜਾ	/pəỳṛa/	bad

ਮਈ	/məi/ F.	May
ਮਸਾਂ	/məsaŋ/	scarcely, hardly
ਮਸੀਤ	/məsīt/ F.	mosque
ਮਹੀਨਾ	/mə̀ina/ M.	month
ਮੱਖਣ	/məkkhəṇ/ M.	butter
ਮੰਗ ਕਰਨਾ	/məṅg kərna/	ask for, order
ਮੰਗਣਾ	/məṅgṇa/	ask for, order
ਮਗਰ	/məgər/	after
ਮੰਗਲ (ਵਾਰ)	/məṅgəḷ(var)/ M.	Tuesday
ਮਜ਼ਦੂਰ	/məzdūr/ M.	workman, labourer
ਮਜਬੂਰ ਕਰਨਾ	/məjbur kərna/	force, compel
ਮੰਤਰੀ	/məntri/ M.	minister
ਮੰਨਣਾ	/mənṇa/	believe : agree
ਮਨਾ	/məna/	forbidden
ਮੰਨਿਆ ਪਰਮੰਨਿਆ	/mənnya pərmənnya/	famous
ਮਰਜ਼ੀ	/mərzi/ F.	pleasure, ' free will '
ਮਰਦ	/mərd/ M.	man (as opposed to woman)
ਮਰਨਾ	/mərna/	die
ਮਾਂ	/maŋ/ M.	mother
ਮਾਤਾ	/mata/ M.	mother (*respectful*)
ਮਾਫ਼ ਕਰਨਾ	/maf kərna/	forgive
ਮਾਮਾ	/mama/ M.	uncle (mother's brother)
ਮਾਮੀ	/mami/ F.	aunt (mother's brother's wife)
ਮਾਰਚ	/marəc/ M.	March
ਮਾਰਨਾ	/marna/	hit, beat : shut (door, window)

ਮਾਰ ਸੁੱਟਣਾ	/mar swṭṇa/	kill
ਮਾਲਟਾ	/malṭa/ M.	orange
ਮਾਲਿਕ ਮਕਾਨ	/malyk məkān/ M.	landlord
ਮਾਲੀ	/mali/ M.	gardener
ਮਿੰਟ	/mynṭ/ M.	minute
ਮਿੱਠਾ	/myṭṭha/	sweet
ਮਿਲਣਾ	/mylṇa/	meet : get, find (*cf.* 16.8)
ਮਿਲਣਾ ਜੁਲਣਾ	/mylṇa jwlṇa/	resemble
ਮੀਂਹ	/míṇ/ M.	rain
ਮੀਲ	/mil/ M.	mile
ਮੁਸਲਮਾਨ	/mwsəlman/ M.	Muslim
ਮੁਕਣਾ	/mwkṇa/	finish, end (*intr.*)
ਮੁਕਾਉਣਾ	/mwkəw̄ṇa/	finish, end (*trans.*)
ਮੁੰਡਾ	/mwnḍa/ M.	boy
ਮੁਫ਼ਤ	/mwft/	free, gratis
ਮੁੱਲ	/mwl(l)/ M.	price
ਮੁੜਨਾ	/mwṛna/	turn, return (*intr.*)
ਮੂੰਹ	/múṇ/ M.	face, mouth
ਮੇਜ਼	/mez/ F., M.	table
ਮੇਰਾ	/mera/	my
ਮੈਂ	/məyṇ/	I
ਮੋੜਨਾ	/moṛna/	turn, return (*trans.*)
ਮੌਕਾ	/məwka/ M.	opportunity
ਯਾਦ	/yad/ F.	memory
ਯਾਦ ਆਉਣਾ	/yad əwṇa/	remember (*cf.* 16.8)
ਯਾਰਵਾਂ	/yárvaṇ/	eleventh
ਯਾਰਾਂ	/yaraṇ/	eleven

ਰਹਿਣਾ	/rəýṇa/	live, stay
ਰੱਖਣਾ	/rəkhṇa/	put
ਰਲ ਕੇ	/rəl ke/	together
ਰਾਹੀਂ	/ráiṇ/	by means of
ਰਾਜ਼ੀ	/razi/	happy, content
ਰਾਤ	/rat/ F.	night
ਰੁਕਣਾ	/rwkṇa/	stop (*intr.*)
ਰੁੱਖ	/rwk(k)h/ M.	tree
ਰੁਪਿਆ	/rwpya/ M.	rupee
ਰੇਡਿਓ	/reḍyo/ M.	radio
ਰੋਕਣਾ	/rokṇa/	stop (*trans.*)
ਰੋਜ਼	/roz/	daily, every day
ਰੋਟੀ	/roṭi/ F.	bread, food
ਰੋਣਾ	/rona/	cry, weep
ਲਈ	/ləi/	for
ਲਹਿਣਾ	/ləýṇa/	descend, go down
ਲਹੌਰ	/ləẁr/	Lahore
ਲੱਖ	/lək(k)h/	lac, hundred thousand
ਲੱਗਣਾ	/ləgṇa/	begin : be attached to (*cf.* 23.6)
ਲੰਡਨ	/ləṇḍən/	London
ਲੱਭਣਾ	/lə́bhṇa/	get, find (*cf.* 16.8)
ਲੰਮਾ	/ləmma/	long, tall
ਲੜਨਾ	/ləṛna/	fight, quarrel
ਲਾਉਣਾ	/ləwṇa/	attach, put on (*cf.* 23.6)

ਲਾਹੁਣਾ	/ləẃṇa/	take off (clothes) : open (door, window)
ਲਾਲ	/lal/	red
ਲਿਆਉਣਾ	/lyəw̄ṇa/	bring
ਲਿਖਣਾ	/lykhṇa/	write
ਲਿਪੀ	/lypi/ F.	script
ਲਿਫ਼ਾਫ਼ਾ	/lyfāfa/ M.	envelope
ਲੁਕਣਾ	/lwkṇa/	hide (*intr.*)
ਲੁਕ ਛਿਪ ਕੇ	/lwk chyp ke/	secretly
ਲੁਕਾਉਣਾ	/lwkəw̄ṇa/	hide (*trans.*)
ਲੈਣਾ	/ləyṇa/	take, get, buy
ਲੋਕੀਂ	/lokiṇ/ M.Pl.	people
ਲੋੜ	/loṛ/ F.	need
ਵਹੁਟੀ	/vəẃṭi/ F.	wife
ਵਕਤ	/vəkət/ M.	time
ਵਖਰਾ	/vəkhra/	separate, different
ਵਖਾਉਣਾ	/vəkhəw̄ṇa/	show
ਵਗਣਾ	/vəgṇa/	flow : blow (of wind)
ਵਜੇ	/vəje/	o'clock
ਵੱਡਾ	/vəḍḍa/	big
ਵੱਢਣਾ	/və́ḍṇa/	cut
ਵੱਧ	/və́d/	more
ਵਰਣਮਾਲਾ	/vərəṇmala/ F.	alphabet
ਵਰਤਣਾ	/vərtṇa/	use
ਵਰਦੀ	/vərdi/ F.	uniform
ਵੱਗ੍ਰ	/və́ra/ M.	year

ਵਲ	/vəl/		towards
ਵੜਨਾ	/vəɽna/		enter
ਵਾ	/va/	F.	wind
ਵਾਂਗ	/vaṅg/		like
ਵਾਪਸ	/vapəs/		back
ਵਾਰ	/var/	M.	day (of week)
ਵਾਰੀ	/vari/	F.	time, turn
ਵਾਲ	/vaḷ/	M.Pl.	hair
ਵਿਆਹ	/vyá/	M.	marriage, wedding
ਵਿਆਹ ਕਰਨਾ	/vyá kərna/		marry
ਵਿਹਲ	/vél/	F.	leisure, free time
ਵਿਹਲਾ	/véla/		free, unoccupied
ਵਿਕਣਾ	/vikṇa/		be sold
ਵਿਚ (ਵਿੱਚ)	/vyc/		in
ਵਿੱਚੋਂ	/vyccoŋ/		from in, among
ਵੀ	/vi/		too, also, even
ਵੀਰ (ਵਾਰ)	/vir(var)/	M.	Thursday
ਵੇਖਣਾ	/vekhṇa/		see
ਵੇਚਣਾ	/vecṇa/		sell
ਵੇਲਾ	/veḷa/	M.	time

English–Punjabi Vocabulary

The same words are included as in the Punjabi–English vocabulary : verbs are given in the root-form.

a /yk/, or usually omitted
(be) able /sək-/
about (with numbers) /kw/ ;
  (concerning) /bare (yc)/
address /pəta/ M.
aeroplane /həvāi jàz/ F.
(be) afraid /dər-/
after /bad/, /pycche/,
  /pycchoṇ/, /məgər/
afternoon /ṣam/ F.
again /fer/, /do vari/
age /wmər/ F.
agree /mən(n)-/
alike /ykko jɏa/
all /sɵb/, /sara/
alone /kəlla/
alphabet /vərəŋmala/ F.
also /vi/
although /pàŋveŋ/
always /səda/
amazement /həyrāni/ F.
among /coŋ/, /vyccoŋ/
Amritsar /əmrytsər/

and /te/
anger /gwssa/ M.
(be) angry /gwsse ho-/
animal /janvər/ M.
answer /jwab/ M. :
  /jwab de-/
any /koi/, /kɏj/
anyone /koi/
anything /kɏj/
anywhere /kyte/, /kɏdre/
appear /nəzər a-/ :
  /nəzriŋ pəy-/
apple /seb/ M.
April /əprəȳl/ M.
army /fəwj/ F.
arrive /pəẃñc-/
as /jyveŋ/, /jys təràŋ/
as many, much /jynnaŋ/
ask /pwc(c)h-/
ask for /məŋg-/, /məŋg kər-/
assembly /səbà/ F. :
  /məjlys/ F. (*Muslim*)
attach /la-/

(be) attached /ləg(g)-/
August /əgəst/ M.
aunt /caci/ F., /mami/ F.

back /vapəs/
bad /khərāb/, /pəy̆ṛa/, /bwra/
bag /thəyli/ F.
ball /khyddo/ M.
ban /pabēndi/ F.
bare /nənga/
bathe /nà-/
bathroom /gwsəlkhana/ M.
be /ho-/, or auxiliary
beard /dáṛi/ F.
beat /mar-/
beautiful /sóṇa/
because /kyoṅky/
because of /kərke/
become /ho ja-/, /bən-/
before /pəýlaṇ/, /pəýloṇ/ :
   (= in front of) /sámṇe/
begin /ləg(g)-/ : /ṣwru kər-/,
   /ərémb kər-/
beginning /ṣwru/ M.
behind /pycche/, /pycchoṇ/
believe /mən(n)-/
beside /koḷ/
besides /chwṭ/
beyond /pəre/
big /vəḍḍa/
bird /pəyñchi/ M.
birth /jənəm/ M.
black /kaḷa/
blow /vəg-/
blue /nila/
book /kytāb/ F.

boot /buṭ/ M.
both /doveṇ/
bottle /botəl/ F.
box /bəkəs/ M.
boy /mwṇḍa/ M.,
   /bəcca/ M.
bread /roṭi/ F.
break (intr.) /ṭwṭ(ṭ)-/ :
   (trans.) /toṛ-/
breakfast /naṣta/ :
   /naṣta kər-/
bring /lya-/
broad /cəwṛa/
brother /pài/ M.
brother-in-law /saḷa/ M.
build /bəṇā-/
burn (intr.) /jəl-/ :
   (trans.) /jəlā-/
bus /bəs/ F.
but /pər/ : (rather) /səgoṇ/
butter /məkkhən/ M.
buy /ləy-/
by /naḷ/

call /səd(d)-/, /bwlā-/
(be) called /əkhvā-/
can, use /sək-/
cap /ṭopi/ F.
car /kar/ F.
(take) care of /sámb-/
carpenter /tərkhāṇ/ M.
cat /bylli/ F.
ceiling /chət/ F.
certainly /zərūr/
chair /kwrsi/ F.
child /bəcca/ M., /bəcci/ F.

cigarette /sygrəṭ/ F.

cinema /synema/ M.(II)

city /ṣəÿr/ M.

clean /saf/, /saf swthra/ :
/saf kər-/

clever /syaṇa/

cloth /kəpṛa/ M.

clothes /kəpṛe/ M.Pl.

coat /koṭ/ M.

coffee/ kafi/ F.

cold /ṭhəṇḍa/ : /sərdi/ F.

college /kalyj/ M.

come /a-/

come down /ləÿ-/

come in /vəṛ-/

come out /nykəl-/

come up /cəṛ-/

committee /kəmēṭi/ F.

compel /məjbur kər-/

consider /səmj-/

cook (intr.) /pək(k)-/ :
(trans.) /pəkā-/

cooked /pəkka/

corn /kəṇək/ F.

country /deṣ/ M.

cry /ro-/

cup /pyala/ M.

cupboard /əlmāri/ F.

cut /kəṭ(ṭ)-/, /véḍ(ḍ)-/

daily /roz/

date /tərīkh/ F.

daughter /tī/ F.

daughter-in-law /núṇ/ F.

day /dyn/ M. (day of
week) /var/ M.

dear /pyara/

December /dəsəmbər/ M.

deep /ḍúṅga/

delay /cyr/ M., /der/ F.

descend /ləÿ-/

desire /ṣəwk/ M.

die /mər-/

different /vəkhra/, /hor/

difficult /əwkha/

direction /pasa/ M.

dirty /gənda/

dismiss /jwab de-/

do /kər-/

doctor /ḍakṭər/ M.

dog /kwtta/ M.

door /búa/ M.

double /duṇa/

dress /ḍres/ M.

drink /pi-/

dry /swkka/

each /hər/

early /jəldi/

earn /kəmā-/

earth /zymīṇ/ F.

easy /səwkha/, /əsān/

eat /kha-/

effort /koṣyṣ/ F.

egg /aṇḍa/ M.

eight /əṭ(ṭ)h/

eighth /əṭhvaṇ/

eleven /yaraṇ/

eleventh /yárvaṇ/

else /hor/

employ /kəm yc la- /

employee /kərəmcari/ M.

employment /nəwkri/ F.

empty /khali/

end (*intr.*) /mwk-/ :

   (*trans.*) /mwkā-/

England /yṅgləÿṇḍ/

English /əṅgrēz/ :

   (language) /əṅgrēzi/ F.

enter /vəṛ-/

envelope /lyfāfa/ M.

especially /khas kərke/,

  /khas təwr te/

even /vi/, /hi/, /i/

even if /pàṇveṇ/

even then /taṇ vi/

evening /ṣam/ F.

every /hər/

every day /(hər) roz/

everyone /hər koi/,

  /səb koi/

everything /səb kẃj/

eye /ək(k)h/ F.

face /múṇ/ M.

factory /karkhana/ M.

fall /pəy-/ : /ḍyg(g)-/

famous /mənnya pərmēnnya/

far /dur/

fare /kərāya/ M.

farmer /zymīndar/ M.

father /pyo/ M. :

  (*respectful*) /pyta/ M.(II)

father-in-law /səẃra/ M.

fear /ḍər-/

February /fərvəri/ F.

few /thoṛe/

field /khet/ M.

fifth /pəñjvaṇ/

fight /ləṛ-/

fill /pèr-/

film /fyləm/ F.

find /myl-/, /ləb(b)-/

  (*cf.* 16.8)

finger /wṅgəḷ/ F.

finish (*intr.*) /mwk-/ :

  (*trans.*) /mwkā-/

fire /əg(g)/ F.

first /pəÿla/

fit /təgra/

five /pəñj/

flow /vəg-/

flower /phwl(l)/ M.

fly /wḍ(ḍ)-/

food /khaṇa/ M., /roṭi/ F.

foot /pəyr/ M.

for /ləi/

forbidden /məna/

force /məjbur kər-/

forget /pẁl ja-/

forgive /maf kər-/

fork /kanṭa/ M.

four /car/ : (all four) /care/

fourth /cəwtha/

free (unoccupied) /véla/ :

  (gratis) /mwft/

free time /vél/ F.

Friday /ṣwkkərvar/ M. :

  /jwma/ M. (*Muslim*)

friend /dost/ M.

from /toṇ/ : (from people)

  /koḷoṇ/

from here /éthoṇ/

from there /óthoṇ/

from where /jýtthoŋ/
from where ? /kýtthoŋ/
(in) front of /sámṇe/
fruit /phəl/ M.

garden /bag/ M.
gardener /mali/ M.
general /am/
generally /am kərke/
get /ləy-/ :   /myl-/,
   /ləb(b)/ (cf. 16.8)
get up /wṭ(t)h-/
girl /kwṛi/ F., /bəcci/ F.
give /de-/
glass /gylās/ M.
go /ja-/
go along /ṭwr-/
go away /cəla ja-/
go back /mwṛ-/
go down /ləý-/
go in /vəṛ-/
go off /cəla ja-/
go out /nykəl-/
go up /céṛ-/
good /cəṅga/, /əccha/
granddaughter /potri/ F.,
   /dótri/ F.
grandfather /dada/ M.,
   /nana/ M.
grandmother /dadi/ F.,
   /nani/ F.
grandson /potra/ M.,
   /dótra/ M.
grass /kà/ F.
great /bəṛa/
green /həra/

ground /zymīŋ/ F.
guest /pərəẃṇa/ M.
gurdwara /gwrdwara/ M.

hair /vaḷ/ M.Pl. : (Sikhs'
   uncut hair) /kes/ M.Pl.
half /ə́dda/ : 1½ /ḍéṛ/ :
   2½ /ṭài/ : +½ (half past)
   /sáḍe/
hand /hət(t)h/ M.
harm /nwkəs/ M.
happy /khwṣ/, /razi/
hard /əwkha/
hardly /məsaŋ/
hat /ṭopi/ F.
have (cf. 13.2)
he /ó/, /é/
head /syr/ M.
heat /gərmi/ F.
here /éthe/ : (to here) /édər/
hide (intr.) /lwk-/ :
   (trans.) /lwkā-/
high /wcca/
hit /mar-/
holiday /chwṭṭi/ F.
home /kèr/ M.
hope /wmɛ̄d/ F.
horse /kòṛa/ M.
hot /gərəm/
hour /kəẏṇṭa/ M.
house /kèr/ M.
how ? /kyveŋ/, /kys təràŋ/
how much ?, how many ?
   /kynnaŋ/
hundred /səw/
hunger /pẁk(k)h/ F.

I /məyŋ/
ice /bərf/ F.
if /je/, /jekər/
ill /bəmār/
immediately /cə̀tpət/,
 /hwne/
in /vyc/, /yc/, /cə/
indeed /hi/, /i/
India /pàrət/
inside /əndər/
instead of /di thaŋ/
invite /səd(d)-/
-ish /jýa/
it /ó/, /é/

January /jənvəri/ F.
job /kəm(m)/ M.,
 /nəwkri/ F.
judge /əndāza la-/
July /jwlāi/ F.
June /jun/ M.
just /zəra/

key /kwñji/ F.
kill /mar swt(t)-/
knee /goɖa/ M.
knife /chwri/ F.
know /jaŋ-/ : /pəta ho-/,
 /pəta ləg(g)-/

labourer /məzdūr/ M.
ladder /pəwɽi/ F.
Lahore /ləẁr/
land /zymiŋ/ F.
landlord /malyk məkān/ M.
language /boli/ F.

last /pychla/
laugh /həs(s)-/
leaf /pəttər/ M.
learn /syk(k)h-/
(at) least /kə̀ttokə̀t/
leave /chəd(ɖ)-/
left /khəbba/
leisure /vél/ F.
less /kə̀t/
lesson /səbək/ M.
letter /cytthi/ F. : (of
 alphabet) /əkkhər/ M.
lie /cù̀th/ M. : /cù̀th bol-/
lie down /ləmma pəy-/
lift /cwk(k)-/
light /jəlā-/
like /vaṅg/
like that /óo jýa/
like this /éo jýa/
like what ? /kýo jýa/
listen /swŋ-/
little /chota/, /nykka/ :
 (a little) /thoɽa/
live /rəýna/
lock /taɭa/ M.
London /ləɳɖən/
long /ləmma/
look /vekh-/
look after /sámb-/
(be) lost /gwac-/
lot of /bəẁt sare/
low /nivaŋ/
luggage /səmān/ M.

make /bənā-/ : be made
 /bəŋ-/

218

man /bənda/ M., /admi/ M. :
 (not woman) /mərd/ M.
manner /təràŋ/ F.
many /kəi/, /bəẃt sare/
March /marəc/ M.
market /bəzār/ M.
marriage /vyá/ M.
marry /vyá kər-/
matter /gəl(l)/ F.
May /məi/ F.
(by) means of /ráiŋ/
medicine /dwāi/ F.
mend /thik kər-/
meet /myl-/
midday /dwpəýr/ F.
midnight /éddi rat/ F.
mile /mil/ M.
milk /dẃd(d)/ M.
million /dəs ləkh/ : ten
 million /kərōɽ/
mine /mera/
minister /məntri/ M.,
 /vəzīr/ M.
minute /mynt/ M.
Monday /somvar/ M.
money /pəyse/ M.Pl.
month /mèina/ M.
more /véd/, /hor/
morning /səvēr/ F.
mosque /məsīt/ F.
mother /maŋ/ F. :
 (respectful) /mata/ F.
mother-in-law /səs(s)/ F.
mount /céɽ-/
mouth /múŋ/ M.
Muslim /mwsəlman/

must (cf. 17.4)
my /mera/

name /naŋ/ M.
near /neɽe/
necessary /cáida e/
need /loɽ/ F.
neighbour /gwáŋɖi/ M.
neither . . . nor . . . /na
 (hi)/ . . . /na (hi)/ . . .
never /kəde nóiŋ/
new /nəvaŋ/
news /khəbər/ F.
newspaper /əkhbar/ M.
next /əgla/
nice /pyara/
night /rat/ F.
nine /nəwŋ/
ninth /navaŋ/
no /nóiŋ (ji)/, /na (ji)/
noon /dwpəýr/ F.
no one /koi nóiŋ/
not /nóiŋ/, /na/
nothing /kẃj nóiŋ/
notice /sucna/ F.
November /nəvēmbər/ M.
now /hwŋ/, /es veḷe/
nowadays /əjkəl/
nowhere /kyte nóiŋ/,
 /kýdre nóiŋ/

o'clock /vəje/
October /əktūbər/ M.
of /da/ : (= among)
 /coŋ/, /vyccoŋ/
of course /zərūr/

office /dəftər/ M.
often /əksər/
oh ! /oe/
old (things) /pwrāṇa/ :
  (people) /bẃḍḍa/
on /te/, /wtte/
one /yk/ : just one /ykkoi/
only /kevəl/, /syrəf/
open (intr.) /khẃl(l)-/ :
  (trans.) /khól-/ : (door,
  window) /lá-/
opportunity /məwka/ M.
or /jaŋ/
orange /maḷṭa/ M.
order /məṅg-/
other /hor/ : (the other)
  /duja/
otherwise /nớiŋ taŋ/
ought to (cf. 17.4)
our(s) /saḍa/
outside /bár/
own /apṇa/

packet /pəykəṭ/ M.
pain /dwk(k)h/ M.
Pakistan /pakystan/
pan /pàṇḍa/ M.
paper /kagəz/ M.
part /hyssa/ M., /pàg/ M.
pen /kələm/ M.
penny /pəyni/ F.
people /lokiŋ/ M.Pl.
perhaps /kyte na/, /kẃdre
  na/
person /admi/ M.
pick up /cwk(k)-/

place /thaŋ/ F.
plant /buṭi/ F.
play /kheḍ-/
poetry /kəvyta/ F.
police /pwls/ F.
poor /gərīb/
porter /kwli/ M.
pot /pàṇḍa/ M.
potato /alu/ M.
pound /pəwṇḍ/ M.
pleasure /mərzi/ F.
prepare /tyar kər-/
price /mwl(l)/ M.
pride /fəkhər/ M.
Punjab /pəñjāb/
Punjabi /pəñjābi/
purse /thəyli/ F.
put /rək(k)h-/, /pa-/
put on /la-/ : (clothes) /pa-/
put out /kéḍ(ḍ)-/
put under arm /kəcche
  mar-/

quarrel /ləɽ-/
quarter /cəwtha hyssa/ :
  +¼ (quarter past) /səva/ :
  −¼ (quarter to)
  /pəwṇe/ : 1¼ /səva/
quick /tez/
quickly /jəldi/
quite /bylkwl/

radio /reḍyo/
rain /mīŋ/
rather /jẃa/
raw /kəcca/

read /pə́ṛ-/

ready /tyar/

reckon /əndāza la-/

recognize /pəchāṇ-/

red /lal/

remember /yad a-/

rent /kərāya/ M.

resemble /myl- jwl-/

restriction /pabēndi/ F.

return (*intr.*) /mwṛ-/ :
  (*trans.*) /moṛ-/

rich /əmīr/

ridiculous /hasohiṇ/

right /ṭhik/ : (not left)
  /səjja/

ripe /pəkka/

rise /cə́ṛ-/, /wṭ(ṭ)h-/

river /nədi/ F.

road /səṛək/ F.

roof /chət/ F.

room /kəmra/ M.

rose /gwlāb/ M.

run /nəs(s)-/

rupee /rwpya/ M.

sad /wdās/

same /ói/, /éi/

same sort of /ykko jýa/

satisfied /razi/

Saturday /ṣənychər(var)/ M.

say /kə́ý-/, /akh-/

scarcely /məsaṇ/

school /skul/ M.

scissors /kəyñci/ F.

script /lypi/ F.

seat /siṭ/ F.

second /duja/ : (of time)
  /skynṭ/ M.

secretly /lwk chyp ke/

see /vekh-/

seem /jap-/, /nəzər a-/

(be) seen /nəzər a-/,
  /nəzriṇ pəy-/

self /ap/

sell /vec-/

send /pej-/

sensible /hwṣyār/

separate /vəkhra/

September /sətēmbər/ M.

servant /nəwkər/ M.

seven /sət(t)/

seventh /sətvaṇ/

several /kəi/

sew /syu-/

she /ó/, /é/

shoe /buṭ/ M.

shop /həṭṭi/ F. : ' shops '
  /bəzār/ M.

short /choṭa/

show /vəkhā-/

shut /bənd/ : /bənd kər-/ :
  (door, window) /mar-/

side /pasa/ M.

sight /nəzər/ F.

Sikh /syk(k)h/ M.

sit /bəyṭh-/ : sit down
  /bəyṭh ja-/

sister /pə̀yṇ/ F.

sister-in-law /saḷi/ F.

six /che/

sixth /chevaṇ/

sky /əsmān/ M.

sleep /səwŋ-/

slowly /həwḷi/

small /choṭa/, /nykka/

smoke /pi-/

snow /bərf/ F.

so /es kərke/

so much, many /enaŋ/, /onaŋ/

so that /taŋ jo/

(be) sold /vyk-/

some /koi/, /kẃj/

someone /koi/

something /kẃj/

sometimes /kəde/

somewhere /kyte/, /kýdre/

son /pwttər/ M.

son-in-law /jwāi/ M.

sorrow /dwk(k)h/ M.

speak /bol-/

special /khas/

speech /boli/ F.

spoon /cəmməc/ M.

stairs /pəwṛiaŋ/ F.Pl.

stale /béa/

stamp /tykət/ M.

stand /khlo-/ : stand up /khlo ja-/

station /sṭeṣən/ M.

step /pəwṛi/ F.

stick /soṭa/ M., /soṭi/ F.

still /əje/

stop (intr.) /rwk-/ : (trans.) /rok-/

story /kàṇi/ F.

street /sərək/ F.

strong /təgra/ : (of tea, etc.) /tez/

study /pə́ṛ-/

such /əjýa/

suddenly /əcəncet/

sugar /cini/ F.

summer /gərmiaŋ/ F.Pl.

summon /bwlā-/

Sunday /əytvar/ M.

sun /surəj/ M.

sunshine /tẁp(p)/ F.

surprise /həyrāni/ F.

sweet /myṭṭha/

table /mez/ F., M.

tailor /dərzi/ M.

take /ləy-/

take off (clothes) /lá-/

tall /ləmma/

talk /gəllaŋ kər-/ : start talking /gəlliŋ pəy-/

task /kəm(m)/ M.

taxi /təyksi/ F.

tea /cá/ F.

teach /pəṛà-/

teacher /wstād/ M.

telephone /təylyfon/ M.

tell /dəs(s)-/

ten /dəs/

tenth /dəsvaŋ/

than /naḷoŋ/, /toŋ/

thank you /tə̀nvad/ : /ṣwkria/ (Muslim)

that /ó/ : (= who, which) /jo/, /jéṛa/ : (conj.) /ky/

that very /ói/

then /odoŋ/, /os veḷe/ :
/taŋ/ : /fer/
there /óthe/ : (to here) /óder/
therefore /es kerke/
these /é/
they /ó/, /é/
thing /ciz/ F. : /gel(l)/ F.
think /soc-/, /sémj-/ : or
use /khyal/ M.
third /tija/
thirst /tré/ F.
this /é/
this very /éi/
those /ó/
thought /khyal/ M.
(be) thoughtful /sociŋ pey-/
thousand /hezār/ :
hundred thousand
/lek(k)h/
three /tyn(n)/ : /trey/
(dial.) : all three /tynne/
throw /swṭ(ṭ)-/
Thursday /virvar/ M. :
/jwmerat/ F. (Muslim)
thus /eveŋ/, /es teràŋ/
ticket /ṭykeṭ/ M.
tie /bén(n)-/
time /veḷa/ M., /veket/ M. :
/vari/ F. : /cyr/ M.,
/der/ F. : for a long
time /kynnaŋ cyr/
(be) tired /thek-/
to /nuŋ/ : (to people) /koḷ/
to-day /ej/
together /rel ke/, /naḷ/ :
/keṭṭha/

to-morrow /kél/ : day after
to-morrow /persoŋ/
too /vi/
towards /vel/
town /şeýr/ M.
train /geḍḍi/ F., /ṭren/ M.
translation /envād/ M.
tree /rwk(k)h/ M., /buṭa/ M.
triple /tiṇa/
true /secca/
trust /peròsa/ M.
trustworthy /peròse yog/
try /koşyş ker-/ : /jeten
ker-/
Tuesday /meṅgeḷ(var)/ M.
turban /pegṛi/ F., /peg(g)/
F.
turn /vari/ F. : (intr.)
/phyr-/, /mwṛ-/ :
(trans.) /moṛ-/
twelfth /bárvaŋ/
twelve /baraŋ/
twice /do vari/
two /do/

uncle /caca/ M., /mama/ M.
under /heṭh/
understand /sémj-/,
/sémj a-/
uniform /verdi/ F.
unoccupied /véla/ :
(= empty) /khali/
until /tek/, /taiŋ/
use /vert-/
(be) useful /kem a-/
usually /ekser/, /am kerke/

vehicle /gəḍḍi/ F.
very /bəẁt/, /bəṛa/
village /pynḍ/ M.

wait for /wḍīk-/
wake up (intr.) /jag-/ :
  (trans.) /jəgā-/
wall /kénd/ M.
wander about /phyr-/
want /cá-/ : /cáida e/ :
  /ji kər-/
warm /gərəm/
wash /tò-/ : (oneself) /nà-/
washerman /tòbi/ M.
water /paṇi/ M.
way /təràṇ/ F.
we /əsiṇ/ : /apaṇ/ (dial.)
wear /pa-/
Wednesday /bẁd(var)/ M.
week /həfta/ M.
well /cəṅgi təràṇ/ :
  (emph.) /te/
(be) wet /pỳj(j)-/
what ? /ki/, /kéṛa/
whatever /jo kẃj/
when /jəd/, /jədoṇ/
when ? /kəd/, /kədoṇ/,
  /kys veɭe/
where /jytthe/ : (to
  where) /jýddər/
where ? /kýtthe/ : (to
  where ?) /kýddər/
where from ? /kýtthoṇ/

whether . . . or . . .
  /pàṇveṇ/ . . . /pàṇveṇ/ . . .
which /jo/, /jéṛa/
which ? /kéṛa/
white /cyṭṭa/
who /jo/, /jéṛa/
who ? /kəwṇ/, /kéṛa/
whoever /jo koi/
whole /sara/
why ? /kyoṇ/
wide /cəwṛa/
wife /vəẁṭi/ F.
wind /va/ F.
window /bari/ F.
winter /syaɭ/ M.,
  /sərdiaṇ/ F.Pl.
with /naɭ/
without /bynàṇ/
woman /tiviṇ/ F., /ystri/ F.
word /ṣəbəd/ M., /ləfəz/ M.
  (Muslim)
work /kəm(m)/ M. :
  /kəm kər-/
workman /məzdūr/ M.
write /lykh-/
wrong /gəɭt/

year /véra/ M.
yes /haṇ (ji)/, /aho (ji)/
yesterday /kél/ : day before
  yesterday /pərsoṇ/
yet /əje/
you /twsiṇ/ : /tuṇ/
your(s) /twaḍa/ : /tera/

TEACH YOURSELF BOOKS

RUSSIAN

Michael Frewin

Russian is always thought to be a very difficult language but, in fact, it is not so much difficult as different. Only half the population of the Soviet Union speaks Russian as their mother tongue — the other hundred million learn it as a foreign language and accept this as natural.

This book aims to give a good working knowledge of the language. It consists of twenty lessons, each containing a reading passage, a section to explain new grammatical points, and exercises which practise the new material in many different ways. A key to the exercises is included and, as well as the grammar notes in each lesson, a summary of all the main forms is given in the appendix.

At the end of the book, a selection of reading passages is provided which are all derived from contemporary Soviet sources and are completely unabridged. They are thus a real guide to the progress the student is making and hence a particularly valuable feature of the book.

ISBN 0 340 21281 0

TEACH YOURSELF BOOKS

SWAHILI

D. V. Perrott

Swahili is a relatively easy language to learn. There are no real difficulties of pronunciation and none of spelling, and it is quite possible for the student working on his own to master the language.

This book covers the whole of the Swahili language without being in any sense a formal grammar. It begins by explaining the construction of a Swahili sentence, using about a dozen of the commonest words, and then goes on to show the changes caused by the different classes of nouns and the various verb tenses. At the end of each graded lesson there is a list of new words and an exercise.

The author, a Former Member of the International Institute of African Languages and Culture, has written a working course in Swahili invaluable both to the student and to the absolute beginner.

ISBN 0 340 05823 4